STEWARDS OF THE POOR

The Man of God, Rabbula, and Hiba in Fifth-Century Edessa

*The work of Cistercian Publications is made possible in part
by support from Western Michigan University to
The Institute of Cistercian Studies.*

ISBN 0 87907 308 X

Library of Congress Cataloging-in-Publication Data

Doran, Robert, 1940–
    Stewards of the poor : the man of God, Rabbula, and Hiba in
fifth-century Edessa / translations and introductions by Robert Doran.
        p. cm. — (Cistercian studies series ; no. 208)
    Includes bibliographical references and index.
    ISBN-13: 978-0-87907-308-4 (alk. paper)
    ISBN-10: 0-87907-308-X (alk. paper)
    1. Sanliurfa Lli (Turkey)—Church history.   2. Syria—Church history.
3. Church history—Primitive and early church, ca. 30–600.   4. Rabbula,
Bishop of Edessa, ca. 350–435.   5. Hiba, Bishop of Edessa, 5th cent.   I.
Title.   II. Series.

BR185.D67   2006
275.65—dc22

                                                    2005036003

Printed in the United States of America

TABLE OF CONTENTS

ACKNOWLEDGMENTS

How I first came across the 'Man of God', I cannot recall but, after working on the spectacular asceticism of Simeon Stylites, I was particularly captivated by him, and then intrigued by his place in the society of Edessa. There are many whom I can remember to thank for their encouragement and support: Sebastian Brock, Peter Brown, Glen Bowersock, Daniel Caner, Susan Harvey, Derek Krueger, Mary Whitby, and my students in Religion 51 'The Holy Wo/Man in Late Antiquity'. Amherst College has always been a warm and generous place to work in, and I particularly thank Dean Lisa Raskin. The staff at the British Library was welcoming and extremely helpful. I also thank the Vatican Library for permission to use the manuscript illustration of Saint Alexius for the cover. I am particularly indebted to Dr Rozanne Elder of Cistercian Publications for her tireless patience and good humor in editing the manuscript. As always, I could not have finished without the support, love, and occasional bemused looks of my family, Susan Niditch, Rebecca and Elizabeth.

ABBREVIATIONS

ACO	Acta Conciliorum Oecumenicorum
CBQ	Catholic Biblical Quarterly
CRAI	Comptes rendus de l'Académie des Inscriptions et Belles Lettres
CSCO	Corpus Scriptorum Christianorum Orientalium. Paris, Louvain.
CSCO Scr.Syri	Corpus Scriptorum Christianorum Orientalium Scriptores Syri
CTheod	Codex Theodosianus *The Theodosian Code and Novels and the Sirmondian Constitutions.* Translated Clyde Pharr. Princeton: Princeton University Press, 1952.
BM	The British Museum
CS	Cistercian Studies Series. Spencer, Kalamazoo.
Evagrius, HE	Evagrius Scholasticus, *Historia Ecclesiastica*
JECS	Journal of Early Christian Studies. Baltimore: John Hopkins Press,
JTS	Journal of Theological Studies. Oxford–London.
JTS ns	Journal of Theological Studies, new series. Oxford–London.
Mansi	Giovanni Mansi, ed., *Sacrorum conciliorum nova et amplissima collectio*
O	J. J. Overbeck, *S. Ephraemi Syri, Rabulae episcopi Edesseni, Balaei aliorumque.* London: MacMillan, 1865.

PG	J.-P. Migne, Patrologia cursus completus, series Graeca
PO	Patrologia Orientalis
PS	Patrologia Syriaca
RB	Revue Biblique
Theodoret, HE	Theodoret of Cyrrhus, *Historia Ecclesiastica*
Theodoret, HR	Theodoret of Cyrrhus, *Historia Religiosa*
TU	Texte und Untersuchungen zur Geschichte der altenchristlichen Literatur. Leipzig–Berlin.
ZKG	Zeitschrift für Kirchengeschichte. Gotha, Tübingen, Stuttgart.

EDESSA AND SYRIAC CHRISTIANITY

E DESSA, 'mother of all the cities of Mesopotamia',[1] lies today in south-eastern Turkey near the border with Syria, and is called Urfa, a name quite close in sound to the ancient syriac name Urhay or Orhay. Mesopotamia translated literally means 'between the two rivers', as Edessa lay east of the Euphrates, between the Euphrates and the Tigris rivers. The name Edessa was given by the seleucid rulers, successors of Alexander the Great, after the macedonian town of that name. After the seleucid retreat from east of the Euphrates, the region was temporarily independent but soon became a pawn between the Roman and Parthian Empires. Eventually, it lost its status as a kingdom and became part of the province of Osrhoene in the Roman Empire, a development that was finalized between December 240 CE and September 242 CE.[2]

---

[1]From a Syriac text dated to 240/241 CE, edited by Javier Teixidor: 'Deux documents syriaques du IIIe siècle provenant du moyen Euphrate', *Comptes rendus de l'Academie des Inscriptions et Belles Lettres* (1990) 144 A. See also, Denis Feissel, Jean Gascou, Javier Teixidor, 'Documents d'Archives Romains Inédits du Moyen Euphrate (IIIe s. après J.-C.)', *Journal des Savants* (January-June 1997) 3–57.

[2]For the date, see Fergus Millar, *The Roman Near East 31 BC–AD 337* (Cambridge, Massachusetts: Harvard University Press, 1993) 479. For the history of Edessa in the roman period, Millar (472–488) is indispensable. For a recent history of early Edessa, see Steven K. Ross, *Roman Edessa. Politics and Culture on the Eastern Fringes of the Roman Empire, 114–242 CE* (London-New York: Routledge, 2001).

Edessa occupied a strategically important position. As one
scholar has described it:

> No power, seeking to maintain control of the region,
> could afford to neglect this site. It lay at the junction of
> ancient highways. One, the road from Armenia, descended
> from the great centre of Amid (Diyarbakr), and debouched
> from the mountains into the plain at this spot. Thence it
> continued southwards to Harran and along the river Ba-
> likh, across the Euphrates, and beyond to the great cities of
> Syria in the west and south. At Orhay [Edessa] the north-
> south meets an east-west road which linked Nisibis, and
> beyond Nisibis, the Iranian countries and India and China
> in the east with the fords of the Euphrates in the west.
> Along this road caravans carried, in Seleucid and also, we
> may presume, in pre-Seleucid times, spices and gems and
> muslin from India, and silk from China to the populous
> towns Asia Minor and the Mediterranean seaboard.[3]

As Hans Drijvers[4] has characterized the region, it was thoroughly
bilingual and had a mixed population; besides those of local origin, there were Persians, Greeks, Jews, and others. 'There was
therefore a permanent interaction between the various population groups which lived densely packed within the walls of the
usually small towns, where privacy was rare.'[5]

When did Christianity come to Edessa? As Sebastian Brock has
noted, 'All the evidence [of Syriac Christianity] for the period
prior to the fourth century is exceedingly limited, and usually
of uncertain interpretation'.[6] The Edessene Chronicle, which

[3]Judah Benzion Segal, *Edessa 'The Blessed City'* (Oxford: Clarendon, 1970)
3–4. See also 136–139.

[4]Hans J. W. Drijvers, 'Syrian Christianity and Judaism', *The Jews Among Pagans
and Christians,* edd. Judith Lieu, John North, Tessa Rajak (London: Routledge,
1992) 124–127.

[5]Drijvers, 'Syrian Christianity and Judaism', 127.

[6]Sebastian P. Brock, 'Eusebius and Syriac Christianity', *Eusebius, Christianity,
and Judaism,* edd. Harold W. Attridge and Gohai Hata (Leiden: Brill, 1992) 221.

dates from the mid-sixth century CE, begins by recounting a
flood which occurred in Edessa in November 201 CE. Among
the damage done was that 'to the sanctuary of the church of the
Christians'.[7] The fascinating Christian, Bardaisan,[8] was born in
154 CE. A member of the court of King Abgar VIII, Bardaisan was
acquainted with greek philosophy and with astrology. With his
son, he wrote numerous hymns in Syriac and has been considered
the father of syriac hymnody. Debate remains over how far he was
influenced by gnostic writers. Later writers—such as Ephraem
the Syrian—attacked his followers for denying the resurrection
of the body and holding a docetic christology. *The Book of the
Laws of the Countries,* probably written by a student of Bardaisan,
consists of a dialogue between Bardaisan and his followers on the
relation between free will and fate. In it, Bardaisan describes the
customs and laws of various peoples, including Jews and Christians, and argues that, although customs, traditions, and fate can
all influence people, human beings still have free will. Thus *The
Book of the Laws of the Countries* suggests that a sizeable christian
community existed in Edessa by the early third century.[9] Several Christians were martyred under the persecutions begun by
Diocletian,[10] and Brock argues for the preeminence of Edessa:

For a list of sources for reconstructing christian history at Edessa, see pages 221–
226 of this article. In what follows, I am deeply indebted to Brock's article.

[7]Ludwig Hallier, *Untersuchungen über die Edessenische Chronik,* Texte und Untersuchungen 9 (Leipzig: Hinrichs, 1892).

[8]On Bardaisan, see Hans J. W. Drijvers, *Bardaisan of Edessa* (Assen: Van Gorcum, 1966).

[9]Hans J. W. Drijvers, *The Book of the Laws of the Countries* (Assen: Van Gorcum, 1965) #46.

[10]See *Acts of Shmona and Gurya* and *Acts of the Deacon Habbib.* A convenient
translation is found in F. C. Burkitt, *Euphemia the Goth with the Acts of the Mar-
tyrdom of the Confessors of Edessa* (London: Williams & Norgate, 1913) 90–123.
For Habbib, see also Robert Doran, 'The Martyrdom of Habbib the Deacon',
Religions of Late Antiquity in Practice, ed. Richard Valantasis (Princeton, New
Jersey: Princeton University Press, 2000) 413–423.

The importance of the specification of standard Syriac as
'Edessene' in fact lies elsewhere, for it provides us with clear
evidence that, at the time when standard Syriac/Edessene
emerged out of Proto-Syriac (perhaps by about 300) and
became the literary language of Aramaic-speaking Christianity throughout the Middle East, Edessa must have been
the most prominent Christian center in the whole area.[11]

By the time Eusebius of Caesarea wrote his *Ecclesiastical History*[12] at the beginning of the fourth century CE, a fascinating story
(HE 1.13) had appeared to consolidate the importance of Edessa
as a christian center. The story tells of letters sent between King
Abgar of Edessa and Jesus. In them Jesus promises to send one of
his disciples to Abgar. After Jesus' resurrection, Judas Thomas sent
as an apostle to Edessa Thaddaeus/Addai who converted Abgar.
The story had immense success from the beginning. Thomas the
apostle also became central to the Christian Church at Edessa.
When Egeria visited Edessa on her pilgrimage in the late fourth
century, Thomas himself was said to have evangelized the city,[13]
and the bones of Thomas were praised by the great Ephræm
the Syrian.[14] In 441, these bones were enshrined in a silver rel-
iquiary.[15] Many scholars hold, without full probative value, that
several works which display marks of syrian origin—*The Gospel of
Thomas, The Acts of Thomas, The Book of Thomas the Contender*—were
composed in Edessa.[16] The Christians of Edessa honored, along
with the bones of Thomas, the letter of Jesus to Abgar, and the
fifth century *Teaching of Addai* retells the story found in Eusebius,
adding that a portrait of Jesus himself was given to Abgar.[17]

[11]Brock, 'Eusebius and Syrian Christianity', 226.
[12]Abbreviated hereafter as *HE*.
[13]Segal, *Edessa,* 66.
[14]*Carmina Nisibena* 42.
[15]Edessene Chronicle 61.
[16]See Brock, 'Eusebius and Syriac Christianity', 225.
[17]See Segal (*Edessa,* 76–78) for the development of the veneration ascribed
to this portrait.

THE MAN OF GOD, RABBULA, AND HIBA

The writings translated here all deal with events in fifth-century Edessa. Two remarkable men were bishops there: Rabbula, from 411/412 to 435/436; and Hiba, his successor, from 435/436 to 457—with a hiatus of two years from 449–451 CE. The two men had been at odds during the christological controversy surrounding Nestorius, bishop of Constantinople. Although Edessa lay within the sphere of influence of Antioch, Rabbula had agreed not with the position of John, the bishop of Antioch, but with that of his opponent, Cyril, bishop of Alexandria. Hiba had supported John and Nestorius. Rabbula exiled Hiba from Edessa, and Hiba in turn called Rabbula a tyrant. Perhaps the appointment of Hiba to succeed Rabbula was an attempt to bring Edessa back under the influence of Antioch. Two of the writings translated here deal directly with the christological controversy.

Besides the theological issues involved, the writings here translated also shed light on the developing role of christian clergy and their position in society. Hiba is accused not only of being a heretic, but also of robbing the poor and appropriating ecclesiastical property for his own personal use. In contrast, the *Life* of Rabbula eulogizes Rabbula for his work on behalf of the poor. Rabbula is said not to have built any churches, but he did build hospitals for the poor and the lepers. The *Life* of the Man of God differs from the *Life* of Rabbula in suggesting that Rabbula had once been a builder of churches, but ceased after learning about the Man of God. Despite this difference, both works emphasize the important role of caring for the poor as the major christian duty of the clergy. Rabbula is said to have held that, whatever the Church had, it had only as a steward for the poor. The Man of God identifies himself with the poor and, at the miraculous disappearance of his dead body, Rabbula is said to have realized that any poor person could be a holy person.

This emphasis on the poor seems absent from the episcopate of Hiba. Is it only by accident that, about two years after Rabbula's death, an altar table weighing seven hundred twenty pounds of silver was donated to the main church in Edessa? Or that, four years later, a silver reliquary was donated to hold the bones of Saint Thomas? These gifts came from Senator, a former consul, and Anatolius, a patrician, powerful men in the Roman Empire. In the proceedings against Hiba, these same two men are blessed by the crowds, so they were regarded as beyond local factional politics. Their gifts do, however, seem to symbolize a change in church leadership policy in Edessa; one cannot imagine the biographer of Rabbula being in favor of Rabbula's accepting such gifts. Were the church leaders to adorn their churches and live like the wealthy elites of the city, or were they to wear the simplest clothing and use all money given to them to help the poor?[18]

In analyzing this issue one may suggest possibly different backgrounds for Hiba and Rabbula. Little is known about Hiba prior to his run-in with Rabbula, except his scholarly work as a translator. He was a member of the edessene clergy, but no mention is made of his being a member of a monastic community. By contrast, the monastic life of Rabbula, even after he became a bishop, is given great prominence in the *Life of Rabbula*. He is a monk-bishop. Although it may be too strong to claim that Rabbula wanted to turn Edessa into a monastic community, the concern he shows for the poor and the sick, his insistence that the clergy see themselves as possessing nothing as their own but as holding goods as stewards for the poor, echo Rabbula's actions in selling all his possessions and giving the proceeds to the poor before entering monastic life. The monk has to be content with what he has, not seek more. The emphasis on Rabbula's need for withdrawal from his episcopal duties to refresh his soul underlines the sense of Rabbula as a monk who has been called to serve the Lord's people. Rabbula's attitude towards his role as bishop was shaped by his monastic vocation. Perhaps it is the lack of such monastic training that led Hiba to have a different view of the role of bishop in a community.

The story of the Man of God fittingly coheres with that of Rabbula. As an example of the advent of a holy person to a com-

---

[18]This discussion has been fruitfully explored by Peter Brown, *Poverty and Leadership in the Later Roman Empire* (Hanover, New Hampshire: University Press of New England, 2002).

munity in the guise of a poor stranger, it reinforces the need for the community and its leaders to be concerned, not with social status and prestige, but with serving the poor.

FACTIONALISM IN EDESSA

Sebastian Brock has pointed to an intriguing difference between the Abgar correspondence found in Eusebius of Caesarea and that found in the fifth-century *Teaching of Addai*.

> A second special interest of the *Teaching of Addai* concerns the nobility of Edessa, several of whom are named as being the first converts to respond to Addai's preaching. The appearance of exactly the same names in the legendary *Acts of Sharbel* and of *Barsamya* suggests that all three documents in fact emanate from the same circles . . . it looks as if the authors of the *Acts of Sharbel* and of *Barsamya* were seeking to promote the view that (a) their pagan ancestors had converted to Christianity at a much earlier date than was in fact the case, and that (b) the upper classes of Edessa had produced a martyr and a confessor long before the (historical) martyrdoms of Shmona, Gurya, and Habbib, who all came from surrounding villages. The first of these aims is clearly shared by the author of the *Teaching of Addai*.[19]

There are hints in the *Life* of Rabbula that the author viewed the nobles of Edessa with suspicion. In attacking Bardaisan, the author states that the edessene nobles had all been followers of Bardaisan and that Bardaisan thought that he would be protected by them as by strong city walls, that 'he could establish his error by the feeble strength of those he helped'. Here the edessene nobles are characterized as feeble and unreliable, offering fickle

---

[19]Brock, 'Eusebius and Syriac Christianity', 228.

protection. In the proceedings in Edessa against Hiba, all the inhabitants of the city come to meet Count Chaereas, sent by the emperor to defuse tensions in Edessa. As he enters Edessa the whole city is said to have signed a petition asking for the deposition of Hiba as bishop, but only some clergy and monks in fact take the oath that the petition was presented on their behalf. Of those vested with authority in the city, Counts Theodosius and Eulogius are named as well as two provincial subordinates of the Master of the Divine Offices, a member of the city's inner committee, Aurelianus, and Abgar, a barrister. Because, as Segal surmises,[20] there were twelve members of the select group of municipal administrators and a much larger group of councillors and presumably more leading families whose families had counts among them, this number seems surprisingly small. It suggests that there was factionalization in Edessa, or, at least, a powerfully interested minority intent on getting rid of Hiba. By using the charge of heresy and thereby backing the theology then in favor in the imperial court, this small group might have been hoping to gain approval and prestige for its actions.

CONCLUSION

These three documents therefore raise interesting questions. First, the *Life of the Man of God* is very different from other examples of syriac hagiographical literature in that the Man of God does no special penitential exercises and performs no miracles. Together with the *Life of Rabbula*, the *Life of the Man of God* shows how flexible the genre was; hagiography was not at all confined to miracle accounts and was deeply influenced by biblical models. Secondly, a presentation of the proceedings against Hiba in the Second Council of Ephesus in 449 CE raises the question of how pervasive was the split between 'Nestorians' and 'Cyrillans'.

---

[20]Segal, *Edessa,* 126.

Hiba could succeed Rabbula as bishop of Edessa and rule for over twelve years without disturbance. Only when circumstances were favorable to a coup were his opponents able to oust him. Finally, these *Lives* should further the discussion of how the role of the bishop was being re-shaped in the late fourth and early fifth centuries. As bishops became more and more a part of the civic structure, they were exhorted to care for the poor, and yet, as building projects demonstrate, more and more the traditional role of city benefactors was thrust upon them. Should bishops lead lives appropriate to the level and prominence of other civic dignitaries, or should they identify themselves with the lowest members of society, the urban poor?

THE MAN OF GOD

THE STORY OF
THE MAN OF GOD

THE DISCOVERY of the story of the Man of God of Edessa reads like a detective novel. The narrative itself—in a nutshell—begins, in either Old or New Rome, with rich senatorial parents who were childless. Their prayers for a son were answered, but, from his birth their son showed himself less than interested in the usual pursuits of the rich elite. On the eve of his marriage, he left town, caught a ship, and eventually landed in Edessa. There he lived among the poor, begging for his daily meager ration of food and praying constantly in the church. Attempts by his parents to find him were unsuccessful and he remained hidden until a church custodian one night found him praying in the church. The custodian dragged his life story out of him. Soon the Man of God fell ill, and the custodian placed him in the local hospital. While the custodian was otherwise occupied, the saint died and was buried in the graveyard for the indigent. The custodian, on hearing that the Man of God had been taken out to be buried, hurried to the bishop of Edessa, told him the story, and beseeched him to come give the holy man the proper honor he deserved. The bishop and his entourage set out, but, when they went to retrieve the body, they found only the rags he used to wear. Thereupon the bishop declared that he would, from then on, concern himself only with caring for the poor.

This sparse narrative, in which the saint performs not a single miracle, did not remain that way for long. From the early Middle Ages on, the story of the Man of God was bound up with the story of the life of Saint Alexius, a life told in almost every european language—English, French, Italian, German, Spanish, Russian. In the narrative of this saint, Alexius was a rich young man born in

Rome to a roman senator, Euphemianus, and his wife Aglaïs. Just married but without having yet consummated the marriage, he left his bride a ring and other tokens before leaving town and going to Edessa. There he lived among the poor, fasting and praying constantly. When a dream revealed his sanctity to a custodian of the church, he left Edessa and, by chance, returned to Rome and lived in his parents' house, unbeknownst to them. As he was about to die, his holy presence was revealed by a miraculous voice. The emperors sent to his father, ordering him to bring forth the saint dwelling at his house. Astonished, the father learned too late that this unknown saint was his long lost son. Alexius' mother and his wife, desolated, came to his body. Many miracles and healings took place at his body. The emperors and the roman pontiff conducted the body to the Church of Saint Peter.

Within the story of Saint Alexis, the story of the Man of God remained hidden. A manuscript which contained the story of the Man of God without the trappings of Alexius was known to the great and indefatigable collector of manuscripts, Joseph Assemani, but it was not until Arthur Amiaud in 1889 published the results of his work on syriac manuscripts pertaining to the life of Saint Alexius that the Man of God narrative was recovered. Amiaud was able to show how the original life had been added to by a further narrative which eventually resulted in the *Life of Saint Alexius*. In the translation below, the seam between the two narratives can clearly be seen.

Pinning down the details of this further development is difficult. At some point, the version which ends with the death of the Man of God in Edessa was expanded with motifs also found in the life of John Calybite. This saint, whose feast day is 15 January, was born at Constantinople of noble parents. He left home and, dressed as a beggar, was sheltered in a hut by his parents who did not recognize him. Only on his death-bed did he make himself known to them. The account of the Man of God's death in Edessa was conveniently re-written so that the saint left Edessa when he saw that he was becoming known in the city.[1] The tradition oscil-

---

[1] From Amiaud on, scholars speak of 'the resurrection' of the Man of God. The term seems to go back to a remark found in the *Acta Sanctorum* that, after

lates between his ending up in Constantinople ('New Rome') or Rome itself. Stebbins, in his study of the origins of the legend of Saint Alexius, points to the fact that Constantinople appears in such ancient texts as the Codex Vallicensis,[2] while the syriac text from the ninth century CE, which Amiaud translates, points to Rome.[3] For our purposes, tracing the later development is unnecessary.

ANALYSIS OF THE STORY

The story of the Man of God is remarkable within the history of syrian saints. While the syrian saints performed prodigious miracles and extravagant feats of asceticism,[4] these are absent from the life of the Man of God. Hans Drijvers once stated: 'A typical example of a Syriac life of a saint is the legend of the Man of God from Rome, who lived his holy life at Edessa'.[5] But the next example Drijvers adduces, Jacob of Nisibis, is precisely that of a saint who works miracles and repels, by himself, enemies attacking the city. Jacob, like Simeon Stylites, is a wonder-worker. The only

---

an account of the Man of God's death in Edessa, he was said to live again *(revixisse* or *redevivum)* [Joannes Bollandus *et alii, Acta sanctorum quotquot toto urbe coluntur* (Paris: Palmé, 1863–) 31:264 (July 17)]. This does not mean 'resurrection', but simply states that the Man of God is found to be alive, so that the narrative could continue with the expansion of the story telling of the Man of God staying at his parent's home. Amiaud's translation 'sa sortie du tombeau' for ܡܢ ܩܒܪܐ may have added to the misunderstanding. Tombs for the poor would not have been single burial plots.

[2]C. E. Stebbins 'Les origines de la légende de saint Alexis', *Revue belge de philologie et d'histoire* 51 (1973) 507.

[3]Arthur Amiaud, *La légende syriaque de saint Alexis, l'homme de Dieu* (Paris: Vieweg, 1889) lxxviii.

[4]For example, Baradatus, who built and for a long time lived in a cage which was not large enough to allow him to stand up and which was open to rain and heat. The life of this saint, and others like him, is found in Theodoret of Cyrrhus, *A History of the Monks of Syria,* trans. R. M. Price (Kalamazoo: Cistercian Publications, 1985).

[5]Hans J. W. Drijvers, 'Hellenistic and Oriental Origins', in Sergei Hackel, ed., *The Byzantine Saint* (San Bernardino, California: Borgo, 1983) 26.

miraculous element in the syriac life of the Man of God occurs
after he has died, when his corpse disappears from among the other
bodies of the poor and only his rags remain.[6] As for his ascetic life,
the Man of God certainly prays a great deal and eats only once a
day. But his diet is fifteen ounces of bread—a good loaf—and three
ounces of vegetables. Boring and sparse, but nothing compared to
the starvation rations of other syriac saints.[7] Simeon Stylites would
not eat for days at a time, and the Man of God's diet seems even
more generous than what Bishop Rabbula ate. The emphasis laid
by the *Life* on the Man of God's regimen is that he lives and eats
like a poor person. He does nothing extraordinary, except be a
poor person. It is this that makes the Man of God extraordinary.

THE GREEK VERSION

In 1933, Margarete Rösler published a greek life of the Man of
God from an twelfth-century CE manuscript housed in Venice.[8]
This version—translated below—is fascinating in its similarity
to, and difference from, Amiaud's syriac text. The title contains
the name Alexius, but the name is not found in the body of the
text, where the main protagonist remains unnamed. The saint's
birth-place is explicitly identified as Rome, no space is given to
his education, but the general outline of the life is basically the
same as that contained in the syriac text. There are, however, three
important differences.

---

[6]Some have tried to see a miracle in the fact that, when the Man of God goes
to the harbor, a ship bound for Syria is suddenly there. See Margarete Rösler,
'Alexiusprobleme', *Zeitschrift für romanische Philologie* 53 (1933) 515. While the
coincidence is providential, it is not miraculous.

[7]See Arthur Vööbus, *History of Asceticism in the Syrian Orient*, CSCO Subsidia
17 (Louvain: Peeters, 1960) 2:261–264.

[8]Margarete Rösler, 'Alexiusprobleme', *Zeitschrift für romanische Philologie* 53
(1933) 508–528.

• First, the custodian is described as a holy man and is made aware of the presence of the Man of God in Edessa through a dream.

• Secondly, the church is identified as that of the Theotokos, the title for the Virgin Mary much disputed in the Nestorian debate. This church was not built in Edessa till 489 CE.

• Thirdly, the bishop is not named and the story ends with the grave-diggers telling the unnamed bishop and his clergy that they have buried the stranger with the poor.

The Rösler manuscript clearly shows that this is where the story ends: the next page of the codex is empty and is the last page in the codex.[9] This last point is particularly interesting in that it shows that, for the author, the story satisfactorily ended at this point. In his discussion of the syriac version, Amiaud held that the story was entirely trustworthy if one eliminated the miracle of the corpse's disappearance, and he recognized that other aspects of the story, e.g. his interaction with his slaves, were a bit exaggerated.[10] It is precisely these details that are missing from the greek version. Rösler, followed in this by Odenkirchen,[11] in his exploration of the origins of the old french version, expended a great deal of effort to show that the greek version is the more 'authentic' version.[12] Rather than following this red herring, we will compare the two tellings of the story and note where the different tellers placed their emphases.

Both the greek and the syriac manuscripts include miraculous events: in the syriac, the disappearing corpse; in the greek, the triple appearance of an angelic figure in a vision to the custodian. But each narrative contains details that set it in a different time period: the syriac during the life of Bishop Rabbula (412–436),

---

[9]Rösler, 'Alexiusprobleme', 508.

[10]Amiaud, *La légende syriaque* (above, n. 3), lxxii.

[11]Carl Odenkirchen, *The Life of St. Alexius in the old French version of the Hildesheim manuscript , the original text reviewed, with comparative Greek and Latin versions, all accompanied by English translations* (Brookline, Massachusetts: Classical Folio Editions, 1978) 29–32.

[12]See Rösler, 'Alexiusprobleme', 514–517.

the greek after the building of the Theotokos church in 489 CE.
These very differences evidence the plasticity of the story and the
way it could be shaped to convey quite different messages.

THE PLOT

When the two tellings are compared, a basic plot line emerges.
A son of rich and noble parents, about to embark on an advan-
tageous marriage, instead leaves his home town and travels to
Edessa. There he lives among the poor, sharing their life during
the day and praying at night. The church custodian comes to
know who he is, but does not reveal his identity. When the Man
of God falls ill, he is placed in a hospital for poor strangers. While
the custodian is detained, the Man of God dies and is buried in
the paupers' burial ground. When the custodian hears about this,
he alerts the church authorities that a rich man had lived a holy
life among the poor of their city.

This sketch of the narrative plot common to both traditions
reveals that the narrative's stress falls on the contrast between
the Man of God's former rich life style and his life among the
poor. The story notes that the beggar does not eat much and
spends his time in prayer, but the real source of amazement is his
voluntary choice of poverty. This is a story about a person who
renounces wealth and voluntarily becomes poor. Such a renunciation is commonly found in saints' lives—see, for example, the
Life of Antony.[13] Having heard the Gospel call, 'Go, sell all that
you have, and come, follow me',[14] Antony does just that. This,
however, is just the beginning of the remarkable life and famous
deeds of Antony. In the life of the Man of God, this is the main
point of the story. The striking anonymity of the main character,

---

[13] *Athanasius of Alexandria: The Life of Antony. The Coptic Life and The Greek Life,*
translated by Tim Vivian and Apostolos N. Athanassakis (Kalamazoo: Cistercian
Publications, 2004).

[14] Mk 10:21; Lk 18:22.

as of the others in the story, means that the plot revolves around the renunciation. The story is less a biography than a parable, a *mashal*.[15] It represents in narrative form the same world-view as that encapsulated in the pithy description Paul gave of Jesus' life style: 'though he was rich, yet he became poor'.[16] It is this basic *mashal* which finds its expression in the syriac and the greek tellings. Hans Drijvers, followed in this by McLeod, was thus correct in noting the symbolic character of the story.[17] Drijvers stressed the notion of the saint as an *alter Christus,* another Christ. Drijvers almost turns the story into an allegory: the saint's prayer at night imitates Jesus' prayer in Gethsemane; the door-keeper is like Peter in trying to prevent the suffering of the Man of God.[18] Such an allegorical reading, however, tends to blunt the powerful thrust of the parable itself on the divine quality of renunciation.

The Greek Version

The greek version presents a bare-bones account, except in two instances. Firstly, at the time of his marriage, the narrator has the saint reflect within himself, 'What is this world? Truly, this way

[15]See the discussion of *mashal* in Susan Niditch, *Folklore and the Hebrew Bible* (Minneapolis: Fortress, 1993) 67–87. On p. 86, Niditch defines *mashal:* 'Drawn from personal memory and experience and built upon the traditions that are claimed by a folk group to be its collective memory, the *mashal* is a form of oblique and artful communication that sets up an analogy between the communication (a saying, an icon, a narrative, a symbolic action, or another form) and the real-life settings of the listeners'.

[16]2 Cor 8:9.

[17]Hans J. W. Drijvers, 'Die Legende des heiligen Alexius und der Typus des Gottesmannes im syrischen Christentum', in Margot Schmidt and Carl Friedrich Geyer, edd., *Typus, Symbol, Allegorie bei den östlichen Vätern und ihren Parallelen im Mittelalter* (Regensburg: Pustet, 1982) 187–217. Frederick G. McLeod, 'The Stranger as a Source of Social Change in Early Syriac Christianity' in Francis W. Nichols, ed., *Christianity and the Stranger. Historical Essays* (Atlanta: Scholars, 1995) 40–44.

[18]Drijvers, 'Die Legende', 192.

of life is vain; rather, blessed are those who serve God'. The same thoughtful note is repeated when the saint recounts his life to the custodian: 'I reflected that what I had [were] the transitory things of this world'. These reflections are not found in the syriac version. Here the author has the saint express a much more general observation about the world than the rejection of wealth and luxury. His words resonate with those of Ecclesiastes:

> 'Vanity of vanities, says the Teacher,
> Vanity of vanities! All is vanity'.[19]

The saint's decision is portrayed as a reflective evaluation of this world. His words could have been spoken by anyone deciding to renounce the world and, in fact, the author explicitly links the saint to other servants of God. Secondly, the custodian is portrayed as a holy man, worthy to receive the vision appearance and revelation of the saint's presence. Like can be known only by like. The author is implicitly encouraging his listeners to strive for holiness so that they can be attuned to the things of God.

The narrative starkness of the ending of the *Life* is striking. There is no divine vindication of the holy man, no repercussions upon the city. But the very bleakness of the ending may provide a clue to its significance, for it puzzles the listener to ask what will happen next. Will the bishop pursue the matter or will he return home, satisfied that he had done his best? What motive had led the bishop to come—the holiness of the Man of God or the fact that his parents were members of the roman aristocracy? The abrupt ending forces the listeners to raise questions about their own lives. Are miracles important for holiness? Does a proper burial with pomp have anything to do with a holy life? The answer the *Life* suggests is 'none'. The Greek life, in this reading, seems geared to those who have chosen the life of asceticism: it reminds them of why they renounced this world, and dissuades them from thinking that the ascetic life leads to anything other than an unknown death. Its author would, in this view, be an ascetic writing an exhortatory example for other ascetics, as well as for himself.

---

[19]Ecclesiastes 1:2.

The Syriac Version

In contrast to the greek, the syriac version has a long introduction which—besides emphasizing the contrast between wealth and poverty/abasement—begins to place the Man of God squarely within the christian heroic tradition. The author uses the traditions of the hebrew Scriptures to contrast the saint's virtues with those of Esau; that is, he links him to Jacob. He sets him on a journey to the heavenly Jerusalem, which Paul, in Galatians 4, associated with Jacob, as opposed to the earthly Jerusalem symbolized by Esau. He especially links the Man of God to Abraham, the father of believers. After thus enfolding the Man of God in the symbolism of the Scriptures, the author develops the special quality of the hero by using traditional tale motifs: the childless parents, the prayer for a child, the birth of the hero, the difference of the hero from his peers. The parents are portrayed, not as holy and faithful, but as wealthy socialites, more interested in money than in God. Noteworthy too is the way the saint's peers are shown as arrogant elites, quick to use their position to intimidate those beneath them on the social scale. His parents want to see him acting like them, arrogant towards his male slaves, sexist towards his female slaves. The antitheses become clear: this world—wealth, status, marriage—versus the heavenly world—poverty, abasement, celibacy.

The Man of God's life in Edessa is described fairly routinely. When the custodian comes across him by accident, the Man of God's reply to a question about who he is epitomizes his position: he is one of the poor, he replies. The difference between the Greek and the Syriac versions become striking at the death of the Man of God. In the syriac, the bishop is named; he is Rabbula, bishop of Edessa from 412–436 CE. When he and his entourage go into the common graveyard for the poor, they find no corpse, but only the rags which he had worn. The reaction of the bystanders is to be expected: great amazement and trembling. In antiquity, such a sign indicated that some sacred person had been present. The gods always let human beings know they had been present, as when Athena 'seeming a seahawk, in a clap of wings' leaves the Akhaians in Pylos astounded and awed.[20] Oedipus, made sacred by his extraordinary actions, takes off his filthy garments and changes; then, 'not war, nor the deep sea overtook him, but something invisible and strange caught him up—or down—into a space unseen'.[21] The theme of the presence and departure of a sacred person is found in *Tobit*, as the angel Raphael journeys with Tobias and then, mission accomplished, tells Tobit and Tobias who he is and then ascends before their eyes.[22] Within the christian tradition, of course, the motif of searchers finding only clothes but no corpse occurs in the Gospel of John when Peter and John race to the tomb of Jesus.[23] Interestingly, no verbal resonance of this gospel scene is found in the departure of the Man of God.

What is most powerful about the ending in the syriac version, is its description of the effect these events have on Rabbula. From that moment on, he devoted himself exclusively to the poor and strangers. This reaction to the past presence of a holy person within his community suggests how the syriac author has shaped the message. Rabbula asks, 'For who knows whether there are many like this saint who delight in abasement, nobles to God in their souls but not recognized by humans because of their abasement?' The author has molded the basic parable so that it becomes a test. The story now is focused not so much on the Man of God as on how one reacts to the presence of the holy in one's midst.

Tests of humans have always been the stuff of folk-tales. This is particularly true where the test revolves around the care for strangers. One finds it constantly in Homer's *Odyssey*. When Antinoös hits the disguised Odysseus with a stool, even his fellow suitors rebuke him:

> A poor show, that—hitting this famished tramp—
> bad business, if he happened to be a god.
> You know they go in foreign guise, the gods do,
> looking like strangers, turning up

---

[20]Homer, *The Odyssey*, 3.371.
[21]Sophocles, *Oedipus at Colonus*, 1658–1662.
[22]Tobit 12.
[23]Jn 20:4–9.

in towns and settlements to keep an eye
on manners, good or bad. (*Odyssey* 17, 458f.)

Within the christian tradition, one finds this test factor emphasized in the scene of the Last Judgement found in the Gospel of Matthew:

I was hungry and you gave me food, I was thirsty and
you gave me something to drink, I was naked and you
gave me clothing, I was sick and you took care of me, I
was in prison and you visited me . . . When you did it
to the least of my brethren, you did it to me.[24]

Here we are in a world where sacred beings can at any moment visit mortals and where mortals are exhorted to treat other humans decently and with respect—just in case. The actions of Bishop Rabbula are thus an expected ending to this type of test narrative, a story which directs its readers to proper moral actions. So we find in Rabbula's canon for monks that the monks are admonished to receive strangers kindly.[25] Priests and members of the community are instructed to take care of the poor,[26] and houses are to be set aside where the poor can find rest.[27] Yet, interestingly, there is no explicit reference in the narrative of the Man of God to the matthean text.

The syriac tradition contains several figures who are identified with the poor. The apostle Thomas, as he is about to die in *The Acts of Thomas*, witnesses to his own life:

Behold, therefore, I have fulfilled your word and accomplished your command; and I have become poor and needy

---

[24]Mt 25:31–46. Sherman W. Gray has thoroughly tracked down how Matthew 25:31–46 was interpreted within the christian community: Sherman W. Gray, *The Least of My Brethren. Matthew 25:31–46. A History of Interpretation,* SBL Diss 114; Scholars: Atlanta, 1989.

[25]Canon 17. These canons, or admonitions for monks, attributed to Rabbula have been collected and translated by Arthur Vööbus in *Syriac and Arabic Documents regarding Legislation relative to Syrian Asceticism* (Stockholm: Etse, 1960) 24–33. Some manuscripts interpret canon 17 to refer only to other monks.

[26]Canons 11–12,24.

[27]Canon 16. See Vööbus, *History of Asceticism,* 2:361–371.

and a stranger and a slave, despised and a prisoner and
hungry and thirsty and naked and weary for your sake.[28]

Here the reference to the matthean text is clear, but so is the
emphasis on being poor and a stranger.[29] Ephraem of Edessa is
described as wearing 'clothes which were of the many-colored
rags of the dust heap'.[30] In his testament before his death, Ephraem
asked to be buried among the graves of the destitute and the
criminals.[31] Within this tradition, the monks called themselves
ܡܣܟܢܐ, 'the poor ones'.[32]

Of particular importance is the way the Man of God is described as ܡܟܝܟ, often translated as 'humble'; I have preferred
'the abased one' or, when the abstract noun is used, 'abasement'.
In the prologue, the Man of God is the destroyer of pride by his
abasement. This use of ܡܟܝܟ resonates with its use in the Suffering Servant song of Isaiah 53:3: 'He was despised and rejected
ܡܟܝܟ by others, a man of suffering and acquainted with infir-
mity'. Also, in the hymn found at Philippians 2:6-11, the theme of
which is that one in exalted status leaves everything to be obedient to God, it is said of Jesus that 'he humbled himself ܡܟܟ ܢܦܫܗ
and became obedient to the point of death'. Aphrahat, in his
homily 'On Humility' (Demonstration 9), refers to this text:

> Our Saviour, exalted and glorious, humbled himself
> (ܐܬܡܟܟ); he was exalted and lifted up to his former
> nature, and glory was added and all things were sub-
> jected to him. Our Savior, because he humbled himself
> (ܡܟܟ), received glory and received increase.[33]

---

[28]*Acts of Thomas* 145.

[29]This, of course, is not peculiar to the syriac tradition. There is the lovely
story of Laurence of Rome who, when persecutors demanded the treasures
of the church, brought forth all the christian poor (Ambrose, *De officiis ministri*
2.28,140; PL 16:141).

[30]J. B. Segal, *Edessa. 'The Blessed City'* (Oxford: Clarendon, 1970) 88.

[31]*Testament* 252, as reported by Vööbus, *History of Asceticism* 2:91–92.

[32]Vööbus, *History of Asceticism* 2:366.

[33]*PS* 1.440 1.26–441 1.5.

Within this homily, Aphrahat draws on biblical examples of humility—Jacob, Joseph, Moses, David, Hezekiah, Mordechai, Daniel, and Mary.[34] But Jesus is the Teacher of Humility (ܡܠܦܢܐ ܕܡܟܝܟܘܬܐ),[35] Christ the King the Humble One (ܡܟܝܟܐ ܡܠܟܐ ܡܫܝܚܐ).[36] The humble are sons of the Most High and brothers of Christ;[37] in whomever humility is found, the gentle and humble one dwells in him (ܐܝܟܐ ܓܝܪ ܕܫܟܝܚܐ ܡܟܝܟܘܬܐ).[38] For Aphrahat, as for Ephræm, ܡܟܝܟܐ is a title for Christ.

The author of this text thus stands squarely within the syriac tradition in his telling of the life of the Man of God. The expanded syriac version of the story asserts that the author was the custodian, but we may see this as an attempt to bolster its authenticity by claiming it is an eye-witness account. The author favors the position of Bishop Rabbula on poverty, and he provides one unexpected observation: that the death of the Man of God took place before Rabbula's eyes became dim. The author thus seems to know details about the persons in the story. Yet the author of the *Life* of the Man of God presents a different picture of Bishop Rabbula from that found in the *Life* of Rabbula. In that life, Rabbula, from the start of his bishopric, was concerned about the poor and did no building; the Rabbula in the Man of God narrative, by contrast, has completed many building activities and desists only because of the revelatory disappearance of the corpse of the Man of God. The author of the *Life* of the Man of God champions the poor, but is perhaps not so keen a supporter of Rabbula.

---

[34]*PS* 1.411, 417.
[35]*PS* 1.420 11.3–4.
[36]*PS* 1.428 11.14–15.
[37]*PS* 1.418 11.17–18.
[38]*PS* 1.429 11.2–3.

TEXTS

I have used Amiaud's critical edition of BM Add 17177, while noting a few changes which I found in checking the manuscript itself. This manuscript dates from the first part of the sixth century CE. Amiaud noted that the first ten or so lines of the manuscript were lost. He replaced them, following BM Add 14655, a manuscript which dates from around the eleventh century CE and which contains the expansion of the life of Alexis in Rome as well as the original life.[39] I suspect he does this because, according to his stemma for the manuscript tradition, these two manuscripts belong to the same branch.[40] I, however, have preferred to follow BM Add 12160, which dates from the last half of the sixth century CE and which does not contain the expansion telling of the Man of God's return to his parents' home in Rome. For the second life, I have followed Amiaud in using BM Add 14655.

For the greek life, I have used the edition by Margarete Rösler of Codex VII, 33, fol. 177r–179r at the library of San Marco, Venice.[41] As Rösler notes, this manuscript dates from the twelfth century CE, and has many scribal errors.

---

[39]Amiaud, *La légende,* ii, vii–viii,∖. Amiaud uses roman numerals in his introduction and syriac letters as numbers for his translation pagination. So transposed, these numbers refer to pages 2, 7–8 of the introduction, and page 3 of the translation.

[40]Amiaud, *La légende,* xv–xviii.

[41]Rösler, 'Alexiusprobleme', 508–511.

THE MAN OF GOD

THE ORIGINAL SYRIAC LIFE

THE ACCOUNT OF THE MAN OF GOD from the city of Rome. He was triumphant and received a crown because of his poverty and toil for Christ's sake in the days of the holy Mar Rabbula, bishop of Edessa.

My friends, let us hear with discerning affection the account of the marvelous man. For we rightly call him an angel of God, as he despised all the pleasures of this transitory world. Now the account of him is like this.

This man was heir to great wealth, but he chose for himself the hatred of wealth. He exchanged it for the love of poverty: not ordinary poverty, but [one][1] of shame and reproach. For he was a destroyer of pride by his abasement, and of abundance[2] by his abnegation, but he was a builder of divestment[3] and of abasement.[4] He was perfect in fasting: from his belly[5] he barred food, and he did not yield to his belly so that he might not be enslaved like Esau.[6]

---

[1]Amiaud, following BM Add 14655, reads 'a true [poverty]' (ܪܕܘܬܐ).

[2]Amiaud reads ܪܒܘܬܐ, 'haughtiness'.

[3]To translate ܪܫܠܘܚܐ, I have used the root meaning of ܫܠܚ, 'to take off, to strip' rather than 'to send'. McLeod emends to ܪܫܠܝܐ, 'eremitical life'.

[4]A resonance to Jer 1:10: 'I appoint you . . . to destroy and to overthrow, to build and to plant'.

[5]Amiaud: 'mouth'.

[6]Gen 25:29-34.

He was a watchful and vigilant guardian of his body because he fled far from marriage and from fornication. For virginity and chastity dwelt innocently in his body as if by agreeable ordinance. Like Abraham, he joyfully separated from his family and his country, for he yearned and was pressing in his petition to be enrolled and recognized in the Jerusalem which is above.[7] What can I add to extol the praise of one whose extreme perfection is so overpowering that no tongue can tell it? The account of such a person is beyond us and is inadequately told by us.

Our account of him begins in this way.

His parents were from the city of Rome, so from this point the inquiry ought to begin. They were rich, renowned for family and for nobility. However, they lacked children. As much as their wealth increased and grew, so with their wealth their sorrow also increased because they could see no heir to their funds and they did not know for whom they were accumulating. For if Abraham, the father of all believers,[8] could say in sorrow to his Lord, 'My Lord, what will you give me, for behold I continue without sons',[9] how much more would those mourn whose mind was fastened on their wealth? Now, through tears, many prayers, and vows, a son was born to them, and our account is about him. He was dear to God, to his parents, to whoever saw him. His parents were relieved from their distress. Now the child was magnified even while still on milk: the privileges of nobility grew up with him, and these honors were his from his parents. When he reached the age for schooling, he went to school in great pomp with a large retinue of servants. However, he not only disregarded these transient things which pass away, but he even did the exact opposite. For he exercised himself in abasement as he quietly gave his attention to his study. While many of his peers sought very hard to corrupt him with the arrogance of knowledge,[10] he did not relinquish his sobriety. Then the parents of the child, as they

[7]Gal 4:26.

[8]Gal 3:7-9; Gen 12:3; 15:5.

[9]Gen 15:2.

[10]The manuscript which Amiaud numbers B reads: 'while very many of his peers played before him'; the manuscripts which Amiaud numbers D E F G H read: 'in the impudence of games'.

did not understand that he was a chosen vessel of God, began to be gloomy and mournful because they supposed that he was unsophisticated and incompetent in the ways of this world. So they secretly schemed that the child might be more worldly-wise and artful. His father ordered his slaves to be unrestrained with him and to accustom him to be assertive. But he rebuked and admonished them by his humble practices, and he turned away from them with a dignified, humble countenance. His mother also provided beautiful handmaids adorned with all sorts of gorgeous worldly ornaments, and she ordered them to wait upon him. The youth did not openly thrust them from his presence, but, with his countenance turned downwards, he assented to be waited upon by them. Afterwards, he ordered them with a dignified word to leave his presence while he remained alone. The mother of this attractive [person] then asked his adorned handmaids if he spoke with them or laughed with them. But they said, 'Not only does he not laugh with us, but we do not even dare to look at him because of his overpowering dignity'.

For a long time he maintained these [customs] in this way. But after time passed and he arrived at the full flower of youth, his parents proposed to betroth him a wife according to custom, which they did. When the time of the marriage drew near, they provided whatever was excellent and magnificent, and set up a splendid bridal chamber. All the city was invited to the wedding feast. But on the very first day of the wedding feast, as the bride was getting ready to come in procession [to the wedding], a holy prompting bubbled up in his soul's mind, and he asked one of his groomsman to go with him to the harbor. The groomsman thought that he spoke in jest. But, when [the groomsman realized that] he truly wanted to do this, he tried to prevent him by saying, 'What! All the city is invited to be merry and rejoice today at your house, and we should seek out places that are deserted? Who will approve of us or who will not scoff at us when we do this? We turn joy to sadness, and great rejoicing is turned to sorrow for everyone who was expecting your joy'. But as hard as his groomsman attempted to detain him, just as hard was that attractive [young man] persuading him that they should go. As his groomsman esteemed him, he was led to the view of the humble one. Together they took two horses and went to the harbor, while no one else accompanied them. He said to his groomsman, 'Stay here, guard this horse for me while I divert myself and then together we will go to the wedding feast'. Since [the groomsman] was unaware of what he planned to do, he did as ordered while entreating him, saying, 'Let us return quickly and not be late and be scoffed at'. Then the blessed one, after withdrawing himself a little way from the groomsman, prayed and said, 'O you who more than matches our requests with your[11] gifts, open for me your door on which I knock,[12] and grant me now [this request] according to my heart'.

As he was praying, behold a ship arrived while he was there, bound for Syria. Immediately he boarded it. By God's providence, a mighty wind came up for the ship and without delay brought it to the port of Seleucia in Syria. Then the blessed one left Seleucia and went all around begging and was brought to a city of the Parthians called Edessa. He remained there in the surrounding area until his death.

Now these were the practices of the blessed one in Edessa: during the day he was constantly in the church and in the martyrion,[13] while he took nothing from anybody. For he decided to dispense with food during the day, so that he could keep his fast until evening.

When evening arrived, he would stand by the door of the church, his hand stretched out, and he would accept alms from whoever was entering the church. When he had received from them what he deemed necessary, he would draw back his hand from taking. Now the ration[14] of his food was about ten minin[15] of bread and two of vegetables. If by chance he would receive more, he would immediately give it to someone else, and from alms he would make alms. There are proofs and attestations con-

---

[11] The third person masculine suffix is used here.

[12] Mt 7:7-8 || Lk 11:9-10.

[13] A martyrion is a shrine dedicated to a martyr and raised over his tomb. It was separate from the main meeting place of the faithful at the church.

[14] Greek τακτόν.

[15] A *min* is about one-and-a-half ounces.

cerning this from many people about the Man of God.[16] He did not dwell apart from the poor. But when night came, after all the poor whom he was with were sleeping, he would rise up. He would crucify[17] himself to a wall or to a column and he would pray. He would enter with the earliest who were coming to church for prayer, and [would stay] until day-break. In this way he filled up every day.

He told no one about his former life and his dignity; not even his surname would he consent to declare in order that his [former] way of life might not become known or be discovered through his name.

Now that groomsman, when he had waited a long time and [his master] did not return to him, went around the whole harbor and made inquiries as he sought him. When he learned that he had embarked on a ship, he returned to the home of the blessed one and announced what had happened. No one can describe the grief and sorrow that seized the parents of the humble one. In keeping with their wealth and rank, they sent into all harbors and countries as they sought him. Now, one of his christian servants was among those who went out on the search for the saint. As they went about in the cities, they came also to Edessa where their master was begging. This [christian] servant of the saint entered and made this man's case known to the praiseworthy bishop Rabbula of Edessa. Not only did [the servant] not find [the blessed one], but he was not even believed because the case was so extraordinary. Since [the servant] was not able to come across him, he left and took himself off to other regions in search of him. The blessed one, however, had recognized his servants when they had entered the church and when they left. But they, although he was begging right in front of them, had not the least idea it was he as there was no sign of stateliness in him because of his extreme poverty. For how could they recognize him in a man clothed in shameful rags and begging? [It is] likely that he even accepted alms from them.

---

[16]Amiaud takes this sentence to be about tests and trials of the Man of God by other people.

[17]Clearly, the meaning is that he would extend his arms in the form of a cross, but the image is striking.

Now, after a long time had passed, one night a pious custodian,[18] one who deserved to see the sight, was going out to see if the time for the liturgy had arrived. As he was going along, he found that humble one in a cruciform position praying while everyone was asleep. He saw this not once or twice but many times during long nights. Then one night that custodian went and stood by him and interrogated him, 'Where do you come from?' and 'What is your occupation?' At first the blessed one did not return an answer to the custodian who was asking him. Finally, it was dragged out of him by the violence of the petition, and he answered and said to him, 'Hey, why are you interrogating me about these things, man? Ask those around you. From them you can learn who I am and where I am from, for I am one of them'. But the custodian could not bear to leave this astonishing (person) uninvestigated. For his mind was afire. He took an oath and put himself under a curse not to leave him alone and not to go away from him until he learned the truth about him. But the Man of God was in torment because he feared the oath and the curse, as he surely was not a heretic,[19] and he consented to reveal the truth to the custodian. But he also exacted an oath from the custodian not to reveal [it] to anyone while he was alive. Then he revealed everything to him as he said, 'That Christian who came some time ago seeking a man was my servant, and he was seeking me'. The custodian, when he heard these things, entreated him greatly and besought him to live with him. When he would not consent, he left him. From then on, that custodian, although he had been doing his work well,[20] improved himself[21] by austere practices. He trained his body[22] more than previously until even

[18]Greek παραμονάριος.

[19]Amiaud translates: 'because he was not fond of quarrels'; Mcleod: 'and also because of his dislike of disputes'. The sentence in fact explains why the Man of God fears the oath. In a world where oaths and curses were seen as bringing about what is cursed, the Man of God fears that the curse will fall from God on the custodian if he does not learn who the Man of God is. If the custodian does not find out who the Man of God is, he will be liable to the curse.

[20]Taking MS ܪܚܝܩ, rather than Amiaud ܠܚܝܩ.

[21]Reading MS ܐܝܟ, rather than Amiaud ܐܝܟ.

[22]Literally, 'stretched out his limb'.

his appearance bore witness to his austere practices as he said to himself, 'If this one who used to live in great luxury does these things, what ought we wretches not do for our redemption?'

Now after a long time, the blessed godly humble one became sick and fell between the columns. The custodian, as he passed here and there and did not see the saint as usual, sought for him diligently. When he found [the blessed one], he entreated him to come into his house with him and be taken care of because of his sickness, but [the blessed one] did not want to do so. So [the custodian] said to him, 'After you are well again, I will let you return to your customs'. But he did not consent. The custodian then said to him, 'Well then, I will bring you to the place for strangers'.[23] After a great deal of persuasion, [the blessed one] just barely consented, while he exacted from [the custodian] an oath to do nothing more for him than [was done] for strangers. [The custodian] lifted him up and carried him there, and he visited him constantly. But God, who always works the will of those who fear him, completed the length of the saint's life, and finished his crown.[24] He protected his humility for him even after his death. For on the day that he was to leave this world for his eternal dwelling, an obstacle arose for the custodian, and he was unable to go as usual to visit the humble one. When the blessed one gave up his spirit, immediately those of the place for strangers, as is their custom, took him out without any fanfare on a stretcher to where they bury strangers hurriedly.

When those who were to bury him had left and had gone a distance, the custodian came and asked after him. When he learnt that he was dead and they had left to bury him, he immediately began to mourn and to groan greatly. He ran to the saintly bishop Rabbula and fell at his feet calling out and saying, 'I beseech you, my lord, remember me and have pity on me'. (Now the light of Bishop Rabbula's bodily eyes was still unimpaired.) Then he and those with him quieted the custodian from calling out and they

---

[23]Greek ξενοδοχεῖον. It has the meaning of 'hospital', but I have kept the literal meaning because of the significance of 'stranger' in the text.

[24]Literally, his garland of victory: a common metaphor for attaining heaven.

asked him, 'What is the cause of this bellowing?' So he told him everything that had happened and besought earnestly that that clean and pure body be honored with great honor and pomp,[25] and be laid in a special place.

The bishop was astonished when he heard these things. Ablaze with fire because he was zealous for virtuous deeds, he at once ordered that they go to where the saint had been taken for burial. Lo and behold, as they were on their way, those porters who had buried him met them as they were coming from where they had buried the victor. When asked 'Where did you bury that stranger?', they told them, 'With his fellow strangers'. The bishop and those with him took those porters along with them to point out the grave. When they arrived at the grave, the bishop ordered that it be opened again, and he and his associates with the porters entered to see the corpse and take it to be honored. They looked, and they saw that the rags[26] in which the saint had been wrapped were laid by themselves in position, but there was no body. Astonished, they sought the corpse throughout the entire burial area, but they did not find it. Only the rags. Great amazement and trembling seized them for a long time. The bishop, when he recovered his composure, said, 'Let us pray'. As he prayed, the holy Rabbula wept and said, 'From henceforth, may the Lord keep me far away from any other business than only to grant relief diligently to strangers. For who knows whether there are many like this saint who delight in abasement, but are nobles to God in their souls, not recognized by people[27] because of their abasement'. From then on the holy lord Rabbula took great pains and was in charge of the strangers.

Consequently,[28] with much diligence he was always multiplying his gifts for the poor and for strangers, and in his speech he was urging the love of strangers. For he desisted from constructing many buildings and turned away from concern for transitory

---

[25]These two words were used to describe how he was sent to school by his parents.

[26]He is earlier described (fol. 123r, col 2) as dressed in 'shameful rags'.

[27]The MS, which has ܢܝܫܝ, is rightly emended by Amiaud to ܢܝܫܝ.

[28]Follow manuscript ܐܬܘܠܝܚܡܒ, not Amiaud ܐܬܘܠܝܚܡܘ.

things. Only for orphans and for widows did he take heed, and he was solicitous for the unfortunate and for strangers. He was solicitous and cared not only for those of his own city, but he also busied himself on behalf of strangers in far-off cities and distant regions. He did not neglect to support them with his gifts so that he might share in God's blessing for those who have mercy. As he began, so the blessed Rabbula ended in the love of strangers.

Now this narrative about the man of God which we told above was publicly proclaimed by that custodian who was the friend of the blessed one. It was also written down by him for a record. For he took care and interrogated the saint with oaths and curses and [the saint] made known to him all his former exalted life and his later abased life and did not conceal anything from him.

Here ends the narrative which is about the man of God.

THE MAN OF GOD

EXPANDED SYRIAC VERSION

HERE IS A LIFE of the same man of God, written at Rome, which recounts his divine way of life and his leaving this world.

Now the life which we told above about the man of God was published by the custodian, who was the friend of the blessed one. But later, after a long time, another Life about this same re-markable man came to us. It dealt with his way of life in Rome, the city where the parents of the blessed one lived. Beyond those things which happened in Edessa and were told by the custodian, it described different events which took place after his death and burial, and the search in the burial ground, his departure—which God knows how it happened—and his arrival in Rome. For the custodian who wrote his life narrated what he learned from the blessed one. But the faithful in Rome wrote the narrative about him, being unaware of the story of his death in Edessa. This happened because, perhaps, the blessed one was not aware how his death was reverenced in Edessa, or perhaps they had not received the story about him from Edessa. They did not write about what they did not know. But this is from the document which they found in the hand of the blessed one at his death [in Rome]. Perhaps this is what he had in mind when he was ill in Edessa, and God did for him in accordance with his desire and in accordance with the supplication of his parents, who were ceaselessly asking God to see their son before their death. So God, in his graciousness, brought it about both that his virtue

27

was not known to human beings during his lifetime, and that his parents were not deprived of a reply to their request to see their son and then die.

This is how those in Rome wrote the story of what happened after his departure from the grave in Edessa and his arrival among them.

When the man of God saw that he was beginning to be known to the people in Edessa, he fled from there and came to Laodicea. When he found a ship bound for Tarsus, he boarded it, saying, 'I am going to Tarsus, to the church of Saint Paul, where I am not known by the people of the city'. Once he had boarded the ship, it was seized by a vehement wind and driven to the blessed one's homeland, the city of Rome. When the blessed one left the ship, he said, 'The Lord God lives, as it has happened that I have arrived at my homeland. No longer shall I be a burden to anyone, but I will go to my parents' house, for today I will not be recognized even by them'. As he left the ship to go there, he said, 'Henceforth, [my] guide is the Lord and may this saying be confirmed by signs'.

He left and went to his parents' house, and he ran into his father as he came from the court with his retinue. The blessed one bowed to him, and said, 'Servant of God, deal kindly with me, poor as I am and a stranger. Let me be in your house, and I will be satisfied with the crumbs which fall from your table,[1] and to be with your household slaves. For it is said, "Whoever gives to the poor, lends to God".[2] May the holy God give and bestow to you the kingdom of heaven. May he bless also whomever you have far from home, and may he accomplish the hope of such a one'.

When his father heard him speak about one far from home, he was greatly moved in his charity to accept him as a servant. For he recalled his only son and that he did not know what had happened to him. At once his father took him and led him to his home, and said to all his servants, 'Whoever of you is willing to serve the stranger, as the Lord God lives, will be set free and will receive from my household property for himself. Moreover, set up his bed and place it in my palace where I enter and leave,

[1]Mt 15:27 || Mk 7:28.
[2]Prov 19:17.

so that I always see him when I enter and leave. Let no one be deprived of his food in order that the stranger may eat, but, by my order, what he needs will come from my own table'. They obeyed. But, when it was evening, the slaves afflicted him and beat and mocked him. They committed many other things like this against him, as they kicked and battered him. When these things were being done to him, he did not become angry. He reflected upon that saying of the Gospel which says, 'Whoever strikes you upon your right cheek, turn to him the other'.[3] The Man of God[4] knew that what happened to him came from the instigation of Satan and that enemy's war against virtue. All the more gladly and readily he endured them, [and with much patience he accepted what came upon him]. For the Holy Spirit was his guide.

For seventeen years, the man of God stayed in his parents' house in utter abasement and poverty while they were not aware who he was. When the time for the putting off of his body and his departure from the world arrived, the Man of God said to the boy who served him, 'My brother, go and bring me paper and ink'. The boy went and brought him paper and ink. The blessed one sat and wrote down all the way of life which he had lived, from the day he left his parents' house up till that very day. He recorded agreements between him and his mother and father, and those spoken by him to his bride when she was sitting in the bridal chamber and when, as they were wrapped in a covering of purple silk, he gave her the ring and the bridal veil. He wrote down all his way of life which he had lived after this. After he departed this world, his parents would know, from the details which he set down, that he was their son.

Then, one day—that is, on the Sunday of Holy Week[5]—as the archbishop, Innocent,[6] was in the church and the god-fearing emperors in the city of Rome, after the celebration of the divine mysteries and after the communion of the people, a voice

---

[3] Mt 5:39.

[4] Literally, 'the son of the man of God'.

[5] The Sunday before Easter.

[6] The manuscript reads ܐܝܠܘܣ, but Amiaud suggests rightly that one should emend it not to ܐܝܠܛܘܣ, that is, Anacletus, but to ܐܝܢܘܣ, that is, Innocent.

was heard from the center of the altar, saying, 'Come to me, all you who labor and carry heavy burdens, and I will refresh you'.[7] Amazement and fear seized everyone. They fell on their faces and cried out, 'Lord, have mercy on us'. They earnestly entreated God. Again a voice was heard a second time, saying, 'Seek the man of God, and let him pray for Rome. For, at dawn on Friday, God will take his charge from him'. The voice was heard again a third time, saying, 'Seek the pure body of the man of God in the house of Euphemianus'. On the Thursday evening, all the people, the god-fearing emperors, Innocent the archbishop, and all the senators gathered together. They came, carrying the life-giving cross, in which there was part of the precious tree of the crucifixion. They went to the holy Church of Peter and Paul, as they sought in love and affection that holy body which had been revealed to them. The emperors, the leading bishops, and all the senators entered the Church of the holy Peter and fell on their faces. They earnestly entreated the Holy Spirit that the holy body might be revealed to them, and, with a clamor, they asked the help of Mary, our Lady, the holy Mother of God, and of the disciples for the world, Peter and Paul, who lay before them in a reliquary. The pious[8] emperors and the archbishops rose up and turned their faces heavenwards towards God. The divine goodness appeared to them from on high and said, 'He whom you seek is in the house of Euphemianus'. Then the pious emperors and the archbishops turned and called Euphemianus to them and said, 'Such a grace is in your house, and you did not reveal it to us?' But Euphemianus said to them, 'As the Lord God lives, I did not know'.

Then immediately, he hurriedly sent and summoned his head slave and said to him, 'Do you know anyone from your group in whom there is grace such as this?' That slave, glancing heavenwards, said to them, as he swore by our Lord Jesus and by the life-bringing cross (upon which he was hung in the flesh for the love of the human race), 'I do not know anyone in whom there is such grace as this. (For I do not lie so as to lose life, and I do not hide such a gift as this, which belongs to everyone. For our

[7]Mt 11:28.
[8]Literally, 'faithful, believing'.

Lord said in the Gospel, "You shall not swear",[9] and again, "What shall a man inherit, if he obtains all the world but loses his soul? Or what shall he give in exchange for his soul?"[10])'[11] Then the pious emperors and the archbishops and all the senate gave orders to go to the home of Euphemianus, and there search for the precious body. Immediately, Euphemianus ordered his household slaves to prepare thrones and seats for the officials of the faithful and honored emperors, and for the leading priests, and to prepare lamps and fragrant, sweet-smelling spices with which to receive the emperors, as was customary. The emperors and the archbishops left and came to the house of Euphemianus. The mother of the man of God spread a clean veil in the window, and was looking out of the window and saying, 'What is this turbulence? What is this commotion? What is being talked about?' The espoused bride rose up secretly and was also looking out and listening to what was being said.

Then, he who served the man of God approached and said before his master, 'Might you be seeking that poor man whom you charged me to serve? For we notice many and great virtues and glorious signs in him. From one Sunday to the next, after he received the divine and ineffable mysteries, he ate two ounces of bread, and so remained fasting all week. All his life-time, he spent his nights without sleep. Also, many times some of the slaves beat and mocked him, and he endured whatever they did to him in great gladness and much cheerfulness'. When Euphemianius, his father, heard this, he went close to where the man of God was lying. When he bent towards him, he did not hear a word or a moan from him. When he uncovered his face, he saw that it was shining like the face of an angel, and that he held a paper in his hand. When the father wanted to take it from the man of God to see what was written on it, the man of God did not agree to give it to him. Then Euphemianius approached the pious emperors and said to them, 'We have found him whom you seek'. He began straightaway to tell them how he had received him seventeen years ago. He also informed them, 'He holds a paper in

---

[9]Mt 5:34.
[10]Mt 16:26.
[11]Amiaud considers the verses in brackets a later interpolation.

his hand, but does not wish to give it to us'. As soon as the pious emperors and the archbishops and all the people heard [this], the emperors ordered a decorated couch to be placed in the center [of the assembly] and the venerable body to be brought and placed on it. The pious emperors and the archbishops and all the people rose up and entreated that dying one placed before them to give them that paper in his hand. But it was not given to them. Then the emperors and the archbishops came close to him and said to him, 'Even if we are sinners, we are the emperors, and this[12] is the father of the inhabited earth. Give us this paper in your hand so that we can see what is written on it'. Straightaway, he gave the paper to them. When they received it, they gave it to the honorable Aetius, head record-keeper of the holy church.

As [Aetius] was reading the paper, as soon as the man of God's father heard the story, he recognized his son. He rose up swiftly from the couch on which he was sitting. He rent his garments, tore his hair, and scattered his grey hairs on the ground. He ran and cast himself on his son's chest; he wept bitterly and said, 'Woe to me, my lord. Why have you acted in this way towards me? You have filled my heart with sadness and grief'. He groaned and said, 'I feel abandoned, deprived of you. I saw you lying there and I heard your voice, but you did not reveal and tell me that you were the one I hope to see again, so that, when I recognized you, I might be comforted by you, and you might restore my life. Woe to me, my beloved son. Woe to me, a poor wretch. What shall I do? Or what shall I say? How shall my heart not be filled with groans, with sorrow and sadness? I see my only son dying. He lies on a bed and he does not speak to me'.

Then his mother, when she heard, set forth like a lioness as she leaves her den and hides her presence, and she came into the midst of the assembly. A great crowd had assembled at her home. She cried out and asked her husband to give her space so that she might fall upon her son. When she came near him, she wept with bitter groans, and said, 'Woe to me, my beloved son,

---

[12] The reference here is not clear. Is it another way of describing the emperors? Or is it a reference to God? The grammar would seem to suggest that the emperors are speaking of their position.

fed from my breasts, the hope of my eyes and the comfort of my life'. She threw herself upon his precious and holy chest, and lovingly kissed him and said in sorrow, 'Why have you acted so towards me, O my son? You filled my heart with grief and great sadness. You have added pain upon the former pain, because I have seen you lying in suffering and misery among the slaves in your father's house, and I did not know that it was you. You hid, and you did not reveal yourself to me, that I might recognize you and be consoled in you, and that you might restore life to me'. Her eyes were continuously shedding tears like fountains.

Then the bride, clad in black, came running to him, calling out and groaning as she said, 'Woe to me, my lord. Why have you acted so towards me? For look how you have filled me with great suffering. Woe to me. I see my turtle dove who alone among men was mine.[13] From now on, how will I be able to see you? For whom shall I wait?'

The emperors and all the people were amazed. Then the sick and the paralyzed came near that holy body, and they were healed. Those who were dumb spoke, the blind saw, lepers were cleansed, and demons banished.

Then the pious emperors carried the couch on which he lay so that they might be sanctified by his holy body. All the people pressed around the couch, so that they were not able to walk. The emperors and the archbishops ordered that much gold and silver be thrown on the road so that all the people would go after their gold [and give space to walk. But the people could not be persuaded even to look at the gold][14] but their whole desire was fastened on the holy one, that they might touch his body. With difficulty, the emperors were able to carry it to the holy Church of Peter. There they celebrated him for seven days, while his father and mother and his bride were in mourning. Afterwards, the faithful emperors ordered a coffin made of gold and precious stones. When it was ready, they placed the precious body of the holy one in it. Suddenly, that coffin discharged a pleasant smelling

[13]Cf. Song 2:14,16.

[14]The words in brackets are lacking in this manuscript, but perhaps fell out through scribal error.

myrrh. Everyone crowded to take some of the myrrh. To everyone who took some of it came much benefit in the grace of our Lord Jesus Christ. Along with him to the Father with the Holy Spirit be praise, now and always for ages and ages. Amen. Here ends the account of the man of God.

THE LIFE AND LIFESTYLE
OF THE MAN OF GOD, ALEXIUS

GREEK VERSION

E WAS THE SON of the Senate leader when there were emperors in Rome. His parents urged him to marry a maiden from the palace, and the emperor was fond of him because he was the only son of his parents. As the time for his marriage drew near, on the day before the marriage the young man said to himself, 'What is this world? Truly, this way of life is vain; rather, blessed are those who serve God'. As he pondered these things, he said to his best man, 'Let us go to the dock by the river'. For a river passes through the city of Rome; the sea is eighteen miles away, and ships go up by means of the river.

When they had gone down, he dismissed his slaves and his best man. On hearing the sailors cry out, 'Who wants to sail to the east?', he asked them where they sought [to go]. They said to him, 'Seleucia in Syria'. Then he boarded the ship with them and immediately they set sail.

When they arrived in Seleucia, he disembarked and immediately sold his expensive garments and the rings which he carried. Besides his own rings, [he also carried]¹ rings he had given as passage money. All the rest he distributed to the poor. Then he

---

¹The grammar here is difficult. One can either leave out τούς δακτυλλίους αὐτοῦ, as Rösler suggests, or, as I have done, take the phrase as an editor's comment to ensure that there were rings enough not to defraud the sailors. I have taken the verb ἐφόρη—which can mean 'he wore' as well as 'he carried'—to govern this editorial comment as well as the previous clause.

departed for Edessa, the city of Syria. Collecting rags wherever
he found them, he made himself a cloak. He used to sit all day
among the poor. When the sun set, he would sit near the door of
the church of the holy Mother of God. Stretching out his hand,
he would receive alms from those entering to pray. From them,
he would acquire twelve *obols;* with ten *lepta* he would buy some
bread, and with the other two *lepta* some vegetables.² He was
content with these, and, indeed, he suffered greatly.

Now, a great disturbance had immediately arisen in the city
of Rome and in the palace: what had happened to the senator's
son? The whole city mourned with his father, the Senate's leader.
There was great and inconsolable mourning in the Senate and
among the prefects. The emperor sent into every region to seek
the senator's son. They even came to the city where he was, but
they did not recognize him because he had so lowered himself,
sitting among the poor and those dressed in rags.

Now the custodian of the church of the most holy Mother of
God was a holy man, fasting every day of his life. One night he
saw someone in a dream telling him, 'Go out to the portico of
the Mother of the Lord and you will see a slave of God. He eats
bread and a few vegetables after sunset, and drinks water from
the pool. He kneels and prays throughout the whole night, but,
when day comes, he sits among his brothers, that is, the poor'.
On seeing the dream the custodian thought that it was an idle
oddity of his imagination. But again, on the following night, he
had a similar vision; and again he disregarded what was in the
vision. Then, on the third night, a fearsome man appeared to him,
saying, 'Do you not wish to obey me and derive profit? Just go,
and do not delay'. So [the custodian] went out in the night and
found him praying, just as it had been indicated to him. [The
custodian] asked him, 'Who are you, honored brother? What is
your way of life?' He said to him, 'I am a human being, a beggar
who receives alms'. When the custodian had pressured him a great

---

²*Obols* and *lepta* were very small coins. A *drachma,* a greek silver coin, was
roughly equivalent to a *denarius,* or a laborer's daily wage (see Mt 20:2). An *obol*
is equal to one-sixth of a *drachma,* and a *lepton,* roughly one-twentieth of an
obol, was worth even less (see Lk 21:2, for the widow's offering).

deal, saying, 'God has shown me your way of life', then the man of God said, 'Let us go into the baptistery of the church. Promise me as I wish, and I will tell you who I am'.

When they arrived at the baptistery, he said to [the custodian], 'Swear to me that you will tell no one during my lifetime anything of what is said by me, or I will not tell you anything about myself. Even so, I will not tell you my name'. Then the custodian gave him complete assurance, just as he requested. So the man of God said to him, 'I am the son of a certain senator, one of the leaders of the Senate of Rome, the only son of my father. Now, I was about to be married to a woman from a leading senatorial family. With the day of my marriage imminent, I reflected that what I had [were] the transitory things of this world. Saying nothing to anyone, I left everyone for the sake of God. I came into this city and have been in it twelve years. I made this tunic for myself from rags, and I sit the entire day among the poor. When evening comes, I sit down at the door of the church and stretch out my hand and receive alms. From what I receive, I keep twelve *lepta* for my own account, and the remainder I give to the poor. From the twelve *lepta,* I buy some bread with ten *lepta* and vegetables with two *lepta,* and from this I live. I drink water from the pool flowing in the middle of the city. When darkness comes, I bend my knees, and I pray to God for the entire night. When the emperor sent orders throughout every city, the slaves of my father were seeking me. They even came to this city, and I received alms from them, not only once but twice. They did not discover me, but I recognized them'.

On hearing this, the custodian glorified God, and he besought [the man of God], saying, 'Come into the deacon's area. Put down a rush-mat and rest there the night'. But he said to [the custodian], 'Is this what you swore to me?' [The custodian] had no further reply, but left him alone in his way of life. As he saw [the man of God] seated among the poor, he praised God. He certainly did not tell anyone anything about him because of the oath he had sworn to him.

When the twelve years were completed, the man of God fell ill, and he lay afflicted with chill and fever. When the custodian noticed it, the man of God said to him, 'Do [me] a favor, and take me to the place for strangers. Tell them, "Take this stranger, a poor man who came from afar and who is sick". When you come to see me, you should first visit [the other strangers]. Come to me in such a way that no one knows that you are coming on my account'. The custodian did just as he told him, and he delivered him to the place for strangers. He made him rest off by himself near the door on a pallet[3] with a rush-mat. Each day, after celebrating morning service, the custodian used run to the place for strangers. He would look in on the strangers and, when he was leaving, he would also look in on [the man of God] and depart for the church praising God.

Now one day the ruler of the city wanted the custodian on some public business. He sent during the night and placed him in the garrison and kept him for three days. As God willed, the man of God died. Released from the praetorium around nine o'clock in the morning, the custodian immediately went speeding to the place for strangers, as was his custom. Not finding the man of God, he said to those there, 'Where is the man who lay [there]?' They told him, 'They went out to the strangers' burial place to bury him'. On hearing this, he tore his garments and went to the church, crying aloud and saying, 'Help, brothers'. Then the bishop enquired, 'What is this?' When the custodian told him the whole story about the man of God, the bishop immediately took the clergy and came with the entire city to the strangers' burial place. [The bishop decided that] the corpse ought to be conducted with prayers and psalmody and be buried in some area of the church to which the custodian belonged. When they arrived at the strangers' burial place, the servants of the place for strangers met them, carrying only the bier. They had buried his holy corpse. When [the bishop] asked where they had laid him, [they answered] him that, when they had found an empty spot, they wrapped him in the rush mat with the rags he was wearing and laid him to rest.

---

[3]Rösler has read εἰς τὸν κρείατον. She translates this: *auf einem Lager*. I have not been able to track down the word κρείατος. I suggest one should read κράβατον, which seems a possible reading of the actual manuscript, and makes sense.

RABBULA

RABBULA OF EDESSA

R ABBULA WAS BISHOP of Edessa from 411/412 to 435/436 CE, and was an important player in the controversy which erupted between Nestorius, bishop of Constantinople, and Cyril, bishop of Alexandria, over the person of Christ. Rabbula, in contrast to most of the bishops connected with the patriarchal see of Antioch, sided with Cyril of Alexandria. In this, he was opposed by an important member of the Edessene clergy, Hiba, who was to succeed him as bishop of Edessa. We are fortunate to possess a *Life* of Rabbula, and it is this which is translated here. Besides the *Life,* there are various sources containing information about him: ascribed to him are rules for clergy, monks, covenanters and lay-people; liturgical hymns, some of which may be authentic; letters from a correspondence between himself and Cyril of Alexandria; and a sermon he is said to have preached in Constantinople. Mention of him is also made in various church documents.

HIS EARLY LIFE UNTIL HIS ORDINATION AS BISHOP

Rabbula was born in Qenneshrin, also called Chalcis ad Belum,[1] the greek name of which derives from the greek city of Chalcis in Euboea. It lay about forty kilometers south-west of Aleppo

[1]On Chalcis ad Belum, see Paul Monceaux and Léonce Brossé, 'Chalcis ad Belum: Notes sur l'histoire et les ruines de la ville', *Syria* 6 (1925) 339–350.

41

(Beroea), one hundred twenty kilometers north-east of Apamea, and about ninety kilometers south-east of Antioch. It was situated in a fertile zone bordering on the desert, in a region dominated by greek cities. The neo-platonist philosopher, Iamblichus, had been born there, and, after teaching in Rome, he returned to the region and resided at Apamea. In the 370s, Jerome, having moved near there to live as a hermit, found one had to use a 'barbarian' speech, presumably Syriac.[2]

Rabbula's family was wealthy, his father a pagan, his mother a Christian. His father, as a member of the wealthy elite of the city, functioned as a priest at pagan ceremonies. We do not know to which god he prayed, probably the god Bel. The *Life* tells us he took part in the sacrifices the emperor Julian had offered on his march against the Persians. Julian left Antioch on 5 March 363. He passed through Beroea (Aleppo), where he sacrificed a white bull to Zeus,[3] before moving on to Hierapolis, which he reached on 9 March. Paul Peeters has argued that the emperor could not have passed through Rabbula's birthplace, and asked whether it was at Beroea or later at Carrhae that Rabbula's father would have officiated.[4] As Glen Bowersock has noted:

> But Chalcis is not at all far from Aleppo and was connected to it by road. A wealthy, pagan priest in Neoplatonist Chalcis would have had every reason to make the short trip up to Aleppo to see the world's first Neoplatonist emperor and Iamblichus' spiritual descendant.[5]

---

[2] Jerome, *Letters* 5.1; 7.1-2; 15.1. See J. N. D. Kelly, *Jerome. His Life, Writings and Controversies* (New York: Harper & Row, 1975) 46–47.

[3] Julian the Emperor, *Letter to Libanius,* 399d. Letter 58 in *The Works of the Emperor Julian,* Loeb Classical Library; trans. Wilmer Cave Wright (New York: Putnams, 1923) 3.200–202. Letter 98 in *L'Empereur Julien. Oeuvres Complètes,* trans. J. Bidez (Paris: Les Belles Lettres, 1924) 1.180.

[4] Paul Peeters, 'La vie de Rabboula, évêque d'Édesse', *Recherches d'histoire et de philologie orientales* (Brussels: Bollandists, 1951) 141.

[5] Glen W. Bowersock, 'The Syriac Life of Rabbula and Syrian Hellenism', in Tomas Hägg and Philip Rousseau, edd., *Greek Biography and Panegyric in Late Antiquity* (Berkeley: University of California Press, 2000) 261.

As a son of a leading citizen of Chalcis, Rabbula received an excellent education in Greek, the language of power,[6] and was being groomed by his father for a position of power. He was later given a distinguished honorary governorship by an emperor, a recognition that he was an influential local citizen.[7] By this time, it would seem, his father was dead, as no further mention is made of him.

Rabbula's Conversion

Rabbula's conversion to Christianity began when, on a visit to some of his estates, he witnessed a healing miracle by a christian hermit, Abraham. When Rabbula told his mother about his new-found interest in Christianity, she led him to Eusebius, bishop of Chalcis ad Belum, who sent him to Acacius, bishop of Beroea. The two bishops had been pupils in the same monastery. Both had been consecrated bishop by Eusebius of Samosata,[8] sometime in the late 370s after his return from exile under the emperor Valens. Both had been present at the Council of Constantinople in 381.[9] While almost nothing is known about Eusebius of Chalcis, we know more about Acacius. He had been a disciple of Julian Sabas,[10] and was consecrated bishop of Beroea in 378. In 381, during the schism among the anti-Arian parties in Antioch, Acacius consecrated Flavian as bishop of Antioch, an ordination opposed by the churches in Egypt and the West, especially Rome which broke off communion with him. Later, he took the side of Theophilus, bishop of Alexandria, against John Chrysostom,

---

[6]Sebastian P. Brock, 'Greek and Syriac in Late Antique Syria', in A. K. Bowman and G. Woolf, edd., *Literacy and Power in the Ancient World* (Cambridge: Cambridge University Press, 1994) 149–160.

[7]See Bowersock, 'Syriac Life', 261–262.

[8]Theodoret, *Historia Ecclesiastica* 5.4.

[9]Mansi, 3:568.

[10]Theodoret, *Historia Religiosa* 2; PG 82:1313.

bishop of Constantinople, at the Synod of the Oak in 403 CE,[11] and he stirred up trouble in Constantinople against John in 404.[12] Later he would be restored to communion with Rome, partly through the mediation of Alexander, bishop of Antioch, and partly because he inserted the name of John Chrysostom on to the ditypchs. In his old age, Acacius was called upon to reconcile John, bishop of Antioch, and Cyril, bishop of Alexandria, after the First Council of Ephesus. This council had been called by emperor Theodosius II to reconcile differing expressions of how the divine and the human were united in the one person of Jesus Christ. Far from succeeding, the council had split between followers of Cyril, bishop of Alexandria, and supporters of Nestorius, bishop of Constantinople, led by John, bishop of Antioch. Both sides had hurled excommunications at each other. The efforts of Acacius resulted in the Formula of Reunion in 433.[13] This future major dispute between Antioch and Alexandria is not at all evident in this early period of Rabbula's life. Rabbula would side with Cyril of Alexandria against John of Antioch, but at this stage of his life, Acacius and Eusebius sent the newly converted Rabbula to the sanctuary of the martyrs Cosmas and Damian at Cyrrhus. The later bishop of Cyrrhus, Theodoret, would be an adversary of Cyril of Alexandria but he would also later sign the Formula of Reunion.

On Rabbula's return to Beroea from Cyrrhus, the two bishops sent him to the solitary Marcian and then to Abraham. Both ascetics lived near Chalcis, and both are known from Theodoret's *History of the Monks*.[14] Marcian probably died around 390, and

---

[11]Photius *Bibliotheca* 59. At the Synod of the Oak, held not far from Constantinople, a council met to resolve issues between John Chrysostom, bishop of Constantinople, and Theophilus, bishop of Alexandria. Theophilus shrewdly accused John of the Origenist heresy, and John was eventually exiled by the emperor.

[12]Palladius, *Dialogues* 9–10.

[13]For a full discussion, see John A. McGuckin, *St. Cyril of Alexandria: The Christological Controversy. Its History, Theology and Texts* (Leiden: Brill, 1994). The Formula of Reunion, also known as Cyril's Letter to John of Antioch, is found on pp. 343–348.

[14]Theodoret *HR* 3; 3.17; English translation by R. M. Price, *Theodoret of Cyrrhus: A History of the Monks of Syria*, III; III.17, CS 88 (Kalamazoo, Cistercian Publications, 1985) 37–48, 44–45.

both Acacius of Beroea and Eusebius of Chalcis, as bishops, are said to have visited him.[15] Marcian's reputation for piety was so great that burial shrines were built for him in Cyrrhus, Chalcis, and other places before his death; he fought against Apollinaris and other heretics, and was an advocate of the Council of Nicæa.[16] Abraham is often identified with the monk described by Theodoret who later became bishop of Carrhae.[17] Theodoret, however, states that Abraham lived near the city of Emesa,[18] which is quite a distance south of Chalcis ad Belum. It is more likely, I suspect, that it is the Abraham with whom Marcian had a disagreement over the time for celebrating Easter.[19]

In describing Rabbula's conversion, then, the author of the *Life* has provided him with a fascinating ascetic genealogy: a well-known monk and opponent of heretics in Marcian, an ascetic like Abraham and Bishop Acacius, 'celebrated for great prudence and sanctity of life',[20] who had overseen the reconciliation between Cyril of Alexandria and John of Antioch over the person of Christ.

Rabbula's Baptism

The author also presents a model Rabbula after his conversion. First, Rabbula makes a pilgrimage to Jerusalem 'to see the holy places'. The fourth century saw an increase in the number of pilgrims traveling to 'the Holy Land'.[21] As Jerome had written: 'I entered Jerusalem, I saw a host of marvels, and with the judgement

---

[15] Theodoret *HR* 3.11; CS 88:42.

[16] Theodoret *HR* 3.17–18; CS 88:44–45.

[17] Theodoret *HR* 17; CS 88:120–125.

[18] Theodoret *HR* 17.3; CS 88:121.

[19] Theodoret *HR* 3.17; CS 88:44–45. There were, however, many monks named Abraham.

[20] Theodoret *HE* 5.27.

[21] See E. D. Hunt, *Holy Land Pilgrimage in the Later Roman Empire (AD 312–460)* (Oxford: Clarendon, 1982); Robert L. Wilken, *The Land Called Holy: Palestine in Christian History and Thought* (New Haven: Yale University Press, 1992).

of my eyes I verified things of which I had previously learned by report'.[22] Georgia Frank has excellently captured the power of such pilgrimages:

> The physical sense of sight was anything but passive in antiquity; it was a form of physical contact between the viewer and the object. For the pilgrim, that gaze extended to the biblical past. The physical sense of sight triggered the 'eye of faith', which in turn perceived a past biblical event as a present reality. . . . Sight and touch remained discrete, but in late-antique Christian piety their functions converged to create the conditions for a biblical realism. . . . That haptic function allowed vision to reach into the past and sanctify the present.[23]

This re-capturing of the biblical past as present is also linked by the author of Rabbula's *Life* with themes prominent in syriac baptismal traditions. Rabbula is said to go down into the Jordan river to be baptized, wearing the robe customary for spiritual brides and, when he is baptized, this robe shines. Sebastian Brock has beautifully explained this by writing that the robe of glory which Adam and Eve lost in Paradise when they sinned, and had to put on garments of skin,[24] is restored at baptism.[25] Brock further explains how the robe of baptism also represents the wedding garment mentioned in Matthew 22:12.[26]

In the account of Rabbula's baptism the combination of the biblical realism (to use Georgia Frank's phrase) in the pilgrimage and the biblical symbolism powerfully shows Rabbula as someone imbued with the Holy Spirit and enmeshed in the life of Christ. One also sees how important liturgy was for this author, a theme to which we will return later.

[22]Jerome, *Apologia aduersus libros Rufini* 3.22, as translated in Kelly, *Jerome*, 124.

[23]Georgia Frank, *The Memory of the Eyes. Pilgrims to Living Saints in Christian Late Antiquity* (Berkeley: University of California Press, 2000) 133.

[24]Gen 3:21.

[25]Sebastian P. Brock, *The Holy Spirit in the Syrian Baptismal Tradition,* The Syrian Churches Series, 9 (Bronx, New York—available at John XXIII Center, Fordham University, 1979) 48–50.

[26]Brock, *Holy Spirit,* 50–52.

Another version of Rabbula's conversion, found in the Life of Alexander Akoimetos 9–23,[27] presents Rabbula as a prominent city councillor and ardent idol-worshiper, and Chalcis as a city rife with idolatrous practices. Alexander burnt down the city's main temple and brought Rabbula to belief by an Elijah-style miraculous fire. After several tests and further miracles by Alexander, Rabbula was baptized at a nearby martyrion outside the city. At his baptism, his cloak was covered from top to bottom with crosses. While there are some points in which the two versions connect—Rabbula as a prominent city official, the miracle at baptism—the differences are so great that Blum's suggestion that this second version was composed to link Alexander with the more renowned Rabbula, and so enhance Alexander's prestige, seems likely.[28]

Rabbula as Monk

Rabbula, too, decided to follow literally the Gospel passage that, to be a disciple, one had to abandon all possessions.[29] For Rabbula, a married man with children, discipleship entailed leaving not only his estates but also his family. His mother and wife took 'the yoke of Christ'—perhaps becoming members of the daughters of the covenant.[30] His children he entrusted to monasteries,

[27]The *Life* was edited by E. de Stoop: *Vie d'Alexandre l'acémète,* PO 6:641–705 (Paris, 1911). An english translation can be found in Elizabeth Theokritoff, 'The Life of Our Holy Father Alexander', *Aram* 3 (1991) 293–318; and in Daniel Caner, *Wandering, Begging Monks: Spiritual Authority and the Promotion of Monasticism in Late Antiquity* (Berkeley: University of California Press, 2002) 249–280.

[28]Blum, *Rabbula,* 36–39.

[29]Lk 14:33.

[30]Within the Syriac speaking church existed committed ascetics, male and female, called the *bnay Qyāmā* and *bnat Qyāmā,* 'sons and daughters of the covenant'. Much of the extant early syriac christian literature was written for such covenanters. In this covenant were those who lived in a state of virginity and those who, in holiness or consecration, lived in the state of married persons but renounced intercourse.

and thus closed to them the door to the advancement in secular society he had had. In giving all his goods to the poor, he imitated Antony, and he did so explicitly to seek solitude as a monk. Alongside this theme of monastic death the *Life* narrates Rabbula's desire for martyrdom. He and his companion Eusebius traveled to Heliopolis/Baalbek to throw down idols. Heliopolis lay over two hundred kilometers south of Chalcis ad Belum. Paul Peeters has ridiculed the notion that just two men should attempt to destroy the famous temple at Heliopolis,[31] but M. J. Lagrange has rightly noted that the two went, not to destroy the temple, but simply to cause enough disturbance to get themselves killed/martyred.[32] Attacks on pagan temples became routine in the late fourth century, particularly after the edicts of Theodosius I, issued on 24 February and 16 June 391, which first prohibited all sacrifices and then basically closed the temples.[33] For the author, this episode before Rabbula became a bishop foreshadows his later actions as bishop in demolishing four pagan temples and re-using their stones in christian buildings, and importantly links the symbolism of martyr to that of monk.

BISHOP RABBULA

Ordination

Like so many other monks, Rabbula was called to be bishop. Rabbula is shown as carefully overcoming his reluctance. As Michael Gaddis states:

---

[31] Peeters, 'Vie de Rabboula', 145–146.

[33] M. J. Lagrange, 'Bulletin: Nouveau Testament', *RB* 40 (1931) 123–124.

[33] CTheod 16.10.10-11. See Garth Fowden, 'Bishops and Temples in the eastern Roman Empire, A.D. 320–435', *JTS* 29 (1978) 53–78. Also Michael Gaddis, 'There is No Crime for Those Who have Christ: Religious Violence in the Christian Roman Empire', PhD Dissertation, Princeton University, 1999.

If 'authority' is understood as a combination of power and legitimacy, then an appearance of dignified disinterest offers a promising way to legitimize one's exercise of that power. Roman emperors in the first centuries of the Principate were expected to assume imperial power only after a carefully choreographed show of reluctance that might include several public refusals—a practice that came to be imitated by many candidates for Christian episcopacy in the fourth century and after.[34]

Rabbula's Life as Bishop

Once a bishop, Rabbula maintained his ascetic practices. Glen Bowersock concludes his fine essay on Rabbula's early life by stating: 'The author has painted an image of the saint in a realistic landscape'.[35] He also remarks, however, that this may be less true of the description of Rabbula's life in Edessa.[36] Here the view of Hans Drijvers, that the life is 'idealized', may be more appropriate.[37] This becomes clear when one notices how this section is structured:

A. Concerns over his Flock:
  (1) liturgy
  (2) clergy
  (3) Covenanters
  (4) lay people
B. Private Devotions
C. Concerns for the City as a Whole
D. Against Heretics
E. Care for the Poor and Lepers

[34]Gaddis, 'There is No Crime', 271.
[35]Bowersock, 'Syriac Life', 269.
[36]Bowersock, 'Syriac Life', 256, n. 7.
[37]Hans J. W. Drijvers, 'The Man of God of Edessa, Bishop Rabbula and the Urban Poor: Church and Society in the Fifth Century', *Journal of Early Christian Studies* 4 (1996) 242.

Section A sets out how a bishop should treat the members of his own congregation. Of note is the emphasis on the sanctity of the liturgy: those who minister have to be holy in order to deal with the holy mysteries; and liturgical leaders should imitate the liturgy of the angels. By placing the liturgy first in his discussion of Rabbula as bishop, the author stresses through Rabbula that it is the liturgy that binds the community. The *Life* states that at Rabbula's death choirs of deaconesses were present to mourn him. Rabbula's rules for Covenanters enjoin the men to learn psalms and the women *madrashe,*[38] and he himself is credited with having composed several hymns.[39] From Rabbula's letter to Gemillinus,[40] bishop of Perrha, we learn how important the Eucharist was in Rabbula's concept of community. Rabbula wrote this letter against the practice of some monks who did not eat any ordinary food, but celebrated the Eucharist and ate the sanctified elements whenever they wished to eat and drink. In horrified response, Rabbula noted that this would imply a daily eucharistic offering,[41] which suggests that Rabbula's practice was to celebrate the Eucharist once a week for the christian community.[42] In Rabbula's opinion, those who act in this way misunderstand what has happened to the eucharistic elements, and turn 'the holy body, which makes the recipient holy' and 'this living bread which bestows life to whoever drinks it' into ordinary food.[43] The letter shows the

---

[38] Rule 20, in Arthur Vööbus, *Syriac and Arabic Documents Regarding Legislation Relative to Syrian Monasticism* (Stockholm: Etse, 1960) 41.

[39] Peter Bruns ['Bischof Rabbula von Edessa—Dichter und Theologe', in René Lavenant ed., *Symposium Syriacum VII,* Orientalia Christiana Analecta 256 (Rome: Pontifical Oriental Institute, 1998) 195–202] has defended the attribution to Rabbula, while Georg Günther Blum [*Rabbula von Edessa. Der Christ, der Bischof, der Theologe* (Louvain: Secrétariat CSCO, 1969) 205–207] has denied it.

[40] There are two fragments of this letter. Arthur Vööbus edited the longer in *Syriac and Arabic Documents,* 61; the shorter is found in Overbeck, 231–238. The attribution of the letter to Rabbula is shown by Vööbus, 'Solution du problème del'auteur de la "Lettre à Gemillinos, Évêque de Perrhé"', *L'Orient syrien* 7 (1962) 297–306.

[41] Overbeck, 232, lines 5–8.

[42] See Blum, *Rabbula,* 113.

[43] Overbeck, 231, line 22; 232, line 4.

centrality for Rabbula of eucharistic thinking whereby partaking of the Eucharist sanctifies Christians. In this regard, as Blum shows, Rabbula carries on the syriac tradition known through Ephræm's earlier writings.[44]

The idealization of the author surfaces in his discussion of Rabbula's desire to replace all the silver and gold liturgical vessels with less ornate vessels. The author has Rabbula frustrated in his desire, and one can glimpse in this scenario the ideal that is being proposed. The liturgy is to form community, but a tiered community. There is a clear hierarchy of clergy, covenanters, and lay-persons. The discussion in the *Life* is, in many respects, a fleshing-out of the provisions of the rules attributed to Rabbula. Monastic legislation reflects the monastic ideal; Rabbula's dealings with the christian community in the *Life* do the same.

Only after describing the bishop's care for his flock does the author turn to Rabbula's care for his own way of life before going on to touch on his concern for the city of Edessa as a whole. Edessa, as we have seen in the general introduction, was a bustling city on an important trade route. All kinds of people resided there. The author argues that Bishop Rabbula actively attempted to restrain unjust oppression. In reading this section, one does well to recall that it is an idealized description: The holy man can heal or harm, bless or curse. Rabbula certainly was ruthless in his dealings with non-orthodox Christians, destroying the church of the followers of Bardaisan[45] and expelling the Audians[46] from their meeting houses. Yet, when one sees the combination of persuasion through love and compulsion through fear, one must recognize it as a trope. Theodoret of Cyrrhus, writing of Abraham, a monk who was to become a bishop, says:

> Spending the whole day on the lawsuits of those in dispute, some he would persuade to be reconciled with each

---

[44]Blum, *Rabbula,* 111–131.

[45]The followers of Bardaisan were accused by Ephraem of denying the resurrection of the body and following a docetic christology.

[46]A rigorist monastic sect founded in Syria by Audius, a deacon of Edessa. Epiphanius (*Pan* 70) considered them heretics and stated that they held that God's form is literally the same as human beings.

other, while to those who would not obey his gentle teaching he applied compulsion. No wrongdoer went away victorious over justice through audacity; to the wronged party he always accorded the just man's portion, making him invincible and stronger than the one who wanted to wrong him. He was like an excellent physician who always prevents the excess of the humors and contrives the equilibrium of the elements.[47]

The image of the physician is found also in the *Life* of Rabbula, and should not be pressed, as Gaddis does,[48] to show Rabbula as violent. The writer is having the bishop carry out the admonitions found in the Second Letter of Timothy: 'convince, rebuke, and encourage, with the utmost patience in teaching'.[49] The apostle Paul had warned the Corinthians to reform: 'Am I to come to you with a stick, or with love in a spirit of gentleness?'[50] As with the prophet Jeremiah, Rabbula's role is see 'to pluck up and to pull down, to destroy and to overthrow, to build and to plant'.[51]

Rabbula's behavior towards pagans may be more complex than that of a zealous hater and destroyer of pagan temples. The author reports that he had four idol temples destroyed, but the sentence[52] contains an adverb which can have multiple connotations and so is difficult to translate ܪܠܝܐܝܬ: does it mean 'freely', 'violently', or 'with authority'? The first two translations suggest willful tyrannical behavior, which I am not sure the author of the life intended. So I have chosen to translate 'with authority'. In this way, the passage would resonate with the comment of the Edessene Chronicle on Jewish synagogues, discussed below, and would show the bishop acting with imperial authority. One wonders, in fact, whether the temples were still in use or whether they had stood abandoned after the decrees of the emperors

---

[47]Theodoret *HR* 17.8. Translation by R. M. Price, *Theodoret of Cyrrhus: A History of the Monks in Syria,* CS 88:123.

[48]Gaddis, 'There is No Crime', 277–278.

[49]2 Tim 4:2.

[50]1 Cor 4:21.

[51]Jer 1:10.

[52]O 203 line 19; see below, page 101.

which, in 392, suppressed the freedom of the pagan cults,[53] and, in 396, the privileges of the pagan priests.[54] Hans Drijvers[55] has collected evidence to show the persistence of pagan practices in Edessa: when the nun Egeria visited the city in 384, the sanctuary of the goddess Atargatis presumably still stood;[56] an imperial rescript of Theodosius I in 382 allowed the citizens to assemble in pagan temples but sacrifices were not permitted.[57] Drijvers quotes from the Chronicle of Joshua the Stylite an entry for the year 497–498 CE:

> While these things were taking place, there came round again the time of that festival at which the heathen myths were recited, and the citizens took even more pains about it than usual. For seven days previously they were going up to the theater at eventide, clad in linen garments, and wearing turbans, with their loins ungirt. Lamps were lighted before them, and they were burning incense, and holding vigils the whole night.[58]

It is clear that Rabbula stood at the beginning of the process of Christianization; his destruction of pagan temples was done for the purpose of re-using their stones for christian buildings. His objection to Christians going to animal games in which, for civic entertainment, 'hunters' armed with pikes would be pitted against wild animals and could be eaten, is in line with the contemporary efforts of Augustine in North Africa, as well as others, to prohibit Christians from attending the theatre.[59]

[53]CTheod 16.10.12.

[54]CTheod 16.10.14.

[55]Hans J.W. Drijvers, 'The Persistence of Pagan Cults and Practices in Christian Syria', in Nina Garsoïan *et alii*, edd., *East of Byzantium: Syria and Armenia in the Formative Period* (Washington: Dumbarton Oaks, 1982) 39.

[56]Drijvers, 'Persistence', 37, citing *Itinerarium Egeriae*, 19.7.

[57]CTheod 16.10.3.

[58]Drijvers, 'Persistence', 39. On the continuing role of pagan rituals, see Ramsay Macmullen, *Christianity and Paganism in the Fourth to the Eighth Centuries* (New Haven:Yale University Press, 1997; Pierre Chuvin, *A Chronicle of the Last Pagans* (Cambridge, Massachusetts: Harvard University Press, 1990).

[59]Robert Markus, *The End of Ancient Christianity* (Cambridge: Cambridge University Press, 1990) 107–123.

As for Rabbula's attitude towards the Jews, it is often said—based on the Edessene Chronicle, that Rabbula seized a jewish synagogue and turned it into a church. However, the Edessene Chronicle actually states:

> In the year 723 [= 411/412 CE] Rabbula became bishop of Edessa. He built the Church of Saint Stephen which had formerly been a synagogue of the Jews. He built this at the command of the emperor.[60]

Hallier, in his commentary on this entry, suggested that one read Audians ܐܘܕܝܐ instead of Jews (ܝܗܘܕܝܐ).[61] However, the emendation seems motivated by a desire to harmonize with the data of the *Life*. The sentence gives no indication that Rabbula forcibly seized the synagogue and thrust out the Jews. Rather, it states he was forced by the emperor to build the church where a synagogue at some previous time had stood. The *Life*, in fact, goes out of its way to show good relations between Rabbula and the Jews. During his lifetime, he made sure they received help when needed and, at his death, they too are shown lamenting.[62]

RABBULA AND SCRIPTURE

Within the *Life* is one sentence which has been the subject of much discussion: 'By the wisdom of God within him, he translated from Greek to Syriac, exactly as it was, the new covenant, on account of its various alterations'. Blum suggested that, given its

[60]Edessene Chronicle 51. The syriac text is in Ludwig Hallier, *Untersuchungen über die Edessenische Chronik mit dem syrischen Text und einer Übersetzung,* Texte und Untersuchungen zur Geschichte der altchristlichen Literatur 9 (Leipzig: Hinrich, 1892) 150.

[61]Hallier, *Untersuchungen,* 106–107.

[62]For an account of earlier relations between the Jews and Christians in Edessa, see Hans J. W. Drijvers, 'Jews and Christians at Edessa', *Journal of Jewish Studies* 36 (1985) 88–102.

unexpected and singular appearance in this context, the sentence may be an interpolation.[63] Whether or not this is true, what is the meaning of the sentence? Did Rabbula provide a completely new translation of the Bible, and, if so, did he work alone or with others? Vööbus has shown how the translation activity in Edessa at that time was usually done by many people.[64] Did Rabbula replace the Old Syriac version with the Peshitta?[65] Or did Rabbula purge the translation of what he thought were tendentious translations?[66] The last suggestion is the most likely: Baarda has shown how the author of Rabbula's *Life* in his citations of the biblical text follows the ancient syriac version in quotations from the Gospels of Matthew and Luke, but a different version, not that of the Peshitta, for quotations from the Gospel of John. He concluded from those facts:

> It seems to me that this revision [of Rabbula's] was not a radical one: the purpose was to have a more accurate translation of the passages that were important in the christological discussions within the Edessene clergy.[67]

This intuition of Baarda is strengthened by an examination of the root ܫܠܡ, particularly in the causative tense, which lies behind the word used in the above passage by the author of the *Life* of Rabbula. This root is used frequently in christological debates, as is shown in the following examples.

Towards the beginning of the letter of Hiba to Mari the Persian, Hiba mentions how he knows that Mari will make known

[63]Blum, *Rabbula,* 106–107.

[64]Arthur Vööbus, *Investigations into the Text of the New Testament Used by Rabbula of Edessa,* Contributions of Baltic University 59 (Pinneberg: 1947); *Studies in the History of the Gospel Text in Syriac* (Louvain: Secrétariat CSCO, 1951); *History of the School of Nisibis* (Louvain: Secrétariat CSCO, 1965) 14–21.

[65]F. C. Burkitt, *Evangelion De-Mepharreshe,* Volume 2 (Cambridge: Cambridge University Press, 1904) 160–165. The Peshitta, a Syriac translation of the Bible, was completed by the fifth century CE and became the standard version of the Syriac Church.

[66]Tjitze Baarda, 'The Gospel Text in the Biography of Rabbula', *Vigiliae Christianae* 14 (1960) 102–127.

[67]Baarda, 'Gospel Text', 127.

to all those where Mari resides what Hiba writes and that the
God-given scriptures will not receive even one change:

ܐܠܗܐ̈ܬܢ ܕܫܘ ܫܚܠܦ ܚܕܐ ܐܦܠܐ ܡܢ ܗܠܝܢ ܕܐܠܗܐ.
ὡς οὐδεμίαν ἐναλλαγὴν αἱ παρὰ τοῦ θεοῦ δοθεῖσαι
γραφαὶ ἔλαβον.[68]

The same root as in the sentence in the *Life of Rabbula* about
Rabbula's translation activity is used in the letter of Hiba. Later in
the letter Hiba will argue from Scripture the difference between
the divine nature and the human nature in Christ.

In later nestorian texts, the Nestorians suggest that their opponents have changed the text of Hebrews 2:9, 'Apart from God,
on behalf of all men he tasted death', to 'He, God, in his goodness,
tasted death for all men'.[69] The Nestorians used a Greek text,
χωρὶς θεοῦ, whereas their opponents had as their text χάριτι
θεοῦ. Most editions of the text have χάριτι θεοῦ. Theodore of
Mopsuestia had earlier ridiculed those who read this latter text:

'It is laughable what they allow here, changing χωρὶς
θεοῦ and making χάριτι θεοῦ'.[70]

Philoxenus of Mabbog, an anti-nestorian writer who died in
523 CE, wrote:

It was into this sort of iniquity that Theodore and Nestorius—the leaders of the heresy of the man-worshippers—
also fell, when they too attempted to alter (ܕܢܫܠܚܦܘ)
some phrases of the Scripture and to interpret others in
the opposite sense. . . . The same applies to the passage
in the Letter to the Hebrews: 'Jesus the Son by the grace
of God'—that is, of the Father— 'tasted death on behalf

---

[68]Flemming, *Akten,* 48, line 16; Schwartz, *ACO* 2.1.3; page 32, lines 14–15.

[69]Luise Abramowski and Alan E. Goodman, *A Nestorian Collection of Christological Texts. Cambridge University Library* MS *Oriental 1319* (Cambridge: Cambridge University Press, 1972) 1:7, lines 5–9 (Syriac); 2:7, lines 23–26 (English).
See also volume 1:5, lines 16–17; volume 2:6, lines 23–24. Sebastian P. Brock,
'Hebrews 2:9B in Syriac Tradition', *Novum Testamentum* 27 (1985) 241, adduces
four syriac manuscripts which have this reading.

[70]PG 66:956.

of everyone'. This they altered (ܣܠܘ) and wrote 'apart from God', taking care to transmit that this Jesus, who accepted death on behalf of us, is not God.[71]

The notion that text-critical choices were often made on theological grounds has been well made by Bart Ehrmann.[72] Here one sees how Rabbula and his circle were actively engaged in promoting one version of the New Testament text which favored their theological stance.

Rabbula and the Poor

The author of the *Life* of Rabbula has Rabbula state:

> According to an honest assessment, we ourselves live from what belongs to the poor . . . According to an honest assessment, to us leaders is allowed as much as the body needs, so that we might use some of it in a simple manner, like the rest of the poor, and not as our body, which desires whatever is hurtful to our spirit, wills.[73]

This encapsulates Rabbula's ministry to the poor. When he gave away all his possessions before becoming a monk, some of them are said to have reached Edessa. The author of his *Life* commented:

> This act foretold that he would receive the city of Edessa as his inheritance. For the mystery of Christ had in advance

---

[71]The text is critically edited by A. de Halleux in *Philoxène de Mabbog. Commentaire du prologue johannique,* CSCO 380, Scr.Syri 165 (Louvain: Secrètariat CSCO, 1977) 52, lines 24–26; 53, lines 2–6. The translation is from the article by Brock, 'Hebrews 2:9B', 236–244.

[72]Bart Ehrmann, *The Orthodox Corruption of Scripture: The Effect of Early Christological Controversies on the Text of the New Testament* (New York: Oxford University Press, 1993).

[73]See below, page 90.

espoused him to Edessa, as to the rest of the regions, with his alms as a pledge, through the agency of her wedding-attendants, the poor.[74]

He is said to have distributed 7,000 *darics*[75] a year to the poor, as well as giving what was needed to his colleagues in the ministry and to those inscribed[76] on the welfare roles of the city. He also sent aid to those in the villages round about. He restored a hospital for men and had one built for women. He was particularly devoted to caring for those afflicted with leprosy. Widows and orphans were under his protection, and he lent money to crafts-people. To pay for all this, he used the accumulated wealth of the church in Edessa, the inheritance of the clergy—who bequeathed what they possessed to the church on their death, and donations from high-placed friends in Constantinople and perhaps Alexandria. At his death, he was called a father to the orphans and a brother to the poor. Susan Harvey rightly notes that Rabbula is properly compared to such other great benefactors as Basil of Caesarea, John Chrysostom, and John the Almsgiver.[77]

RABBULA AND HERESY

The author of the *Life of Rabbula* placed Rabbula's actions for his christian community, his own devotions, and his concern for the city as a whole before discussing his theological stance. The author

[74]See below, page 71.

[75]The *daric* was a gold coin, weighing about eight grams, used within the Persian empire. When the Jews returned from the Babylonian exile, they are said to have donated 61,000 *darics* of gold plus some silver to rebuild the Jerusalem temple (Ezra 2:68-69—although a different number is given at Neh 7:70-72).

[76]For this translation, see Susan Ashbrook Harvey, 'The Holy and the Poor: Models from Early Syriac Christianity' in Emily Albu Hanawalt and Carter Lindberg, edd., *Through the Eye of a Needle. Judeo-Christian Roots of Social Welfare* (Kirksville, Missouri: Thomas Jefferson University Press, 1994) 49, n.27.

[77]Harvey, 'Holy and the Poor', 51. The whole article by Harvey is recommended.

introduces this final section by proposing that Rabbula's behavior is modeled on that of biblical heroes. In dealing with the community at large, Rabbula was compared to the wise King Solomon.[78] In dealing with heretics, the models change to Moses,[79] Joshua,[80] and Josiah,[81] leaders who had fought vigorously against their opponents. The heretical groups dealt with by Rabbula are also mentioned in a longer list of heretics attacked by an imperial law of 30 May, 428.[82]

The author rightly judged that, for Rabbula as for Chaucer's parson, 'first he wrought, and afterwards he taught'.[83] Blum has shown in his analysis of Rabbula's sermon in Constantinople that Rabbula's emphasis lay on the power of grace to perform good deeds.[84]

> For the fount of all teaching is grace, through which Our Lord teaches his Church. . . . For Our Lord's life on this earth and his suffering, which is redemption for us all, gave us a solid help which strengthens our weakness so that there is not only knowledge in us, but also the power for the practice of his commands'. (O 239, lines 12–14; 240, lines 9–13)

> 'So whoever loves, does not dispute but obeys, does not investigate but believes'. (O 241, lines 17–18)

These words from Rabbula's sermon resonate with the exasperation the author shows Acacius displaying when Rabbula tries to dispute with him.

The distrust of theological investigation evinced in the sermon at Constantinople at first seems at odds with Rabbula's actions in the christological controversy of the 430s. Blum has shown that Rabbula did not participate in the First Council of Ephesus in

[78] O 191 1.15; below page 90.
[79] O 191 1.24; page 91.
[80] O 192 1.7; page 91.
[81] O 192 1.8); page 91.
[82] CTheod 16.5.65.
[83] *Canterbury Tales* Prologue.
[84] Blum, *Rabbula,* 133–137.

431.[85] Perhaps he was already weak or even blind.[86] Any weakness did not, however, prevent his strenuous participation in the controversy which followed. Blum has catalogued his letters and actions. In the spring of 431, before the Council of Ephesus, Rabbula was corresponding and debating with Andreas of Samosata. By the beginning of 432, Rabbula was openly hostile to supporters of Nestorius, as Andreas noted in a letter to Alexander of Hieropolis. Sometime later in 432, an Antiochene synod advised the bishops of Osrhoene to withhold communion from Rabbula. About that time, Rabbula wrote to Cyril of Alexandria, and during the events leading up to the reconciliation between John of Antioch and Cyril of Alexandria that led to the Formula of Reunion in 433, Cyril wrote to Rabbula advising him of the unacceptability of the first proposal made by Acacius of Beroea, Rabbula's old mentor. After the Formula of Reunion, in which John of Antioch had renounced Nestorius, Rabbula was vigorous in the attacks on the writings of the dead Theodore of Mopsuestia. Blum has argued that Rabbula and Acacius of Melitene were the instigators of the attack on Theodore's works among the Armenians. These attacks led to the letter of Proclus, bishop of Constantinople, in which Proclus did not explicitly condemn Theodore, but did speak of the one *hypostasis* of the incarnate Word and which was clearly in support of the position of Cyril of Alexandria.

What drove Rabbula in this controversy? Hans Drijvers has suggested political shrewdness as the basis for Rabbula's anti-Nestorian policy:

> The emperor had abandoned Nestorius, and his obedient servant immediately did the same. . . . Rabbula served only two lords, Christ and the emperor, and had cut all his family ties.[87]

Such a political stance would resonate with Rabbula's having held a distinguished honorary governorship before his conversion.

[85]Blum, *Rabbula,* 160–165.

[86]Blum (*Rabbula,* 152, n.2) quotes Theodore Lector (*HE* 2.40; PG 86/1:205A) to the effect that Rabbula was blind in the spring of 431 when he wrote to Andreas of Samosata.

[87]Drijvers, 'Rabbula, Bishop of Edessa', 152.

But does such a motive completely explain why, even after the Formula of Reunion, Rabbula persisted in his effort to expunge the very source of Nestorianism, which he found in the writings of Theodore of Mopsuestia? What led Rabbula to attack Theodore? In the letter to Mari, Hiba ascribes it to an enmity which Rabbula secretly had towards Theodore because Theodore had rebuked him openly in a synod. The much later writer, Bishop Barhadbsabba would elaborate this story: when Rabbula defended himself against charges that he beat his clergy by referring to the incident when Jesus whipped the money-changers in the Temple,[88] Theodore is said to have quoted against him the way the incident is treated in the other Gospels,[89] where there is no mention of whipping, but only a statement that the Lord spoke to them.[90] Most scholars think the story of this Nestorian partisan untrustworthy;[91] I, however, am inclined to think that it is perhaps not far off the mark in tracing the dispute back to biblical interpretation.

One of the many virtues of Georg Blum's analysis of Rabbula is his exploration of the traditional elements in Rabbula's thinking. Blum points to the similarity between Rabbula and the earlier great syrian theologian, Ephræm, vis-à-vis the Eucharist;[92] on the superiority of faith over knowledge;[93] in their emphasis on the unity of Christ.[94] This strong conviction of the unity of the Word made flesh made Rabbula expressly accept for Mary the title 'Mother of God' in his sermon at Constantinople,[95] and which allowed him, as well as Cyril of Alexandria,[96] to speak

[88]Jn 2:13-16.

[89]Mk 11:15-19 and parallels.

[90]Barhadbsabba, *Cause of the Foundation of the Schools*—as in the edition of A. Scher, *PO* 6:380–381.

[91]Blum, *Rabbula,* 167, n. 14.

[92]Blum, *Rabbula,* 123–126.

[93]Blum, *Rabbula,* 135–137.

[94]Blum, *Rabbula,* 145–148.

[95]O 242, 17: ܐܠܗܐ ܝܠܕܬ ܡܪܝܡ. See Blum, *Rabbula,* 138, n.3, for a textual emendation in Overbeck's text.

[96]See John J. O'Keefe, 'Kenosis or Impassibility: Cyril of Alexandria and Theodoret of Cyrrhus on the Problem of Divine Pathos', *Studia Patristica* 32, ed. Elizabeth A. Livingstone (Louvain: Peeters, 1987) 358–365. See also Henry

sometimes of how the Word experienced suffering: 'Although by his own nature He could not suffer, his body by his own free will suffered'.[97] According to his biographer, he rebuked Nestorius for holding that it was the slave born of a woman who suffered. Rabbula's concern that there was an unconfused union of deity and humanity in Jesus and one single agent of the deeds done by Jesus as recorded in the gospels allowed him, with Cyril, to accept the Formula of Reunion.[98]

What was most important for Rabbula, I believe, was his view of the Eucharist. What Henry Chadwick said in his seminal article about Cyril of Alexandria's views on the Eucharist could be said also of Rabbula:

> The eucharist is central for the comprehension of Cyril's religion. Every week, he writes, we hold our sacred meetings behind closed doors, and, as to the disciples, Christ comes among us all both visibly and invisibly: invisibly as God, visibly as being again in the body. And there he allows us even to touch his holy flesh, in the ὁμολγία καὶ ἀνάμνησις of his death and resurrection. Here is the heart of Cyril's religion, the dynamic which imparted such intense religious fervour to his monophysite monks. Every eucharist is a reincarnation of the Logos who is there πάλιν ἐν σώματι, and whose ἰδία σάρξ is given to the communicant.[99]

In Rabbula's view, as we noted above, the Eucharist should be celebrated once a week for all the christian community. Eucharistic thinking is central to Rabbula:

> Therefore it is not only bread in the body of the Messiah as it seems to them, but in the bread is the body of God,

Chadwick, 'Eucharist and Christology in the Nestorian Controversy', *JTS* ns 2 (1951) 158–162.

[97]O 244, 7–8.

[98]Blum (*Rabbula,* 181–182) notes how Andreas of Samosata reported that Rabbula had agreed to the formula (*ACO* 1.4.2, p. 136).

[99]Chadwick, 'Eucharist and Christology', 155.

which cannot be seen, as we believe and as we receive it
distinctly as body.[100]

It is by receiving the Son of God in the Eucharist that the Christians receive the blessed life leading to resurrection. As Frederick
G. McLeod has shown:

> . . . this study into the eucharistic thought of Theodore [of
> Mopsuestia] points out a sacramental and theological shift
> that took place in the late fourth and early fifth centuries
> regarding how one ought to speak about the reception of
> baptism and the eucharist, and how one ought to explain
> them. . . . Theodore interpreted the Pauline statements
> about baptism as meaning a transformation into the one
> body of Christ, and interpreted the eucharist as a spiritual
> transformation into the 'human' body and blood of Christ.
> This manner of speaking about the eucharist scandalized
> Cyril. He took it as literally signifying that it was only
> Christ's human body. While not denying the value of Theodore's general approach to exegesis, Cyril held that Christ's
> human nature spiritually participated in God's nature because it was the Word's body. Those receiving the eucharist
> were also sharing in it in the same way. He was convinced
> that a person could be united to God not only by being
> one with Him in his or her activity but also in what we
> describe today as a mystical union that does not absorb and
> submerge one's individuality in the Godhead.[101]

Like Cyril, Rabbula was scandalized at Theodore's interpretation, and hence his reaction against both Nestorius and Theodore
of Mopsuestia. The liturgy had been central to Rabbula, as evidenced in his canons on the liturgy;[102] on relics;[103] on liturgical

---

[100]O 235, 17–21.

[101]Frederick G. McLeod, 'The Christological Ramifications of Theodore of
Mopsuestia's Understanding of Baptism and the Eucharist', JECS 10 (2002) 75.

[102]Canons for the Monks 16.20; Canons for the Priests and Covenanters
20.27.

[103]Canons for Monks 22–24.

vessels;[104] for the maintenance of churches;[105] and on the proper reception of the Eucharist.[106] In relating the *Life* of Rabbula, the author emphasizes through the sign at Rabbula's baptism the saving significance of the ritual, and, in ordering his life as a bishop, places first his concerns over the liturgy. As we noted above, in his letter to Gemillinus, Rabbula insisted that the Eucharist was no mere bread and wine, but a holy body and a life-giving blood. He, like Cyril, could not see the soteriological role of Christ's humanity in Nestorius and Theodore,[107] and so opposed them vehemently.

TEXT

The *Life of Rabbula* is found in one manuscript, British Museum Additional 14652, dating from the sixth century CE. The manuscript also contains the 'Canons for Priests and Covenanters' and the 'Canons for Monks' as well as the sermon Rabbula is said to have preached in Constantinople. The *Life* was edited by J. J. Overbeck in 1865,[108] and re-issued by P. Bedjan in 1894.[109] A German translation was made by G. Bickell in 1874.[110]

[104]Canons for Priests and Covenanters 32.

[105]Canons for Priests and Covenanters 39.54.58.

[106]Canons for Monks 20; for Priests and Covenanters 31.33.49.52. See Peter Bruns, 'Die Kanones des Rabbula', in H. J. F. Reinhardt, ed., *Theologia et Ius Canonicum* (Essen, 1995) 471–480.

[107]Chadwick, 'Eucharist and Christology', 158. For an excellent development of Theodore's understanding of the Eucharist as a transformation into Christ's body seen as an organic whole; as the human nature was united with the divine nature in Christ, Christians so united in this organic body of Christ will share in Christ's immortal, resurrected life, see McLeod, 'Christological Ramifications', 63–72.

[108]J. J. Overbeck, *S.Ephraemi Syri, Rabulae episcopi Edesseni, Balaei aliorumque opera selecta* (Oxford: Clarendon, 1865) 154–209.

[109]Paul Bedjan, *Acta martyrum et sanctorum,* volume 4 (Paris: Harrassowitz, 1894; rpt. Hildesheim: Olms, 1968) 396–470.

[110]Gustav Bickell, *Ausgewählte Schriften der syrischen Kirchenväter Aphraates, Rabulas und Isaak von Ninive* (Kempten: Kösel, 1874) 155–211.

THE HEROIC DEEDS OF
MAR RABBULA, BISHOP OF
EDESSA, THE BLESSED CITY

MY BROTHERS, in zeal for the love of Christ, through writing we are depicting before your love an icon of the excellent way of life of Mar Rabbula the bishop, the pride of our city, so that he might be to us and to every generation a paradigm that stimulates [us] to imitate his virtues. He appeared as a competitor in the stadium of righteousness, and in the harsh battles against the powers was found victorious.[1] By his wisdom he overcame the cunning of the slanderer, and he sagely despised the world and its desires. He trod underfoot the might of the devil with his warlike strength, and with his self-control he subdued the body and its passions. He overcame Satan, his adversary, in his contest. Those whom he [Satan] led astray he turned back to the truth. With the vigor of his self-control he trod underfoot the cunning lures of the sweet enticements of sin. He helped people with his words and aided many with his deeds. With his endurance he made glad and astounded the angels, and with his faith he praised and magnified his Lord. He found himself[2] and kept possession of his life. The spirit of God rested on him throughout his life until he [Rabbula] raised up a crown of integrity out of all his contests against baseness, and he was adorned with a good, god-worthy end. Therefore, we rightly ought to set down the pleasant memory of

[1]Cf. Eph 6:12.
[2]Mt 10:3.

the godly way of life of this famous hero so that it might be for us and for every generation a representation of his heroic deeds, a paradigm which stimulates them to imitate [those deeds]. [May it be with this narrative] just as with the stories of the excellent patriarchs, those famous heroes in the Old and in the New [Testament]: representations of their virtues rise up in the pigments of the letters which are embodied in the holy Scriptures.

Now, this blessed Rabbula had been a pagan from his youth because his father was a pagan and a priest—when he marched to war against the Persians,[3] the wicked Julian himself had offered sacrifice to demons through the agency of Rabbula's father. His mother, however, was a believer. She was constantly waging war with her husband to convert him to the worship of Christ, but she could not overcome his rebellious will to convert him to the truth. Her husband also tried to entice her, a believer, in all kinds of ways, but he could not enslave to sin the freedom she [had] in Jesus. Therefore, each kept his and her own separate opinion. From them was born the one victorious in everything, Rabbula the zealous one, a second Josiah,[4] if this analogy we are drawing to the glory of the saint is appropriate.

His mother entrusted him to a christian nurse, who suckled him. When he grew up, he was—as a child of rich nobles in their city, Qennishrin—instructed in greek letters. Early on, his mother chose a christian wife for him. Although his wife and his mother were constantly urging him to change from his father's paganism to belief in Christ, he would not be urged by them. For he was strongly attached to the distinguished honorary office which the emperor had granted to him.[5]

[3]The emperor Julian, who is called 'the Apostate', became emperor in 361 CE on the death of his cousin, the Christian Constantius I. He attempted to restore the cult of the gods, but was unsuccessful. Because of increasing threats from the Persians, who had captured Amida at the entrance to Armenia in 359, Julian decided to wage a campaign against the Persians. He left Antioch on 5 March 363. Although at first successful, he died on 26 June 363, when the Persians counter-attacked.

[4]2 Kgs 22–23.

[5]As Bowersock states, 'the recognition of influential local citizens by honorary titles was a deeply rooted feature of imperial administration that reached

Now an excellent reason called him to journey to his landed estates near the wilderness of Qennishrin. On the border of one of his landed estates there was the single solitary monastery of Abraham the recluse. [Rabbula's] servants and the inhabitants of that place were telling him, 'Brethren known as strangers dwell in that monastery, and amazing works of healing have been done through them by Christ, the God of the Christians'. As Rabbula listened, the news of Abraham's signs startled his hearing, and the report of his exploits fell on his soul like an acclamation.[6] As the fire of the love of the divine name of Jesus hastened into his heart, his mind began to doubt his paganism. Forthwith, by the providence of God, that fire quickly led him to see that blessed one, Abraham, so that, with his own eyes he might see the mighty wonderful works of Jesus, whom he had previously hated. It was just as Paul, at his origin, had been sought after by [Jesus]: with the snare of a heavenly voice Jesus began binding Paul to the yoke of the cross, as Paul bowed down.[7] As Jesus snatched Paul from Judaism to his truth, so he also snatched Rabbula from paganism to Christianity. Because signs are urgently required for those who do not believe, the good Lord, concerned about his servants, arranged beforehand the bait of life, as he did for the Samaritan woman[8] and for Nathanael.[9]

By a little sign from Jesus, Rabbula was caught for life. A woman whose flesh had been dried up from a severe chronic illness came towards the victorious Abraham, and her limbs were restored to health. When the blessed Rabbula saw this marvel, he went away amazed in his soul about what had been done, and he began to doubt his paganism because of the mighty deed of Christ. As he himself told us, he was saying to himself in his heart, 'If it is a disgrace for you

---

back to the high Roman Empire' [Glen Bowersock, 'The Syriac Life of Rabbula and Syrian Hellenism', in Thomas Hägg and Philip Pousseau, edd., *Greek Biography and Panegyric in Late Antiquity* (Berkeley: University of California Press, 2000) 262–263.

[6]For this translation, see Bowersock, 'Syriac Life', 260. Literally, the Syriac reads 'hooks', 'anchors', but Bowersock has pointed out that the Greek behind the Syriac was a well-known acclamation.

[7]Acts 9:1–7.

[8]Jn 4:7–30.

[9]Jn 1:45–50.

to deny the shameful gods of the Greeks and to acknowledge a crucified God, see how the remembrance of the crucifixion affects your soul at the healing of this woman. Be true to yourself'.

When his mother saw that his appearance had changed and she heard from those who had been with him about the divine deed performed in his sight, she hastened in her joy to blessed Eusebius, the bishop of her city. She informed him about her son's action, and he rejoiced. After the bishop had sent for him and explained to Rabbula many things about Christ from the Scriptures, he thought others might help support what he had said. Because of this, he rose up diligently and led him off and brought him to the noble Acacius, bishop of the city of Aleppo. They were brothers in Christ and had been instructed together in the precious monastic way of life.

When Acacius heard the cause of their coming, he rejoiced greatly. He felt compassion for Rabbula, and began to say to him, 'My son, you are not able to understand the true power of the truth unless you know that whatever you know is error'. Rabbula answered and said to him, 'How am I able to know that whatever I know is error, if this truth, in its brightness, does not clearly differentiate truth and error for me?' Then Acacius opposed him strenuously for this retort and said to him, 'You are able to know the truth even if you know that you still do not know it'. Then Rabbula said, 'This statement—"I know that I do not know the truth"—is not a positive statement about what the truth is, but rather an argument concerning error, that it is error. I myself seek that truth so that I may know'. Acacius said to him, 'Believe in our Lord Jesus, that he is the Son of God, and that truth is wisdom enough to hold you near him'. Then Rabbula said, 'From where can I understand whether Christ is the genuine truth that I myself am anxious to know?' Eusebius said to him, 'The truth will make itself known to you if you renounce your own understanding and have the need of his understanding'. Rabbula said, 'But how can I forget[10] those things which I remember even though I do not want to?' Eusebius said, 'When you begin to make dwell in yourself the constant memory of Jesus, all the evil things which

---

[10]Same root as 'error'.

are stirring in you will see him and will flee from you like darkness dispelled before rays of light'.

When many things about the faith had been spoken of between them, he vowed that he would go to pray at the shrine of
the heroic martyrs Cosmas and Damian. Eusebius and Acacius
provided him with a prayer and, rejoicing, sent him away. While
he was standing in the church, he saw an acquaintance of his who
had been born blind, but who was now able to see. Rabbula marveled at the power of the cross. He was especially amazed at the
marvel God worked in his very own person, for the Lord opened
his lips and Rabbula offered a new song,[11] a song to God, to the
Father and to the Son and to the Holy Spirit. He gave alms there.
As he meditated on those things that he had seen and heard, he
changed his way of life as he rejected from his soul his error up
to the present. Then Rabbula went to Acacius and revealed to
him how, as he stood and prayed, God made a song spring forth
in his mouth, and Rabbula professed his faith in Jesus before him.
When Acacius heard, he rejoiced that Rabbula believed and said
to him, 'My son, in whoever's heart the fire of the love of God
is active, all desires, with all the thorns of sin, are set on fire by
this love and burnt up.[12] Such a person will be purified sevenfold
from these desires and will be made clean'.

The bishops Acacius and Eusebius led him to the monastery of
the holy Marcian the recluse, and to the blessed Abraham, whom
we mentioned above. By a fertile discourse they strengthened his
mind and persuaded him to stay.[13] Rabbula promised them and
said, 'Because I truly have put my hope in the Lord and believe
in the Son of God, I have vowed all of myself to God, and I will
completely forsake the world. I will perfectly cleave to God and I
will shut myself up in a monastery like you. But I desire this, that I

[11]Ps 40:3; 51:15; Rev 5:9.

[12]Mk 4:7; Heb 6:8.

[13]Brockelman suggested that, in view of the following trip to Jerusalem,
ܢܬܥܡܕ should be emended to ܢܬܥܡܕ = 'that he be baptized'. However, the
manuscript clearly reads the former. After his baptism in Jerusalem and his
disposal of his possessions, Rabbula goes to dwell/stay ܥܡ with Abraham (fol.
90r), and this echoes the use of 'stay' here. The trip to Jerusalem is thus part of
his program before entering the monastery.

may go to Jerusalem and see the holy place and be baptized in the
Jordan where Christ was baptized as a model[14] for us'. When the
fathers heard this, they rejoiced and dismissed him with prayers
and sent him on his way.

When the blessed Rabbula entered Jerusalem,[15] he prayed in
front of Golgotha with many tears and sorrow.[16] He entered the
tomb of Our Lord and the cave where he was born[17] and he went
up to the place of the Ascension.[18] He gave alms to the poor. He
went down from there to the Jordan; at once he petitioned the
priests and recited before them the creed, and they anointed him
and baptized him. As soon as he came up out of the waters, the
special remedy of the blood of Christ with the mark of the crosses
was seen shining forth from every part of that whole garment that
was wrapped around his body—as was the custom for spiritual
bridegrooms of Christ. When they saw this great marvel, all who
were there marveled and trembled and were seized by fear. In
their trepidation, they fell down and knelt in prayer before God.
With uplifted voice they praised God for all the mighty works
that they had seen. After he took part in the holy mysteries of the
body and blood of Our Lord and was initiated into the full divine
mystery,[19] Rabbula returned to his city, rejoicing in his faith and

---

[14]Literally, 'type'. Mt 3:13-17.

[15]The sites listed here refer to all standard pilgrimage sites in the post-Con-
stantinian era. In the Church of the Holy Sepulchre, built by Constantine the
Great, was the grotto of the Holy Sepulchre. Not far from this was a large, open-
air courtyard in which there stood a cross; the rock of the cross with its courtyard was the church called *Ad Crucem,* one of the stational churches, that is, a
church visited during the stations of the cross procession on Good Fridays. The
Church of the Nativity at Bethlehem was also constructed during Constantine's
time. On top of the Mount of Olives stood the Church of the Ascension, built
by the roman matron Poemenia before 378 CE. Egeria, who made a pilgrimage
to the holy places at the beginning of the fifth century CE, mentions all these
places in her diary. Egeria, *Diary of a Pilgrimage,* Ancient Christian Writers 38,
trans. George E. Gingras (New York: Newman Press, 1970).

[16]Mt 27:33.

[17]Lk 2:7.

[18]Mt 28:16; Lk 24:51.

[19]Before they were baptized, catechumens had to leave the church after the
homily and before the eucharistic prayer.

exulting in his hope, overflowing in his love and intoxicated in his mercy, and rendering thanks to God.

As soon as the blessed Rabbula was baptized and went back to his city and entered his home, he made preparations as he had vowed. He was like a wise merchant who set forth after precious pearls. When the merchant found the pearl of his hope, he went and sold whatever he had and bought it.[20] So Rabbula distributed to the needy his gold and his silver and all that he possessed; his alms extended even as far as to the saints and the poor in Edessa. This act foretold that he would receive the city of Edessa as his inheritance.[21] For the mystery of Christ had in advance espoused him to Edessa, as to the rest of the regions, with his alms as a pledge, through the agency of her wedding-attendants, the poor. For he wisely understood in his soul that the decorations of this world and the anxiety of riches, like briars and thorns, choke the seed of the word of God in the unwary, and it does not produce fruits.[22] Because of this, he labored to hurl from himself all the hard burden of the chains of riches,[23] so that the word of God that he received might easily sprout up within him and yield fruits thirtyfold and sixtyfold and a hundredfold.[24] Thus with joy he accepted the command of Our Lord: 'Whosoever does not leave behind all his possessions cannot be my disciple'.[25] He diligently distributed and gave all that he had to the poor so that his righteousness would stand firm forever. He even sold his estates and he properly distributed to the needy the money he received from their sale, so that, by means of them, his deposits to the heavenly treasury, along with their profits, might mount up. There his treasures would be kept safe for him. He set free all his slaves, both those born in the house and those bought by money, and he provisioned and sent away in peace each and every one of them. He instructed, taught, and brought some of them to the monasteries. As for his blessed mother, she rejoiced when he took

[20]Mt 13:45.

[21]I.e. the Church. See the connection between mystery, Christ and the Church in Eph 5:32; Col 1:27; 2:2.

[22]Mt 13:3-9.

[23]Cf. Mt 19:16-30.

[24]Mt 13:18-23; Mk 4:3-20.

[25]Lk 12:13-21; 14:26-27, 33.

all that she possessed, and then she took the yoke of Christ. He did likewise to his wife. He taught his still young children, and entrusted them to the monasteries. Thus he emptied himself of all that he had possessed so that he might possess the Lord of all possessions.

When he had separated himself according to the command of Our Lord from his mother and from his wife and from his sons and from his daughters and from his estates and from all his possessions and from the villages dependent on him and from his slaves and from his friends and from all that the world possesses,[26] according to the command of Our Lord he took up his cross in a secret manner,[27] and set out after him completely. As soon as he had stripped off the world, with its life and all that is in it, he set out alone for the desert in the glowing desire for the true love of Christ, so that he also might be tested by the slanderer as by the example of Our Lord.[28] He desired, like a warrior in the field, to encounter battles with the fierce passions, to strive in a wrestling match with his nature and its habits, and, like a spiritual athlete, to contend with principalities and with powers and with evil spirits, from within and without.[29]

So he went and dwelt in the desert monastery of the blessed Abraham, whom we mentioned above. The blessed Rabbula had been drawn at the beginning, by the small radiance of one of Abraham's signs, to leave the darkness of paganism for the light of the truth. When Rabbula had lived with him for some time in a noble way of life, he strongly urged Abraham that he might take for himself a small dwelling-place near Abraham and live in it as he pleased. So Abraham assented to his argument, and Rabbula took up residence in the monastery. His brother dwelt with him, as did others. Among them was the blessed Eusebius, whom the holy Rabbula made bishop of Tela, the well-known, victorious[30] city. Their way of life was like that of all monasteries. They were

[26]Mt 19:29.

[27]Mt 10:38; 16:24; Mk 8:34; Lk 9:23;14:27.

[28]Mt 4:1-11; Mk 1:12-13; Lk 4:1-13.

[29]2 Cor 10:3-4; Eph 1:21; 6:10-20;1 Tm 4:7-8; Gal 6:16-17.

[30]Tela also had another name, Nikephorion, and so the adjective 'victorious' here is most likely a reference to this alternate name, which means victorious. I thank Professor Glen Bowersock for this insight.

like the church of the apostles because whatever they had was held in common.[31] Many times they joyfully kept vigil without nourishment. One day, as usual, the bread of their monastery ran out. While he was giving thanks to his Lord who had made him worthy to rejoice in bearing such sufferings as these, grace sent them bread for their needs at sunset. Be amazed then, and astonished at the strength of mind of blessed Rabbula. For he saw that grace and he said, 'Because God is aware of my weakness, that I am not strong in afflictions, he did this to test me'. In this judgement, he accepted and gave that nourishment to others at evening time, as Rabbula and his companions slept hungry.

When he saw that people were beginning to visit him as someone who had left behind the world and desired solitude, who hated himself and loved God, he concealed himself from them so that he might not be hindered by their visits from his steady regime of righteousness. He removed himself to the inner desert, as also the blessed Anthony had done.[32] He found a small opening in the ground and, beside it, a trickling stream of water which emitted moisture enough for one. This, then, was what he did there alone: constant prayer, the liturgy of the psalms, and the reading of the Scriptures. For these are the righteous rules both of all the monasteries where there is order, and of everyone who belongs to Our Lord. For he went there so that the thought of God might never be interrupted from his soul. For, as the blessed one himself related, the evil one aroused against him there all his many and varied conflicts, as well as fearsome reptiles; and he multiplied shapes. Satan fought with him openly. He made swarm around and above him snakes and scorpions to cause him fear, basilisks and asps to frighten him; but all of them were conquered by the power of the sign of the cross. When Satan did not prevail over its strength, he would overturn a pitcher of water into which that tiny trickle of water was dripping just enough for his needs. These tests, with which Satan was violently fighting against him to cause him pain, profited his noble righteousness. They made him be vigorous in his prayer, earnestly making supplication and

[31]Acts 4:32.
[32]Athanasius, *Life of Antony*, 49.

strongly imploring God to save him from all evils. By inner and outer self-control, he bravely withstood the evil one and was ready to resist all evil impulses with all good impulses.

As he stood in prayer, so as not to break off his conversation with God, he suddenly saw a band of Arabs approaching. He was glad, for he thought that the time for his crowning had already arrived. They, however, took him to be a dying man living in a barren hole, and they despised him. They left him alone, took only his food and his garments, and departed. He also praised his Lord for the following: he was amazed by the fact that a man who was coming as a kindness to bring him bread for his need, met them and they did not harm him. In both these events his self-control was victorious. As he was living this angelic way of life in his body and in his soul, his mind dwelling in God's presence like the angels in their heavenly worship, the members of his monastery learnt where he was and how he was [living]. They came and took him back to them through supplication.

Then, because the desire for martyrdom was glowing like a fire in his heart, he rose up and led the blessed Eusebius, and the two of them journeyed to Baalbek, a city of pagans. In their divine zeal they entered the city's temple of idols to throw the idols down and be counted worthy for martyrdom.[33] For they went there, with no assurance of returning alive, but they dared to do this in the hope that the pagans would torture and kill them, and they would become martyrs by being killed. Now their desire for martyrdom was not deficient,[34] but they were preserved for the future prepared for them by God to flourish in the episcopate. For the pagans smote them mercilessly until they thought Rabbula and Eusebius were dead. Afterwards the pagans threw them like corpses from a lofty height with many steps, and their limbs were battered on them as they went down each one of the steps; one step led down to the next and dropped the two men in such a way that, still alive, both men were hitting every step until they reached the ground. They returned to their dwelling

---

[33]The word for 'martyr' also means 'witness'.

[34]Text reads ܟܒ̈ܝ, not ܟܒ̈ܝ. One could also translate as: 'their sufferings were not inferior to martyrdom'.

place, rejoicing that they were deemed worthy for God's sake to bear the marks of the sufferings of Christ in their body. So they endured the afflictions of death as they proposed; they did not, however, die in martyrdom as they expected. They were martyrs from their will as they desired, only their slaughter was lacking because they were preserved to give the crown to many.

HOW BLESSED RABBULA BECAME BISHOP OF THE CITY OF EDESSA

When my lord Diogenes, bishop of Edessa, passed away, the bishops, with Alexander the patriarch, gathered at Antioch along with Acacius, bishop of Aleppo, to consider whom they might appoint bishop of Edessa. The spirit[35] of Jesus allowed[36] in their hearts, 'It is right to elect Rabbula for that place because I delight in him'.[37] The spirit, by the mouth of priests, said about Rabbula what it had about David, 'I have found Rabbula my servant who will be useful in my service. I will anoint him with the oil of my holiness by your hands.[38] My hand will help him and my arm will strengthen him. I will cast away from his presence the enemies of truth, and I will break those who hate the truth.[39] I have also brought about prophetically that he tread under foot the raging of heretics. My faith and my grace are with him, and by my name his horn will be so exalted from such a witnessing as this that the spirit of Jesus will be set firmly in people's souls'.

The bishops sent speedily to snatch him from his monastery. They brought him to Antioch and they made him bishop. They did not allow him to say and petition—as many do in outward show, 'I am not able to bear and endure the burden of office'. For

---

[35]'Spirit' here is feminine.

[36]Bedjan reads ܠܡܣܪ, 'convinced their hearts'. However, the manuscript reads ܠܡܣܪ, which seems to reflect the language of Acts 16:7.

[37]See Is 42:1.

[38]1 Sam 16:12-13; Acts 13:22.

[39]Ps 89:20-24.

he did not even agree to use outwardly those standard expressions which men, whoever they are, cry out as they adduce pretexts, 'We do not accept because we are not competent'. For he was a spiritual person, and anxious that his mind not reprove him in anything. He judged everything uprightly in his noble soul, so that neither humans nor God would reprove him in anything. He feared to contend, saying, 'Am I able to stand against God?' He judged his soul and said, 'Since I have not allowed any desire for this position to gain power in my mind, nor aroused desire for it in my heart, I believe without hesitation that this whole affair truly is from God. Therefore, I will willingly bear in my weakness the hard yoke of governance and the precious sacrament of the priesthood. Let his will be done and his pleasure be fulfilled. Just as I obeyed his word and went forth after him out of this wicked world to keep his commandments, so now I also accept his command faithfully and I will go back in his strength within the world. May I only do his will'.

Now, when Edessa heard the news of the priesthood of its pastor, Rabbula, they hastened to go out to meet him in gladness, and they received him in peace. When he entered [the city] and sat upon the throne of the priest, all the people of Edessa applauded him greatly and acclaimed him with their voices. From the first he demonstrated his excellent diligence concerning the precious rules of the liturgy of the church. 'If the priests of Israel served with reverence and honor in the temporal tent, how much more ought we especially serve as priests with reverence and love in the church of God that he bought with his blood?'[40]

By the wisdom of God within him, he translated the new covenant from Greek to Syriac, exactly as it was, on account of its various alterations.[41] He straightaway ordered that many silver vessels, which had been fashioned with care for the serving of ten tables of clerics, be sold. He distributed equitably the price they fetched for the use of the needy. He gently persuaded the clerics to use clay vessels. He also determined to sell the liturgical vessels of silver and gold which the churches had and to give

[40]Acts 20:28; 1 Pt 1:19.
[41]See the discussion in the Introduction to Rabbula.

the prices they fetched to the poor, as he said, 'It is clear to those
who know that adorned liturgical vessels of gold and silver are
not especially necessary for the glory of God, but that the spirit
of God rests in pure hearts'. Yet his order was neglected because
of their contempt. At the request of many, he was restrained from
doing this because the vessels were the offerings of their earlier,
now deceased, fathers, who had offered them to God for the
redemption of their spirit.

He exhorted his clergy like a father to his own sons and instructed them like a head to its members. He urged them affectionately and spoke in this way: 'You know, my brothers, that,
because we are standing higher in the glorious exalted position
of the priesthood, all the people who stand below us give heed
to us and are guided by us. Therefore, let us not in any way be
a stumbling-block to anyone. Let us not put a blemish on our
ministry, thereby disgracing the ministry of our Lord. Let us never
do anything for which we are despised by our own heart or by
people and especially by God, but in everything let us show
ourselves as ministers of God in all the things that are worthy of
God, as the Apostle said.[42] Let us be adorned with all the comely
beauty of true righteousness, and let us provide in our persons
the example of our deeds, witnesses to those who see us that our
promised hope is certain. Because of this, I am beseeching you,
in the gentleness and in the humility of Christ, before all else to
withdraw from the company of women. Let not one of you ever
be persuaded to let his brother's daughter or his sister's daughter
dwell with him. If possible, and it is not a burden to you, not even
one's mother or one's sister should dwell with any of you, as is
appropriate for purity. Above all, do not disgrace your position of
honor with the service of handmaids or of secular slaves. Let your
independence be held in honor by your brothers, sharers with us
in communion, as is becoming to saints. Alternatively, in the case
that one of you dwells with a companion [priest], may you serve
one another as is befitting to christian love. Except because of
the necessity of illness or the distress of pain, abstain completely
from flesh and fowl, along with bathing; not even in the case

---

[42] 2 Cor 6:4.

of ordinary food should you have concern for an abundance of bodily nourishment lest its pleasure smite you with pestering desires. Let the love of silver or the desire for possessions, something foreign to our ways, not even be mentioned among you. Let not fine clothing or elegant garments diminish the honor of your modesty, but instead of these may you persevere in fasts and prayers and in holy deeds. Let none of you yield himself to what is appropriate to the world or to the contentions of its adherents, but may you be occupied with the reading of the holy Scriptures. Do not delight in frivolous idleness and wander randomly in the streets of the city and take pleasure in idle talk without profit, as empty-headed people [do]. Instead, be assiduous in the ministry of the church of God by day and by night and at all times. In all your conversations, show forth the proof of good servants so that at the sight of you everyone will be assured that the promise of God is believed in your soul'.

Like the prophet, he testified to them by his word as he said, 'If you obey me and listen to me, you shall not only eat the fatness of the earth, but you will contemplate the blessed state of heaven. But if you do not obey me but resist, here and now you will be despised by us before all men, and you will be condemned to the judgement of Gehenna before angels and in the presence of all the ages'.[43]

Those whom his love did not convince gently, fear of him subdued forcibly. For he deservedly trampled the proud among them so that they might repent, and the lowly among them he especially honored so that they might be comforted. He contemned and frequently humiliated those who were walking contemptuously and exalting themselves above their neighbors by their riches, so that they might feel suffering. He exalted and loved exceedingly those who, with complete integrity, led their lives in such a way as to be looked down on through the willing desire for[44] poverty. To them he entrusted the leadership of the church. His concern was that those, who, by his power, were being appointed to the ranks of the priesthood, might be perfect in these virtues, and in

---

[43]Mk 8:38.
[44]I have taken ܐܘ as emphatic, rather than disjunctive.

many more than these. He anxiously agonized for a long time to uncover, by his inquiries, reasons to trust men as genuine whom he could bring to the service of Christ. He was mentally tough and prepared boldly to give his right hand up to be mercilessly cut off[45] rather than to stretch it out rashly upon the head of a man concerning whom he had not received confirmed testimony. He was fulfilling in deed the word of the Apostle;[46] he would in no wise be persuaded to place his hand easily upon a man, lest he participate in a stranger's sins. On the contrary, by the laying on of his hand, he would bring to the holy sacraments of the priesthood one who was free from the desires of his soul and body. With uplifted voice he would proclaim before all the church the names of all those whom he sought to bring into the clergy. By the word of God, he charged all his hearers that, if they knew anything about the candidates that was foreign to God, they should make it known. Besides this, he used to inquire secretly about them with all kinds of inquiries, even inquiring about them from themselves whether they should be rejected for any reason. He truly took care in every way so that, like the pure sacrifice and acceptable offering of Abel, the first priest,[47] men without blemish might be offered by his hand to God.[48] Such was his concern that, as much as is possible to human nature, the priests in their liturgy might be equal to the likeness of the heavenly angels.

Now who can tell of his constant admonitions concerning the chaste covenant of men?[49] For in all the years of his life in the priesthood—twenty-four years—he did not cease from this exhortation. We cannot set down and record the great care of his daily admonitions during his lifetime. He charged and threatened them to withdraw completely from intimacy with women. He ordered and admonished them to not eat flesh or bathe while healthy. He advised and instructed them not to be choked by the

---

[45]Mt 5:30; Mk 9:43.

[46]1 Tm 5:22.

[47]Gen 4:4.

[48]Lev 22:20.

[49]Note that the phrase is not what would become the technical term for a community of male ascetics, *bnay qyama*.

business of the world.[50] He forbade them to lend in usury and in money contracts.[51] He coaxed them with affectionate words to love one another. He advised them that, if possible, each might dwell with his companion.[52] He admonished and beseeched them to be occupied in fasting and to be persevering in prayer.[53] He urged them to show themselves in everything through their deeds and words to be disciples of Christ, and he gave orders in his speech about clothing and shoes and trimming the hairs of their heads so as not to appear wanton.

He was admonishing the entire covenant of women[54] at all times that, because of the veil of chastity, the face of the bride of Christ should absolutely not be seen in the market-place by men's eyes, that they should not at all exhibit the signs of wantonness on any of their clothing, that one of them should by no means go to the assembly or to some appropriate place without the accompaniment of many others. He wanted all the daughters of every deaconess to dwell with her in continence, in holiness, and in modesty. 'The unity of the many can be the preserver of them all'.

He was anxious by every means to snatch people from sin and make them partakers of righteousness. As a diligent shepherd who carefully tends his flocks, he was taking care of this spiritual pasture for the rational flock that was entrusted to him by God. He feared to leave off even a little from solicitude for it, lest, in taking pains about himself alone, perhaps even one soul might perish and be found missing from his people. With great vigilance he kept diligent watch at all times and prayed for [his people]. He was worn out by his anxiety that there be no evil in [his people], either in private or in public. In his love, he took [it] upon himself to be as an abomination[55] if in this way his herd would perform good [deeds]. Such was his goodwill towards his herd.

---

[50]Mk 4:19.

[51]Ex 22:25.

[52]Ps 133:1.

[53]Mk 9:29.

[54]Note that the phrase is not *bnat qyama,* the later technical term for female ascetics [see n. 49].

[55]See Rom 9:3.

At all times in his prayer to God, he labored with great pain on behalf of his people. With his words in the spirit, he fed his flock in the strong meadows of the holy Scriptures. With his words of life, he diligently gave it to drink the divine learning, as from a gentle rain. He preserved what was heavenly by his threats, healed what was sickly with his consolations, and strengthened what was weak by his exhortations, so that he might not ever cause anyone to wander from his flock because of his negligence. For his soul trusted in the blessed hope that a reward was kept for his toil, according to testimony of God, who said to him in that parable of the talents: 'O good and faithful servant, you have been faithful over a little, I will place you over much. Enter into the joy of your Lord'.[56]

His excellent ordinances towards the priests of the villages and the monasteries and the covenant are more than can be told. As far as our strength holds, we will refer to them as needed. By the grace of God, his word was seasoned at all times with salt,[57] and was able to impart grace to all those who faithfully received it. His word was believed by his hearers because they saw his actions. His deeds and his words gave profit to everyone at their sight and sound, and as true witnesses were accepted by everyone. His word was fearsome in its reproof and weighty in its correction; it was beloved in its exhortation and profitable to those who truly heard him. For his lips were speaking from the fullness of his heart,[58] and they were encouraging everyone [to perform] splendid deeds [like] his. He did not deign to dazzle by his word, but only to say how a person might be turned to God, from evil deeds to deeds of righteousness. It was not out of a lack of knowledge of these [dazzling skills] and the like, but from a concern about what was most excellent and profitable for people. For he never agreed to employ the embellishments of polished words in his expositions. He did not speak in church so that the excellence of his wisdom might be made known and that he might take praise to himself, like others rejected by their hearers.

[56]Mt 25:21.
[57]Col 4:6.
[58]Mt 12:34.

Rather, he took pains to circumcise by his sharp word the heart of his hearers from evil deeds to good, and he was anxious that they not reject the praise of God because of his words. As if he was recalling in his homily the powerful sound of the prophet Jeremiah, so trumpet-like he proclaimed in the ears of his people that they should separate themselves from iniquity and sins, which bring forth dissoluteness.

He also corrected those who were hastening to the unseemly and disreputable games in the theater and in the circus to look on with lust. By his authoritative words, he completely did away with the foul sight of wild beasts who shed the blood of human beings in the stadium. He rightly threatened and said, 'God forbid that it should happen in a city of believers that human beings, who eat the flesh of God in their faith and drink his blood, should in the games see the flesh of humans eaten impiously by evil beasts'. By his word, he pointed out to them the scabs of sins which, unperceived, ruled their souls in the guise of pleasure. As he himself suffered on their behalf in his love for them, so he truly felt pain because of those who, to the ruin of their lives, acted very badly by not obeying. He did not speak out perfunctorily to testify to the people that they should turn from their evil deeds in order that, because he gave a warning, he might save his own soul, but he preached so that what God confessed by the mouth of the prophet might be fulfilled: 'If you bring forth precious from worthless, you will be like my mouth'.[59] Thus he labored with all his strength.

As for those who were beaten back from the profession of celibacy and virginity by the sores of sins in their flesh, we need only repeat in his words the pains of sadness which stirred him in his heart on their account. When he would hear that someone who had been healthy in a well-ordered way of life had fallen sick through some evil deed, was he not with that person in the pain that he suffered on his account? Or if a report came to Rabbula that a disciple of Christ caused scandal against his profession[60] or

---

[59]Jer 15:19.

[60]The term used is ܩܝܡܐ: perhaps the vow to enter the covenant of men or women is meant.

was scandalized in his faith, was not Rabbula in pain because of this as if he was being burnt up by fire? At all times, as a skillful doctor, he discerned what he might appropriately use against the various types of diseases of the soul. Sometimes, as if with sharpened iron, he cut the pus of the ulcer with a merciful correction appropriate to the reprimand for impiety, so that he might cause suffering and restore life. Sometimes, as if with strong herbs, he was able to kill off the folly by the threats of his words and heal the stubbornness of the disease to bring the sinner to penitence and help. Sometimes, as if with cooling medicines, he healed the sickness of desire by the calm persuasion of his affectionate commands, which were suitable to the correction of the offender, to strengthen and restore [him]. In every way his concern was only that, by his learned care, they come back to the compunction which restores life.

In these and more ways than these, he faithfully demonstrated his solicitude for his flock. For truly he feared the just judgement threatened by God against those shepherds who took care of themselves but neglected their flocks. He truly believed that in the end an honest reckoning would be made with those shepherds, according to the word of Our Lord which he attested to them: 'He to whom much is entrusted, even much is required from him'.[61] Thus, with all his strength, his heart was diligent to admonish, train, and rebuke everyone with full authority, either by word or deed, in season and out.[62] Yet, his physical strength was not as robust as the prompting of his will. His goodwill was stronger than his physical strength, and the consciences of the upright bear witness [to this].

The excellent deeds of the person of my lord Rabbula, the bishop, were constant in these following customs. At times, he was worn out by much fasting. Even his nourishment was like a complete fast. Not only did he allow no laxity in his soul by varying his menu, but even at meals he never agreed fully to satisfy his hunger. He broke his fast with three ounces of bread and one plain, shriveled fruit in his belly, while he abstained from oil and wine. From the day that the name of Christ was invoked over

[61]Lk 12:48.
[62]2 Tm 4:1-3.

him, nothing could overwhelm him and persuade him to satisfy his hunger. By his endurance, he waged constant war against all desires. He was absolutely not overpowered to desire even the slightest thing and taste it, but always he was lifted up and very exalted in his victory over these weak passions, which can abase [even] the strong, under the stern subjection of the necessity he imposed upon [these passions]. To everyone he taught, in his own person, a strenuous, but not ostentatious, fast, and also a plain diet. When he was urged to receive the great magnificence of various foods brought to him in faith by many people for his use, he would send them to the sick, to the afflicted in the hospitals, and to those suffering diseases as they dwelt alone in solitude. As for the contemptible material of his worthless table, all of it was comprised of glass platters, and clay dishes with wooden spoons.[63]

He also trained the members of his household in the same way, as far as they were able. They, too, were zealous, willing to embody in themselves the likeness of his virtue. They spent much of the night with him in constant vigils of psalms and prayers, while during the day they toiled, visiting the oppressed and studying in his presence. Every day they fasted with him. Their need was satisfied by two meals of dry pulse and vegetables. Even the worn-out color with which their faces as well as his own were adorned sufficed to indicate at a glance their straitened way of life. As men who ate from one meager table, their countenances were wasted away to a pale pallor. Even when a bishop, he was diligent to maintain the hard travails of his monastic way of life. The gift of the spirit of the priesthood was for him a helpful partner towards all the virtues. This fact is quite amazing: of the men who dwelt with him for twenty-four years in his monastery, not one of those who served with him in that long stretch of time was able to enter to him customarily with ease, or to speak to him with ease. Everyday their awe of him increased. Their minds trembled from fear of him, as if they were coming into his presence for the first time. It was not that they were made to quake by someone stern and awesome,

---

[63]As we noted earlier in the *Life,* Rabbula had tried to get rid of silver and gold liturgical vessels. Here the utensils of his own table are described as those used by poor people.

but they stood in reverence, as in the presence of one who is wise and venerable. His nobility was not diminished by anything base in their sight; he never willingly gave even an occasion for them to be scandalized in their conscience. For he who even in his own eyes was not conscious of anything impious, how much more [was he] so noble and honorable in the eyes of his companions and of all men? Thus he was both revered and beloved.

Now those members of his monastery, with all his own clergy, were always bound to him by the word of God so that they would accept absolutely nothing from men in the likeness of a present or an honorarium. He even made all the priests of his diocese subject at all times to the punishment of suspension, so that they would not dare to bring anything at all to one of his companions or to one from all his clergy. 'In the case that they bring us a present calling it a blessing, we, who are held in honor by them, rightly should give [the blessing]. In the case of an honorarium, this is a mockery as we, who possess the authority, appropriately confer honor. But in the case of a gift from compulsion, we, who would be supported by them, should have no part [in such a transaction].[64] Therefore, on every count it is we who are under an obligation to give, and not to receive'.

What monk can be compared to him as regards his high degree of privation? In mind he was a monk, and his habitual clothing

---

[64]The previous three sentences are extremely cryptic. I have been influenced in my translation by the canons for clergy and the 'men of the covenant' attributed to Rabbula, canons 5, 6, and 8, and greatly helped by Sebastian Brock, and stirred on by Daniel Caner. I understand them as specifying the earlier absolute prohibition against accepting anything. The first case is particularly problematic as the syriac word ܪܘܚܐ often means 'bribe'. Canon 5 states that the priests and deacons and *periodeutae* should not take a bribe ܪܘܚܐ from anyone, especially those who are engaged in a lawsuit. 'Bribe' is particularly appropriate in the case of lawsuits, and for something illegal. It seems, however, that in the present case Rabbula is more concerned with stating that his people should not take blessings, as they are the ones who give blessings. His clergy should not be under any obligation to non-members, who might be trying to curry favor with them. I have therefore opted for the more general meaning of 'present', which the root meaning of ܫܘܚ would allow. To rephrase the text: rightly we give blessings, we don't receive them, and anyone who sends us one is trying to win our favor, i.e. bribe us.

was a hair tunic and a modest mantle. At the liturgy of the church, he used to wear in winter the one cloak he possessed, and, in summer, one sleeveless vestment. His humble bedding consisted only of a mat, a coverlet, and under his head a small pillow cut from a monk's cloak sufficed.

As for the form of his prayer before God, the fixed times of the liturgy were not sufficient for him. Because of this, he used now and again to set apart a week for continual prayer. He would shut himself off from converse with humanity in the cell of his monastery, concealed from the sight of his attendants. He even stopped reading so that, by refraining from the sound and noise of men, in the quiet stillness of his thoughts his reason might be completely tranquil, his mind aroused in the remembrance of his Lord, his intellect fervent in the spirit of his God, and his prayer might profit him in his solitude. In this way, he offered an acceptable sacrifice[65] of purified intercession to his Lord in his secret[66] temple, as he lifted up through the hands of his soul the record of the sins of the world to receive from before the Lord the pardon of their sins through His boundless mercy. In that stolen stillness of a few days of prayer, who knows how to relate the amazing transformations by which his mind was renewed by the spirit of God?[67] Only the perfect who, like him, were instructed in the hidden secrets of prayer. Doubtless it was easy for the perfect, from the perception of his words, to distinguish the hidden signs performed by the grace of God in his heart. As that which the devourers of the love of God truly hunger after and its drinkers thirst for again,[68] so was he more and more driven by the good desire for the mercy of his Lord. Forty days a year he would leave the city and the constraints of its affairs. He would fervently flee and go far away and perch in his monastery in the desert of Qennishrin, so that there he might entreat earnestly in prayer and strongly implore that his requests be answered.

[65]Rom 12:1.

[66]See Mt 6:6.

[67]Literally, 'the amazing transformations which from the spirit of God were renewed/gained new strength in his mind?'

[68]Sir 24:20–21; Prv 9:5; Is 55:1; Rev 22:17.

Whenever he represented the people before God in prayer, his eyes never ceased from weeping mournfully until he stood up from his kneeling. The flowing multitude of his tears was so great that the sight of it saddened even the fierce and merciless. From the fervor of his spirit, tears poured forth to descend from his eyes to his breast whenever he sat down on his throne in the liturgy. He served in God's presence wisely, fearing the honor of the priesthood because our human nature is guilty, yet confident in true love according to the will of God.

Now the heavenly discipline of this angel-in-the-flesh was shown in this way: many different remedies of healing were distributed to the sick because of the strength of his prayer, and his faith drove out from people grievous afflictions from evil spirits. His word truly examined all whom he knew so that, whether he was deservedly angry with someone or decidedly in agreement with that person, God was conversing with him. Because of this, the reputation of his prayer alone was sufficiently fearsome peacefully to resolve the strife of a man and his companion. How many times would the people, because of the fervor of their faith in him, rend his garments in their desire, and exchange the garments among themselves like *hnana*[69] so that a blessing might be transferred from his clothing to many of them? Also, many from the city and from the whole province trustingly named their sons and even their daughters with the honored name of Rabbula for a blessing. For his flock kept close under the wings[70] of his name and of his prayer for protection, and implored its full healing to attain a long life. He was a powerful city wall which strongly surrounded all his district, one which was never broken down by any of the deceitful affairs of the devil. Those who dwelt within its fortified precincts conducted their lives in good order and in tranquil security through their trust in him.

---

[69] *Hnana* literally means 'pity, mercy, compassion'. However, it came to refer to a mixture of oil, dust and water mixed with the relics of saints or with earth from holy places which was then used to anoint the sick.

[70] Mt 23:37.

By his authority he kept men away from plunder or oppression or merciless demands. Who would dare to plunder a poor man or defraud the needy or trouble his neighbor when fear that the judgement of God, through Rabbula's zeal, might be brought to light against him for his chastisement. The rich man who dealt evilly with a poor man quaked at the mere mention of him and was rebuked. Someone who in his accounting defrauded one poorer than himself quailed and was frightened through fear of Rabbula's name. Everyone hastened to transact his business with his neighbor with an honest accounting so as not to be reproved before Rabbula in a lawsuit. The greedy mouth of defrauders was bound by the muzzle of Rabbula's justice, so that their unjust oppressions could not openly attack the poor, and the ravenous hands of rapacious men were tied by the bands of his honesty, so that their coercive strength could not oppress the weak. Who was there among the nobles of his city or among those who, to do evil, take refuge in the respected houses of powerful people who lifted up his head and proudly boasted and, suddenly, was not entirely crushed by the heel of [Rabbula's] strength so that he was sorry for acting rashly? Or who was there among the judges . . .[71] of his day. . . who determined . . . against Rabbula's decision and did not God swiftly . . . overtake that judge with punishment so that he repented because he had acted foolishly? Or who . . . among all the people in power [was not haughty whose pride] exalted him over Rabbula's humble style of living . . . and did not speedily. . . the righteousness of God act so that he repented that he had sinned. All the orphans and widows in his district, because of their trust in him, dwelt as in a tranquil harbor, because, through their refuge in him, they were not harmed unexpectedly by the tossing waves of savage plunderers. In his day, not only were soldiers restrained from hurting a craftsman or harming the field-laborers, but they were even forcibly brought by his nobility to honor the monastic habit[72]—however despicable to the eye—in the one who wore it. For God so instilled the fear and the love of him in all men, whatever their rank, that many, out of fear and shame, were preserved through him from a multitude

---

[71]Part of the last eight lines in the right bottom of fol. 107 are missing.
[72]Literally, 'christian attire'.

of sins . . . was difficult/stubborn[73]. . . . that someone be found in his jurisdiction . . . world so that the status of marriage . . . should be spoiled out of contempt. . . . Then one of two sisters . . . while he/she[74] had . . . the first who departed. . . . Or he did not allow a man to marry the daughter of his brother or the daughter of his sister. Above all, it was absolutely impossible for a man to divorce his wife for any reason when Rabbula became cognizant of it, for such a divorce is foreign to the will of God.

He did not omit to examine anything that was brought to his hearing. How many times did even the memory of the power of his divine zeal suffice to pre-empt and restrain many from the hateful onset of evil deeds which were being prepared? In his day, who among the infatuated would openly lift up his gaze lustfully to look closely on a lovely modest face? For when he simply recollected the holiness of the pure one, the earth would shake beneath him and the heavens above him and, with a gentle coolness, his body would become calm and rested. Who was there among the disciples of Christ who clothed themselves in clean and washed garments, so as vaingloriously to appear important on the streets of the city? Who, when he saw the dignity of Rabbula as he stood representing the people in such humble attire, would not be so ashamed of himself that he despised his desire? Who was there among the greedy, enslaved to the evil power of the belly's desire, who would presume to eat greedily or drink intemperately when he remembered the table of this splendid person, whose hunger was never satiated? The fear of him set some people right, and the desire to please him preserved others. As for the lovers of money, wasting their lives in the nothingness of commerce, if some one of them noticed honestly that, by means of that steward of God, grace was distributing in one year seven thousand *darics* to the poor—as well as what was needed by his colleagues in the ministry and for all those inscribed on the welfare roles of his city—did that person not at once judge

---

[73]The state of the manuscript does not allow one to decide on the proper connotation of the syriac word.

[74]The state of the manuscript does not allow one to decide if the suffix here is masculine or feminine.

his soul and find himself guilty? Would he not hate his fault and run, like that just one, to help out with the gifts of his alms, so that, in all things, he might imitate the compassion of God?

In all the years of his life, he did not consent to build anything on earth, except for half of the northern nave of the church of the community of his city, which he was forced to do because it was damaged, and that he fixed up in a few days. 'According to an honest assessment, we ourselves live from what belongs to the poor. The poor are sustained not by what belongs to us, but by the righteousness of God. For whatever the Church possesses, she inherits from believing persons for the sustenance of orphans and widows and the needy. According to an honest assessment, to us leaders is allowed as much as the body needs, so that we may use some of it in a simple manner—like the rest of the poor—and not as our body, which desires whatever is hurtful to our spirit, wills'.

There is much to say about the acuteness of his knowledge and the clarity of his understanding; he understood the affairs of each person by his words. Because he was filled with the spirit of God, false words were not able to hide the face of truth to lead him astray by lies. From the spirit of wisdom of God in him, the mind of those who were being judged before him was so shaken that they would speak the truth, even if unwillingly, as their speech was tripped up in their mouth from fright. It was superfluous to seek further for a witness for the condemnation of the accused. For he was able, by himself, to discern by his examination who was guilty and who innocent, so that judgement was pronounced by him not perversely, but rightly. As if he were someone into whose mind people's thoughts crept, so, by his inquiry, he arrived at their secrets to know the truth. Wisdom and intelligence and greatness of heart were given to him in great quantity by God, as to Solomon.[75] On the one hand, his justice was boundless. It worked with authority and power against the scornful, hardened in their pride to commit injustice against the poor. On the other hand, there was no limit to the riches of his kindness, which poured forth abundantly upon the poor in body and in spirit who, by their endurance, were victorious in the crucible of poverty. In

[75] 1 Kgs 4:29.

his justice and in his mercy, he was always guided only as God willed. In his generation and in his time, he was another Moses, as his righteous zeal was detested and hated by evil-doers, and his humble manner despised and contemned by the boastful.

He was like Moses not only in these qualities, but in every thing. In his difficult conflicts with a multitude of religions he imitated Joshua bar Nun,[76] and especially the zeal of Josiah.[77] It was said of him, as it was to Joshua: 'Be strong and act bravely and do not fear, because I am with you to help you'.[78] Just as Joshua bar Nun and Josiah had found the land of Canaan planted throughout with the thorns of paganism, so he found all the land of Edessa thickly grown with all the thorns of sin. Especially flourishing in Edessa was the evil teaching of Bardaisan,[79] until it was condemned and vanquished by him. This accursed Bardaisan, by his artifice and by the sweetness of his melody, had earlier seized to himself all the nobles of the city, so as to be protected by them as by strong city walls. The foolish man thought, as he strayed and caused those with him to stray, that he could firmly establish his error by the feeble strength of those he had helped. However, Rabbula, this wise ploughman of the fields of the heart, not only was vigorous to uproot from his field the hindering tares and to leave the growing grains of wheat (for this was easy), but, in his wisdom, he was also diligent to change those weeds to grains of wheat (for this also was necessary).[80] At the time of Joshua, the powerful sound of the trumpets blown by Joshua and his people shook the walls of Jericho and they tumbled down; Joshua slew

[76]Joshua bar Nun was the successor of Moses (Num 27:18-23). Josh 3:9 states that God was with Joshua as with Moses, and Israel is said to have revered Joshua as they had Moses (Josh 4:14). He had recommended that, confident in God's help, the Israelites should attack the land of Canaan (Num 14:6-10). The Book of Joshua depicts him as leading the assault on Canaan and its conquest and allotment.

[77]Josiah, son of King Amon, ruled Israel from 639–609 BCE. According to 2 Kings 23, he initiated a religious reform to remove all traces of foreign worship and to centralize worship of God in Jerusalem.

[78]Dt 31:23; Josh 1:9.

[79]See the discussion of Bardaisan in the introduction to the *Life of Rabbula*.

[80]Mt 13:24-30.

the people of Jericho and devoted their possessions to the Lord.[81] In contrast, Rabbula, this victorious captain of the host of Jesus Christ, with a gentle and loving voice was able, through the power of his God, to destroy noiselessly their place of assembly and carry off all its treasure and bring it to his community—he even took its stones to use! He gently persuaded those people for whom he fully cared, and leniently subdued them. He made [them] return to the solid truth of the Church of the apostles as they renounced and anathematized their error. Then he baptized them in Christ and made them partakers in his liturgy. In this manner he prevailed by his teaching over many of the sects and he subdued them to the truth. Thousands of Jews and myriads of heretics he baptized in Christ during all the years of his priesthood.

In the armor of the spirit which he wore,[82] he was able to subdue even the Arians to the truth of the sublime Trinity. For he pulled down their prayer-house and brought them to his own. He joined the people who were with them to his flock as together we assigned equal praise to the one essence, the three persons of the Father and the Son and the Holy Spirit.

As for the Marcionites,[83] I cannot even with many words declare how great was his solicitude towards them. Through his diligence, the most victorious great healer, with the help of his God, healed this putrid, gangrenous ulcer of the error of the Marcionites by his patience with them. For God made dwell in them fear of the holy Rabbula; they accepted his truth faithfully as they renounced their error.

---

[81]Josh 6.

[82]Eph 6:11-17.

[83]Marcion was a second-century Christian who was expelled from the christian community of Rome in 144. He died around 160 CE. Inspired by his reading of Paul's epistles, Marcion passionately believed in the newness of the revelation in Jesus, and in the new creation inaugurated by Jesus. He was led to reject physical creation and its creator-god, the god of the Hebrew Scriptures, as a god of justice, while embracing the God of Jesus, a God of mercy and love. His rejection of the Hebrew Scriptures led him to reject those christian writings which thought favorably of the them. Consequently, he rejected the Gospel of Matthew and emended the Gospel of Luke and the pauline epistles. His dislike of the god of this creation led him to adopt a very rigorous ascetic life-style, including abstinence from marriage.

In this way, by means of his divine wisdom, he brought even the insane Manichees[84] to a sound mind of discerning knowledge. They confessed just as he desired; they believed in the truth, were baptized in Christ, and added to his people. Also, as long as they existed, whenever he found the foul error and unclean tradition of the Borborians,[85] he mercifully cast them out to [distant] abodes. There is great folly among them, and it is abominable for pure lips to speak of their foul teachings to purified ears. Because of this, he determined that they never be found in his district.

As for the Audians[86] and the Sadducees who are heretics, who had separated themselves from contact with the Church as anathematized by the truth and had begotten for themselves a false priesthood in the likeness of the true one, straying, blind to the truth, after babbling visions: that true shepherd acted towards them so as to take care of his flock. He scattered their assemblies. He made them strangers to the church they had adorned and he expelled them from it. In their place he settled brothers who

---

[84]Mani came from a christian family, but early in his life began to receive revelations from his 'heavenly twin'. He vigorously preached his beliefs until his martyrdom in the 270s CE. Mani believed in two equal and opposed forces, the kingdom of light and the kingdom of darkness. Through a complex process, the kingdom of darkness had succeeded in capturing within itself some of the particles of light, and it was the duty of all to recognize that they had these light particles in themselves and to return to the kingdom of light. Jesus had come from the kingdom of light as a revealer, to awaken people to knowledge. Manichaeism, the movement which looked back to Mani as its founder, became a world-wide religion, reaching from Africa—Augustine of Hippo was a Manichee in his early years—and Rome to western China. Fervent Manichees were rigorous ascetics.

[85] ܒܪܒܘܪ̈ܝܐ most likely to be identified with the gnostic group known as the Borborites as described by Epiphanius in *Against Heresies* 26.1–17. The name is attested at the heading at 26.1.1 and at 26.3.6, where the name is explained as arising from their filthy perversity, i.e. from βορβορος, 'mud, filth', and appears to be a pejorative play on the name Barbero, another name for Barbelo, the second principle in the gnostic system. Epiphanius accuses the Borborites of many sexual perversities.

[86]The Audians are discussed by Epiphanius in *Against Heresies*, 70. Epiphanius praises their life-style, but criticizes their literal interpretation of 'made in the image of God', by which God's form is the same as man's. He notes that they celebrated Easter at Passover after the fashion of the Jews. It is most likely this last point that enables the author of the *Life* to call them the Sadducees of the heretics.

were partakers of our sacrament. Those who repented he made partakers in his own flock.

In this manner, he showed his care even for Messalian heretics. He brought them to his own place and instructed them in Christ. They accepted his teaching with joy as they renounced their error. This true shepherd was diligent to imitate the love of the heavenly father, as his love towards God was perfect.[87] He demonstrated his care in actions equally towards the good and the wicked. Because of this, he did not neglect even the stubborn people of Israel, but at all times he showed his especial care for them in his actions. For not only did he not deprive them from partaking of the alms of his kindness, but, every year, many of them gladly consented to receive the sign of life, the baptism of Christ, because of his constant exhortations to them.

The blessed Rabbula broke the arrows and bows of the haters of the truth with the shield of his faith,[88] and he conquered the enemy of truth with the weapons of God he held. He subdued with the trampling of truth all the shoots of error, and he wiped clean through the remedy of his teaching the abominable spots of the blasphemies of apostates.[89] He made all his flock one wholesome body of the perfect human.[90] From that time, he started to rest a little and refresh himself because of the gains he had wrested in his battles with erroneous teachings. He began to be anxious only for his own soul and for the household of his faith in matters especially of being perfected, cautioning and admonishing and exhorting those who were perfect, 'It is necessary that we earn heavenly gains with deeds of righteousness as long as we are in the world, so that the true leader might be present to us for a good end, and that we come boldly with him into the kingdom of heaven'.

As he so admonished and instructed his household with these words, and stirred up others with many [words] like these to deeds and to words, there was—as is reported by trustworthy

[87]Cf. Mt 5:44-48.
[88]Eph 6:16.
[89]2 Pt 2:13; Eph 5:27.
[90]Here the author seems to be using the language of Eph 2:14-16 to speak of his christian community in Edessa as a part of Christ's body.

people who learned about it—one bitter plant, the blooms of whose youth the fire of lust had consumed until it grew old and was worn out and was destroyed by death. Its pampered body rotted and became dung in the earth. From this plant, the spirit of lying bred one accursed sprout, Nestorius, the wicked pupil of that Theodore.[91] This lying spirit put into his mouth fatal fruits which blinded with a hidden death. Nestorius first received an accursed seed from the teaching of Theodore and from his close relationship with him. Because it [the seed] insulted human piety, it was choked in the earth of his wicked heart and covered over. When, on some pretext, he seized for himself the exalted throne of the high-priesthood in the great imperial city,[92] he showed himself to be a fool as he proudly went astray. The result was that, through the powerful strength of his authority and the assistance of the nobles of the empire, he easily turned everyone towards his blasphemies. From then on, he presumed to speak calumny against the Most High and he slandered the one who bore him. Now I tremble even to mention the blasphemies that he dared to utter: 'The blessed Mary did not beget God, but she begot a human'. 'If Mary begot the Son, Elizabeth begot the Holy Spirit'.[93] In the insolence of his rebellious[94] heart, he was not moved even to revere the word of the Apostle, which said, 'God sent his son and he was from a woman and he was under the law'.[95] He was shameless in his arrogance, so that he allowed only that the Son indwelt in Jesus as the Spirit indwelt in John. Again, 'That slave who was born from a woman[96] suffered according to his nature

[91]Theodore, bishop of Mopsuestia, who died in 428 CE. He was known as 'The Exegete' because of his commentaries on the Scriptures. His anti-arian polemic led him to insist that the humanity assumed by the divine Logos was a true subject of the human actions of Christ; yet Theodore also took care to emphasize the union between the divine and the human in Christ. Although he died before the nestorian controversy erupted, he was seen by the opponents of Nestorius as the source of Nestorius' thinking, and Theodore was condemned at the Council of Constantinople in 553 CE.

[92]I.e. Constantinople.

[93]See Lk 1:13-17. We do not know if Nestorius ever argued in this fashion.

[94]Overbeck has ܟܝܢܐ, whereas the manuscript reads ܟܝܢܗ.

[95]Gal 4:4.

[96]Phil 2:7-8.

those things which happened[97] to him'. 'The Son who dwelt in him did those signs that He willed'. Therefore, so as [to do] no more to relate the error of that excommunicate, these suffice to make known to the wise the greatness of his impiety. He so railed against his[98] life as impudently to declare, by the distinction of his words, two different sons, one of nature and one of grace. When the holy Rabbula heard of the blasphemies the rebel Nestorius was speaking, his heart was smitten with fear and he was shaken. He early on apprehended, through the wisdom of God in him, what hateful harm would swiftly come upon the flock of Christ through that shameful prelate.

From then on, Rabbula began to speak against his error as he showed how his words truly derived from the trustworthy witness of the divine Scriptures. 'The holy Mary truly begot God. "For behold" the prophet Isaiah said, "A virgin will conceive and bring forth a son and they will call his name Immanuel",[99] which is translated "Our God is with us". And behold, Jeremiah proclaimed, "Our God is seen on earth and lives among men".[100] And behold, the apostle Paul puts a seal on the words of the prophets; he made known that the birth of his Lord in the flesh from the seed of the house of David, and he declared that the same is the son of God.[101] Behold, John explains in his gospel that "the Word became flesh and dwelt among us" and "we saw his glory, the glory as of the only-begotten who is from the father".[102] For John said, "In the beginning was the Word" and "the Word became flesh",[103] without [saying]—God forbid!—that His nature

---

[97]The manuscript has a singular verb instead of a plural. Could this be a sign of translation from an original greek saying of Nestorius?

[98]It is unclear whether the third person singular masculine suffix refers to Nestorius (i.e. his insolence would cause him to lose eternal life) or to Jesus (i.e. he railed against or derided how Jesus had brought life to humans by the union of the divine and human in one person).

[99]Is 7:14.

[100]Bar 3:37.

[101]Rom 1:3-4.

[102]Jn 1:14.

[103]Jn 1:1,14.

was changed. He, the Lord of all, assumed the likeness of a slave,[104] in that He became a complete human while this did not destroy that He was God. The unity of his divinity and of his humanity was preserved. One was the nature and the person of the eternal Son as He had been before he was embodied. He suffered in the flesh by his will, He who by nature could not suffer. Because of this, he died in the body but he is alive in the spirit. He preached to the souls shut up in Sheol,[105] and afterwards he rose in the glory of his father and ascended to heaven, the place where he had been from eternity and for ever'.

Thus our blessed father was stretching out and shooting these spiritual arrows from the bow of his faith by the vigorous string of his true speech. Although they passed through the ears of the people harmlessly and encouraged [them], yet they struck the heart of any opponent to cause him pain and to move him to regret.

At this time, an honorable cause summoned him to go up [to Constantinople] and publicly to confute the ancient error of the recent Jew, Nestorius, that rejected silver still gilded in the priesthood, still puffed up by the pride of pomp and sitting upon the exalted throne of office. Face to face in the sight of the whole church gathered together, with a lofty unashamed voice, Rabbula proclaimed straightforwardly the word of truth. He corrected the perversity of the false teaching of [his opponent] by the true profession of his own faith. Now, after we have written his life, we will set down—for the persuasion of many and for the benefit of everyone—that discourse which the blessed one spoke in the tyrant's ears in the great church in Constantinople so that it may be seen openly by everyone and how his discourse, spoken from the robust witness of his pure conscience, gave great confidence. He did not neglect to uncover that one's error and make known his own truth even to the pious Christ-loving emperors and to all the imperial nobles who hold office. They received him with fear and love and with great honor, as if he were an angel[106] of God or the last of the apostles. From the fervor of their love towards him,

[104]Phil 2:7.
[105]1 Pt 3:19-22.
[106]Manuscript has plural.

they insisted affectionately in faith on kissing his hands so that
they might be blessed by him and have profit. From afar, the noble
report of his excellence in God had stirred them to good deeds.
Often they, and some even more distant than they in the upper
kingdom of Rome, had sent many thousands of gold pieces for the
support of the poor. Much more profitable, however, was being in
close view of him, and much more pleasurable was his conversing
with them. In his homily, he exhorted them to everything that was
good. Now, he had gladly received the gold sent to him from afar.
But when the emperors and the honored ones in person brought
a great deal of gold, with ornaments and clothing, to him, and
they asked him to receive their offerings, he was fearful and said,
'Although truly the actions which forced me to come up here are
evident, perhaps it might seem to them that I sought for myself
a false pretext by which I could come before them and take gifts
from them'. Then, because he would not be despised by any one
of them for any reason, and he would not for anything pawn his
freedom, he was more precious in their eyes and was believed.

As we said before, he showed Nestorius to be wrong and un-
masked his error. He testified to the people about him, and he
declared his own true faith. He persuaded and enlightened the
emperors by his truth, and he exhorted and strengthened the
nobles by his teaching. By words and by actions, he abundantly
helped all who saw him in the cities through which he passed as he
went there and back, until he arrived with love at his own city.

There he remained, continually fighting against that ungodly
person who had recently appeared until that Good Shepherd,
who suffered in place of his sheep, was aroused against him with
an upright judgement by means of faithful and holy bishops from
the south and the west. By the guidance of the Holy Spirit, they
decided to expel him from the rank of the priesthood.[107] He was
preserved for the just judgement of God, in which he will be
answerable along with those who agreed with him.

---

[107]This refers to the summoning by emperor Theodosius II of the First
Council at Ephesus in 431 CE. For a discussion of the council, see the Introduction to Hiba.

Because it is impossible for me to show the battle of our father against this error in a prolonged narrative, or even to declare in a few words the contest of the blessed one for the sake of the true belief of the Church; the forty-six letters that he wrote to priests and emperors and nobles and monks will suffice. These—if grace assists—we will labor to translate from Greek into Syriac so that they may make known to those who come across them what sort of divine zeal was burning and inflaming him, as if by a fire. He was a faithful son of Paul in his hope and in his love.[108] Even if he did not pray that he be accursed from Christ on behalf of his brothers and his kinsfolk in the flesh as the apostle had,[109] Rabbula was anxious, ten thousand times over if it be possible, to be offered in sacrifice for the sake of Jesus in the place of his spiritual brothers and kinsfolk, and that this should occur publicly, which the times did not allow. He spent the days of his life in this world in the constant sufferings of the cross through the willing pain and the voluntary afflictions that were manifested in his person.[110]

Not only was he like Paul in these matters, but also as regards the great favor which was entrusted to Paul by the earlier apostles to take care of the poor.[111] Rabbula was concerned to perform this service too. He kept it as diligently as if he, along with Paul, had received from the apostles this commandment to care for the poor. Who can relate the great care he had for the sustenance of the poor, especially the lofty love he possessed for the poor holy ones? Now, each of the solitary dwelling-places of the monasteries of pious men—who steadily lived the life of a recluse and whose bones, even after their departure were a sweet fragrance in Christ—possessed, at his command, a solitary cell for him. He wished that, as often as he came to visit them, he might be helped in his faith by those who had fallen asleep in peace and especially that he might help their disciples with his exhortations. In the cell he would silently dwell alone to persevere in prayer acceptable

[108]See Rom 5:1-11; 8:18-39; 1 Cor 13.
[109]Rom 9:3.
[110]Lk 9:23.
[111]Gal 2:9-10; Acts 11:29-30; 2 Cor 8:1-4; 9:1; Rom 15:26; 1 Cor 16:1-4; Acts 24:17.

to God and so that his prayer might profit him. Although many and frequent were the offerings of his alms to all people at all times, he also particularly desired to offer himself as a sacrifice to Christ on behalf of all people. According to the desire of his good will towards God and people, he supported his fellow poor out of what belonged to his Lord for as long as he lived in the world according to the will of God. Even after his departure, he left them a good inheritance of prayer, and he entrusted them to the grace of God, the mother of all, so that, from her,[112] the necessity of their needs might be fully supplied every day. Because the fire of love for Rabbula lives on in their hearts, and the precious memory of the beloved name of Rabbula is preserved, her support and her flame reflect the fire of love in their hearts. Because of this, all the needy obtain the supply of their necessities through his good name, as from a gracious fullness. As soon as his friends hear the sweet name of Rabbula, love of him is inflamed in their hearts. Their compassion bubbles up and they give alms. The recipient rejoices, and the giver is helped, and God is praised as, in this way, the work of our father Rabbula towards his Lord is preserved because it is said among Christians, 'Blessed is the servant on whose account the name of his master is praised'.

Because of the love of the poor which he had in his soul, he worked an excellent change in the hospital of his city. What before had been nominally but not really [a hospital] he deemed truly worthy to be [supported] for the glory of God, and to serve appropriately to honor God. He set apart for the hospital certain estates from the wealth of his church so that, from their harvests, what the hospital expended in order to exist might be provided. An opportunity was provided to many to leave riches and property to the hospital in their wills, so that, from them, a thousand *denarii* might be the total income for the hospital in one year. Thus, there was relief for the weak and benefits for the healthy through the provision of his word. Who was there from those whose conscience was foul who did not earnestly desire to feed from the variety of meals for the sick provided through

---

[112]Here grace is personified, and, as 'grace' is a feminine noun, so grace is seen as feminine.

the diligence of his decree? It was impossible for someone to have known through [any sign of] negligence that the sick and those smitten with sores had been placed there, because of the care and the cleanliness upon them by his decree. For their beds were pleasant with soft bedding placed upon them; no dirty or vile linen was there, or ever seen upon them. Trustworthy and truly caring deacons were put in charge by him for the relief their ministration brought and for the provision of what was needed. Along with them were sober brethren full of love who did nothing different for them than what the deacons did.

He acted in the same manner in the hospital for women, which had not even existed at all. By his decree, one had been quickly constructed out of stones from four temples of idols in his city which had been with authority destroyed at his command. He wisely appointed a trustworthy deaconess with women who were daughters of the covenant, so that they might fulfill modestly and readily their ministry of comfort.

From the love of God, which blazed and burnt like a fire compassionately for his fellow human beings, he especially manifested his great care upon the poor lepers who dwelt in isolation outside the city, hated and despised. He put in charge of them a steadfast deacon, who dwelt beside them, with trustworthy brethren appointed to minister to them. Everything necessary for their need came continually from the church inside, while Rabbula himself at all times refreshed their souls by action and by word. Through the action of his charismatic gift, he healed the suffering of their diseases; through the word of God he comforted their mind, that it not be choked by distress. How many times, as a comfort to their souls, did he place the peace of a holy kiss upon the rotting lips of men whose bodies were putrefying, and strengthen them so that their mind not lose hope because of the chastisement of God towards them? He urged them to praise our Lord especially because of their afflictions, as he said, 'Recall, my brothers, how it is written that Lazarus, because he endured evil, was esteemed worthy to lie down on the bosom of Abraham in the place of the kingdom'.[113]

---

[113]Lk 16:19-31.

By all these things and the many which we mentioned previously and the rest that we are not able to relate, the true priesthood of that famous and splendid person was triumphant. The wicked and the presumptuous trembled at his righteousness, and the weak and the poor were supported by his charismatic gift. He inclined his ear gently to the wronged and, in his zeal, he avenged the defrauded. Through his word and deed, he urged on the honorable. He gave help at all times to the abased to exalt them. He embodied in his own person the deeds of the law, and he wrapped the commandment of his Lord like a garment[114] around his soul. The examples of the mercies of his God were seen in him, and he gave abundantly to the limit of his power.[115] All the families of the people of Edessa gloried in him and boasted about him. He gloried his Lord and grew strong, as he saw publicly the saving actions of God, and he did not at all rely upon his own righteousness.

After all these things, as often happened to him, he fell ill in his body. It was at the beginning of the month of Tammuz,[116] when he had completed twenty-four years and three months of his life in the episcopate. Let[117] us consider and truly be enlightened by this marvelous sign done to a man who had always been ill in various ways. On the day that this last illness fell unexpectedly upon him, he had a sudden revelation and he said in the presence of his attendants, 'The time of my repose has come upon me'. Then he showed by his actions how he had truly been told secretly in spirit that he had arrived at the end of his life. He suddenly sped up his distribution of the gift that he customarily gave every Conun; [this time he gave it] in Tammuz.[118] He immediately sent his alms through his deacons. To the north and the east he gave what he customarily did. He sent others who carried his gift to those who lived in the west and in the south, who dwelt

---

[114]ܚܠܘܩܐ, 'long outer garment', not ܚܝܐ, 'life'.

[115]Perhaps 'to the boundary of his jurisdiction'.

[116]In the Hebrew lunar calendar, Tammuz is the fourth month of the year, equivalent to June/July.

[117]The letter ܘ is correctly rubbed out from the manuscript.

[118]Conun is roughly equivalent to December/January. Rabbula thus changes the time of distribution by about six months.

in the hope of the gift of God. He even sent to the holy poor who dwell in the desert of Jerusalem—it also is written of the blessed Paul that he collected a gift for them.[119] Others went out to the territory of all the cities that were under his authority; others distributed to the priests and the community of men and women in his diocese. He gave to the mourners [ascetics] and to the monks in his territory and he distributed to the poor in the villages throughout all the area of Edessa, while others distributed in his city to all the needy, to the monks, and to the community of men and women. He also distributed, as he willed, to the widows and the lepers and he left more for them in his will. He forgave all the debts which he had inherited, and he tore up the deeds by which he had lent a great deal of gold to the craftsmen. He gave from his hand a bounty to all the clergy equally. He completed all his good will and finished all his honorable desire. He saw that he had opposed the world and its impediments, he held in light esteem the evil one and his flattery, and he had despised the body and its allurements. Then he lifted up his voice confidently, because of the good witness of his excellent deeds, as he glorified in the Lord, as the victorious Paul had said, 'I have fought a noble contest and I have completed my course. I have kept my faith and, from this time henceforward, a crown of righteousness is preserved for me which my Lord, who is a righteous judge, will bestow on me on that day.[120] And in his hand I place my spirit'.[121] He said these things as he prayed while suffering at the time of his death. He signed his face with the cross and he blessed lovingly those who were standing in his presence and he surrendered his soul to the Lord gladly.

When, on the seventh day of the month Ab,[122] the news of his death suddenly spread in his city, doubtless even its walls shook and its high buildings tossed to and fro at the sound of the terrible wailing of its inhabitants. In the pain of lamentation, the voice of one man was entwined with that of his neighbor

---

[119]Rom 15:25-26.

[120]2 Tim 4:7-8.

[121]Lk 23:46.

[122]The month roughly equivalent to July/August.

and went out, never stopping. For the whole city was a single lamentation, divided among the eighteen groups of deaconesses inside the church's courtyard and that of the lamentation of the Jews outside, while the entire city—in the streets, the courtyards and inside the church—mourned him with mournful wailings, producing bitter groans and sorrowful tears.

The priests—with all the members of the covenant and the lay-people, along with the Jews—mourned for themselves as they said, 'Woe to all of us entirely, because we are deprived of such a lover of God and a friend of humans! We are orphaned of such a true shepherd and a righteous leader! We are dispossessed of such a provider of good things and one who cared about justice! We are separated from such a schoolmaster of truth and one upright in his faith! We are bereft of such a counselor of noble deeds and an exhorter to what is excellent!'

For they were asking, 'Who will follow in his footsteps, with his deeds? This merciful physician in whose mind the sufferings of his fellow human beings shrilly cry out? He was a father to orphans in his love towards them, a brother to the poor in his care over them, a companion of the mourners through his ascetic practices, and a friend of the saints with his excellent discrimination. Truly he had been anxious over the lives of all men'. So they said these things as they made themselves weep, and, as their souls mourned, they related stories like these.

On the next day, they hastened to cover his pure body in a wooden coffin made from materials inside his dwelling, so that his holy body might not be torn apart by the hands of all the people pressing forward in their love to take from him a relic in their faithfulness. They accompanied him with psalms and poems[123] as he was borne in a distinguished manner to the haven of his grave in the cemetery.[124] There the worn-out ship of his blessed old age descended, carrying inside it the great cargo of righteous-

---

[123]Literally, *madrashe* or 'hymns in stanza form, where all the stanzas of a particular hymn will be constructed on a single syllabic pattern chosen out of the great many syllabic patterns available'.(Sebastian Brock in his introduction to his translation of the hymns of St. Ephrem: St. Ephrem the Syrian, *Hymns on Paradise* [New York: St.Vladimir's Seminary Press, 1990] 36.)

[124]κοιμητηριον, in particular a burial place for strangers.

ness. From this cargo, he will distribute help to those who ask the Lord in faith, through his name, to give them a merciful gift from the treasury of his mercy by means of His truthful treasurer. For behold, there at his grave the sick are being healed, there the healthy are being helped, there the devils are being driven out, and there the distressed are being comforted. There the poor are provided for and the rich are profited. He shows that even his cold corpse is a fount of profit because of the fervor of the spirit which rested in it. He was put in charge—with his Lord's permission—over the sum total of his possessions so that from them he might easily distribute good things to all who, as needy, approach him. He fully gathered his own riches for himself, and all the toil of his exertions is entirely preserved with him until his body is raised and is renewed and his soul is united with it and is so glorified so that, perfected, he will shine in glory, because of his exertions, on the day of the glorious revelation of the Son of God, the Saviour of all. May he, by the gift of his mercy, make all of us worthy by his compassion to stand on his right side in the peaceful shelter of our victorious father. There may Rabbula speak on our behalf to his Lord confidently and not be ashamed[125] of us, 'Behold, here I am, my Lord, and the children you gave[126] to me. We worship you and we praise your father and we glorify your Holy Spirit, now and for ever and ever. Amen.'

[125]Mk 8:38.
[126]Heb 2:13. Cf. Is 8:18; Jn 10:29.

HIBA

BISHOP HIBA,
SUCCESSOR TO RABBULA

THE SECOND COUNCIL of Ephesus, pejoratively named the Robber Council because the proceedings were viewed by Pope Leo I as illegally manipulated,[1] opened on 8 August 449 in the Church of Mary. The council had been convened by Emperor Theodosius II to re-examine the case of the monk Eutyches. Eutyches had gone beyond the theological position of Cyril of Alexandria's Twelve Anathemas, in which Cyril had spoken of the divinity and humanity of Christ as forming one nature [mia phusis].[2] Eutyches affirmed that the human nature [phusis] in Christ had been changed. Eutyches held that there were not two natures after the union.[3] For this opinion, Eutyches had been condemned in 448 by the bishop of Constantinople, Flavian, but he had appealed to the councils of Rome, Jerusalem and Alexandria. The emperor, Theodosius II, convened a council to meet at Ephesus. The patrons of Eutyches,

---

[1] Pope Leo the Great, *Ad Pulcherium*, Epistle 95.2; PL 54:943B.

[2] For an excellent discussion of the meaning of *phusis* in Cyril and the problems it caused, see J. A. McGuckin, *St. Cyril of Alexandria: The Christological Controversy. Its History, Theology, and Texts* (Leiden: Brill, 1995) 207–222.

[3] At first, Eutyches was thought by imperial officials to teach that the body of the Saviour was not consubstantial with that of other humans (Schwartz, *ACO* 2.1.2, p. 120, #107), but he later distinguished between a σῶμα ἀνθρώπου, 'the body of a human', which Christ did not have, and a σῶμα ἀνθρώπινον, 'a human body' derived from the Virgin Mary, which Christ did have (Schwartz, *ACO* 2.1.1, p. 142 ,#522). See R. Draguët, 'La Christologie d'Eutychês, d'après les Actes du Synode de Flavien, 448', *Byzantion* 6 (1931) 441–457.

in particular Dioscorus, bishop of Alexandria, and Chrysaphius, counselor of Emperor Theodosius II, succeeded in organizing the council, and Dioscorus ran it efficiently. Opposition was silenced, and Eutyches was quickly declared orthodox.

Then began action against opponents: Bishop Flavian of Constantinople was mishandled and thrown into prison. He died soon afterwards, and his death was later attributed to his mistreatment.[4] Under the 'protecting' eyes of soldiers, the convened bishops at Ephesus had deposed Flavian as well as Eusebius of Dorylae, who had first denounced Eutyches to Flavian. On 22 August, proceedings were begun against four other bishops: Irenaeus of Tyre; Theodoret of Cyrrhus; Domnus of Antioch; and Hiba of Edessa. Hiba had already been arrested and held in prison, where he learned of his deposition. To round out this history of Christian Edessa, I have translated the proceedings against Hiba.

HIBA BEFORE HE BECAME BISHOP

Hiba succeeded Rabbula as bishop of Edessa. Nothing is known of his origins, but he must have received a good education. He was a member of the school of Edessa,[5] and 'he is said to have composed an exegetical and apologetic work as well as *madrāšē* and homilies'.[6] He was given the epithet 'the Translator', and was involved in the translation of the works of Theodore of Mopsuestia from Greek into Syriac.[7] During his trial, he was accused of having Theodore's works with him. John, bishop of Sebaste in Armenia, claimed that Hiba had become sick from heresy while

---

[4]Henry Chadwick, 'The Exile and Death of Flavian of Constantinople: A Prologue to the Council of Chalcedon', *JTS* ns 6 (1955) 17–34.

[5]On the difficulties involved in tracing the early history of the school in Edessa, see Arthur Vööbus, *History of the School of Nisibis,* CSCO 266 (Louvain: Secrétariat du Corpus SCO, 1965) 10–13, 61–65.

[6]Vööbus, *History of the School of Nisibis,* 12.

[7]That Hiba was not the only one involved in the project is argued by Vööbus, *History of the School of Nisibis,* 15–17.

a priest, possibly a reference to his translation activity. There is no doubt of Hiba's attachment to Theodore of Mopsuestia, as is clear from the letter he wrote to Mari the Persian.

Hiba's letter to Mari also makes clear his opposition to Rabbula, whom he calls the 'tyrant' of Edessa and who, Hiba claimed, set out to expunge the influence of Theodore of Mopsuestia from his diocese. As we noted in the introduction to the *Life of Rabbula,* Rabbula seems early to have attacked the theology of Nestorius, bishop of Constantinople and student of Theodore of Mopsuestia. After the First Council of Ephesus in 431 CE, Rabbula must have extended his attack on Nestorius to include Theodore. One might ask whether all of Theodore's works were suspect, or only the doctrinal works. Whatever the case, a letter of Andreas of Samosata to Alexander of Hierapolis, written about the beginning of 431 CE, states that Rabbula had put under interdict anyone who read Theodore's works or possessed codices containing Theodore's works.[8] Hiba was exiled from Edessa around this time.

A Formula of Reunion, agreed to in 433 by both John, bishop of Antioch, and Cyril, bishop of Alexandria, put an end to the schism between the two see cities, and, more importantly for Hiba, recognized that there were two natures in Christ.

The letter of Hiba to Mari, written after 433, but before the death of Rabbula in 436, gleefully describes the discomfiture of those who, like Rabbula, had persecuted their opponents. The tone of the letter and the fact that Hiba had been expelled from Edessa by Rabbula some time after the First Council of Ephesus would not have led anyone to expect that Hiba would succeed Rabbula to the bishopric of Edessa, but he did.

No doubt his elevation to bishop was not without opposition in Edessa, particularly from the clergy close to Rabbula. Certainly, if the situation in Edessa reflected that outside it, hostility against Theodore of Mopsuestia was growing.[9] John, bishop of Antioch,

[8]Schwartz, *ACO* 1.4.2, p. 86.

[9]See the discussion in Louise Abramowski, 'Die Streit um Diodor und Theodor zwischen den beiden ephesinischen Konzilien', *Zeitschrift für Kirchengeschichte* 57 (1955–56) 252–287; Robert Devreese, *Essai sur Théodore de Mopsueste* (Vatican City: Bibliotheca Apostolica Vaticana, 1948) 130–152.

complained to Proclus, bishop of Constantinople, that certain monks would even disrupt liturgical services to press their theological agenda.[10] In 438 CE, Proclus sent to the eastern bishops a statement of faith, the Tome to the Armenians, as well as a collection of texts attributed to Theodore of Mopsuestia, along with a letter of the Emperor Theodosius II enjoining the bishops to keep the peace. The eastern bishops were asked to subscribe to this credal statement, and to denounce the passages from Theodore.

In his letter, Proclus singled out Hiba, bishop of Edessa, as a fervent follower of Theodore. When John, bishop of Antioch, and bishops associated with him, including possibly Hiba, convened in August, 438, they complained of harassment against them and against the now-dead Theodore. Their appeal that peace be restored and no action be taken against those who had died in the faith of the Church was accepted by Proclus, Cyril of Alexandria, and Theodosius II. Even so, Cyril thought that Theodore, if he were still alive, should be condemned.[11] When the eastern bishops continued to honor Theodore, Cyril undertook to write a tract against him, only fragments of which survive. This tract was answered by Theodoret of Cyrrhus.

What was happening in Edessa at this time can be gleaned from an interaction between Hiba and his accuser Samuel. It took place during the Council of Chalcedon (451). Samuel had stated in the Second Council of Ephesus that he had broken off communion with Bishop Hiba after hearing him say, 'I do not envy Christ that he became God, etc'. Now—at the Council of Chalcedon—he noted that this action had been taken about three years prior to the Council of Chalcedon, that is, about 448 CE.[12] In response to Samuel's accusation, Bishop Hiba then referred to another incident between himself and Samuel. Hiba specified that, after this earlier incident, Samuel remained in communion with him for ten years. The incident therefore can be placed to 438,

> Hiba: 'When you [Samuel] said, "The Life died", did I not immediately say to you, "Friend, If you say this because

[10] As quoted in Devreese, *Essai,* 143, n.2.
[11] Schwartz, *ACO* 1.5, pp. 314–315.
[12] Schwartz, *ACO* 2.1.3, p. 27, #89.

the flesh of the Lord is life-making and our Christ is life,
I also confess [it.] But if you point to the divinity, I do
not accept [this statement.]', and were you not in communion with me for ten years?'[13]

An appropriate setting for Samuel's statement would be Good
Friday, the commemoration of the day on which Christ died.
The statement, however, smacks of theopaschism: how could
God, Life itself, die? Hiba makes the distinction between what
can be said of the divinity and what of the humanity in Christ,
a distinction recognized by the Formula of Reunion. If the incident did in fact occur on Good Friday, it would have occurred
during the increased activity against the writings of Theodore of
Mopsuestia by Armenian monks and by Cyril of Alexandria, but
before the interchange of correspondence between Proclus and
John of Antioch in August 438 CE which ended in the restoration of peace.

Cyril of Alexandria, in his twelve anathemas against Nestorius,[14] had condemned anyone who made a distinction between
texts reflecting the human nature and those reflecting the divine
nature of Christ, but he later—in his letter to John of Antioch
in the Formula of Reunion of 433—grudgingly accepted that it
was not unorthodox to make such a distinction between texts.
He quotes the words John had written to him:

As to what is said about the Lord in the gospels and apostolic writings, we know that some theologians make
some common, as applying to one person, and distinguish
others, as applying to the two natures. They teach that
some are appropriate to God in accordance with Christ's
divinity, while others are lowly in accordance with his
humanity.

---

[13]Schwartz, *ACO* 2.1.3, p. 28, #96.

[14]The twelve anathemas are found in the Third Letter of Cyril to Nestorius.
A translation can be found in McGuckin, *St. Cyril* (above, n. 2): the Letter, pp.
268–275; the anathemas, pp. 273–275.

He then writes:

> When we had read your holy words and we saw that we
> ourselves think similarly—for there is 'one Lord, one faith,
> one baptism'[15]—we glorified God, the saviour of all, and
> we rejoiced with one another that your churches and
> ours have a faith in agreement with that of the inspired
> Scriptures and the tradition of the holy Fathers.[16]

In his later *Second Letter to Succensus,* written between 434 and
438, Cyril would insist that this difference of natures was very
theoretical:

> This objection is yet another attack on those who say that
> there is one incarnate nature of the Son. They want to show
> that the idea is foolish, and so they keep on arguing at every
> turn that two natures endured. They have forgotten, how-
> ever, that it is only those things that are usually distinguished
> at more than a theoretical level which split apart from one
> another in differentiated separateness and radical distinction.
> Let us once more take the example of an ordinary man. We
> recognize two natures in him: for there is one nature of the
> soul and another of the body, but we divide them only at
> a theoretical level, and by subtle explication, or rather we
> accept the distinction only in our mental intuitions, and we
> do not set the natures apart nor do we grant that they have
> a radical separateness, but we understand them to belong to
> one man. This is why the two are no longer two, but through
> both of them the one living creature is rendered complete.
> And so, even if one attributes the nature of manhood and
> Godhead to the Emmanuel, still the manhood has become
> the personal property of the Word and we understand that
> there is One Son together with it.[17]

---

[15]Eph 4:5.

[16]Schwartz, *ACO* 1.1.4, p. 17, lines 17–25.

[17]*Second Letter to Succensus* (Letter 46.5); PG 77:245A–B; Schwartz, *ACO* 1.6,
pp. 161, line 26; p. 162, line 11. The translation is that of McGuckin, *St. Cyril,*
362–363. The whole tortured development behind the reunion is discussed
fully by McGuckin (*St. Cyril,* 110–125).

John J. O'Keefe has rightly drawn our attention to the way in which this letter of Cyril answers the objections of his opponents, and to the fact that the strongest argument he had to answer was the charge that his doctrine implied divine suffering.[18] His opponents

> do not understand the economy, and make wicked attempts to displace the sufferings to the man on his own, foolishly seeking a piety that does them harm. . . . The God-inspired scripture tells us that [the One Son] suffered in the flesh[19] and it would be better for us to speak in this way rather than [say he suffered] in the nature of the manhood, even though such a statement (unless it is said uncompromisingly by certain people) does not damage the sense of the mystery.[20]

In this last clause, Cyril would seem to allow room to Hiba's statement, but to have preferred to say what Samuel had said: the Life died, the Word suffered. As O'Keefe states: 'Cyril's christology . . . develops from the narrative of the economy of the Word, a narrative that implies the Word experiencing suffering'.[21]

HIBA AS BISHOP

From 438, then, till Easter, 448 CE, no further attacks seem to have been made on Hiba. During this time, Hiba carried out some construction of churches:

> [He] founded the Church of the Twelve Apostles in the eastern quarter of the city. A chronicler declares that 'for

---

[18]John J. O'Keefe, 'Kenosis or Impassibility: Cyril of Alexandria and Theodoret of Cyrus on the Problem of Divine Pathos', in Elizabeth A. Livingstone, ed., *Studia Patristica* 32 (Louvain: Peeters, 1997) 358–365.

[19]1 Pt 4:1.

[20]*Second Letter to Successus,* 4–5.

[21]O'Keefe, 'Kenosis', 365.

its splendour and remarkable proportions it had no equal
in the world'. It was popularly called the 'new Church',
by others the 'Great Church'.[22]

Hiba also built, outside the eastern gate of the city, a church/
martyrion for Saint Sergius.[23] Already existing churches were also
adorned during Hiba's episcopate. In 437–438, a great silver altar
weighing seven hundred twenty pounds was presented to the
Cathedral Church. Four years later, the bones of Saint Thomas
were placed in a silver reliquary erected by Anatolius.[24]

The attack on Bishop Hiba was renewed in 448. By then, Eutyches was much in favor at the court of Theodosius II, and action
was being taken against his perceived enemies. Early in 448, an
edict was sent out that nestorian works were to be burnt;[25] and,
Irenaeus, bishop of Tyre, an old friend of the Antiochene party,
was deposed.[26] About this time, a group of disaffected clergy went
to complain of Hiba to Domnus, bishop of Antioch. Eulogius,
a priest of Edessa, stated that they had been present in Antioch
when an orthodox, imperial edict was published in the city. This
may have been the edict to burn 'nestorian' works. When their
cause faltered, some of the anti-Hiba party went to Constantinople and, on 26 October, succeeded in having an imperial decree
issued in which new judges were appointed to try the case of
Bishop Hiba. The imperial commissioners held their meetings
during February 449. Before they met, however, the climate had
changed: the bishop of Constantinople, Flavian, had condemned

[22]J. B. Segal, *Edessa, 'The Blessed City'* (Oxford: Clarendon, 1970) 183.

[23]Saint Sergius, along with his companion Saint Bacchus, were soldiers who
were most likely martyred under emperor Maximin Daia in 312 CE. Rusafa,
a town in the Syro-Mesopotamina plain, was identified as the place of their
martyrdom, and the cult spread rapidly. See Elizabeth Key Fowden, *The Barbarian Plain: Saint Sergius between Rome and Iran* (Berkeley: University of California
Press, 1999). For a different dating, see David Woods, 'The Emperor Julian and
the Passion of Sergius and Bacchus', *JECS* 5 (1997) 335–368.

[24]Anatolius was military commander of the eastern frontier. See J. P. Martindale, 'Anatolius 10', *The Prosopography of the Later Roman Empire Vol. 2. AD
395–527* (Cambridge: Cambridge University Press, 1980) 84–86.

[25]*Codex Justinianus* 1.1.3.

[26]Martindale, 'Irenaeus 2', *Prosopography* (above, n. 24), 624–625.

Eutyches at a synod held in November 448. Just after Easter, on 30 March, the emperor Theodosius II summoned a council to be convened at Ephesus on 1 August 449.

The case against Hiba was not proven. Sixty-six clergy from Edessa—one bishop, fifteen priests, thirty-nine deacons, eleven sub-deacons, and two lectors—had sent a letter to the judges which denied that Bishop Hiba had ever made such heretical statements as had been charged against him.[27] Hiba promised to anathematize Nestorius and his writings in the episcopal church in Edessa, and the judges tried to make the enemies friends so that they might celebrate Easter together on 27 March.[28] There are conflicting reports about the judgement of the court: at the Second Council of Ephesus: the three judges stated that, after the lawsuit, they agreed not to have fellowship with Hiba;[29] at the Council of Chalcedon, however, the three bishops stressed their role as mediators of the crisis and insisted that they had brought the parties to communicate with one another.[30] Just after the celebration of Easter, riots appear to have broken out in Edessa, and Hiba left, or was chased out of, the city.[31] Since Edessa was an important strategic center for the Romans,[32] it was imperative that Edessa be calmed. On 12 April, Count Chaereas[33] entered the city and began a formal investigation into the cause of the rioting two days after his arrival. At this meeting, thirty-eight clergy (ten priests, twenty deacons, eight sub-deacons, and eleven monks) presented a petition asking for the deposition of Hiba. The petition was apparently based on the letter of Hiba to Mari.[34]

[27]Schwartz, *ACO* 2.1.3, pp. 35–37, # 141.

[28]Schwartz, *ACO* 2.1.3, pp. 14–16, #7.

[29]Johannes Flemming, *Akten der ephesinischen Synode vom Jahre 449. Syrisch mit Georg Hoffman's deutscher Übersetzung und seinen Anmerkungen* (Berlin: Weidmann, 1917) 14, fol. 9v.

[30]Schwartz, *ACO* 2.1.3, pp. 14–16, #7.

[31]Flemming, *Akten,* 22, fol. 16v.

[32]See Segal, *Edessa,* 115–119.

[33]Provincial governor of Osrhoene. See Martindale, 'Chaereas', *Prosopography,* 282.

[34]Flemming, *Akten,* 22, fol. 16r. It is impossible to know how many might have signed the letter sent to Beirut and later changed their minds, as many of the names are common names. It would seem that the main spokesman against

Chaereas dispatched a full report to Protogenes, praetorian prefect
for the East.[35] Riots again broke out a few days later, and Chaereas
dispatched another report, this time to Flavius Martialis, Master of
the Divine Offices.[36] Hiba was arrested, and moved from prison
to prison.[37] On 22 August 449, he was condemned, deposed, and
exiled. He was replaced as bishop by Nona, but re-instated by the
Council of Chalcedon in 452 CE. He died in 457, and nothing is
known of these last years.

Within these proceedings against Hiba at the Second Council of Ephesus, one finds references to the appearance, in 448
CE, of some edessene clergy before Domnus, the arch-bishop
of Antioch,[38] and to the trial before the three bishops, Photius,
Eustathius and Uranius, in Beirut and Tyre.[39] Also listed are the
accusations against Hiba made in the Second Council itself,[40] and
within these accusations is found a fuller account of the meeting
of some edessene clergy with Domnus.

THE CHARGES AGAINST HIBA

Within this document, primarily in the accusations shouted out
against him to Chaereas as well as in the statement by disaffected
edessene clergy before Domnus of Antioch,[41] Hiba is accused
not only of heresy, but also of other offenses. Hiba is accused of
simony; of ordaining unworthy candidates to the priesthood and
episcopacy, among them his nephew Daniel, who was alleged
to have had an improper relationship with a married woman,

Hiba in Edessa, the priest Micallus, may have changed his opinion, as this name
appears unusual and is not found in the proceedings against Hiba in Beirut.

[35]Flemming, *Akten,* 20–32, fol. 13v–fol. 23r.
[36]Flemming, *Akten,* 32–54, fol. 23r–fol. 38r.
[37]Schwartz, *ACO* 2.1.3, pp. 16–17, #1.
[38]Flemming, *Akten,* 40, fol. 28v.
[39]Flemming, *Akten,* 24; 38–42, fol. 16v; fol. 28r–fol. 30v.
[40]Flemming, *Akten,* 56–60, fol. 40r–fol. 42r.
[41]Flemming, *Akten,* 56–60, fol. 40v–41v.

Challoa; of using liturgical vessels and vestments for his personal everyday use; of not using as intended all the money collected for ransoming captives, but of keeping most of it and giving it into the keeping of his brother, Eusebius. These charges are not explicitly addressed in these Acts, as the Council of Ephesus was first and foremost concerned with orthodox teaching. Domnus summarily dismissed them, and at Beirut, Hiba was advised to set up the same administrative apparatus to handle business affairs as was in place in Antioch.[42] Daniel is said to have relinquished the episcopacy. Perhaps he knew that the deck was stacked against him, and he preferred to leave rather than defend himself to no point. As for the charge of ordaining unworthy candidates, its veracity depends on the criteria used for determining who is and who is not worthy.

Important for our consideration is that many of the charges are couched in terms of the individual use of community property: Abraham was originally a poor deacon, but became rich from the Church; Daniel led a life of luxury and in his will left great riches to his nephews and to Challoa, riches taken from the Church; Hiba plundered the poor and the sanctuary to become rich; he diverted funds given for the ransom of captives for his own and his family's use; he even wore liturgical vestments for personal non-liturgical use. All these charges stand in startling contrast to the picture painted of Rabbula by his biographer: Rabbula had only one cloak, he ate minimally; he built nothing save hospitals for the poor and the wretched; he told his clergy that they should consider everything that came to them as given by the poor. In his will, Rabbula made provision for the upkeep of the poor. Behind these accusations against Hiba, one suspects there lies a paradigm of how a bishop should behave. He should not dress well nor should he live like the wealthy. Rather, he should live like a monk. It is the clash of paradigms between Rabbula and Hiba that underlay the violence of the accusations.

---

[42]Schwartz, *ACO* 2.1.3, pp. 15–16, #7.

THE CHARGES OF HERESY

The Emperor and the Council of Ephesus in 449 were mainly concerned with the question of Hiba's orthodoxy. His allegedly heretical statements are the following:

> 1. 'I do not envy Christ that he became God, for when/ because he became, I became. For he is from my own nature'. (An alternative to the causal clause of the first sentence is: 'for he is honored, I am honored'.)

> 2. God the Word had known in his fore-knowledge that Christ would be justified from his deeds and, because of this, He dwelt in him.[43]

> 3. Hiba contrasted John 1:1 and Matthew 1:1, saying, 'Is not this one, and this another?'[44] He is also said to have stated that the Jews crucified a mere human.[45]

> 4. At his resurrection, Christ became immortal.[46]

> 5. 'Gehenna is a threat written [to cause] fear'.[47]

I shall discuss these in reverse order.

Number 5: Gehenna

Rabbula had written cryptically to Cyril of Alexandria : 'It is not safe to write in a letter their [Theodore of Mopsuestia's and Nestorius'] reasonings about Gehenna'.[48] One also finds in the

---

[43]Flemming, *Akten*, 42, fol. 30r.
[44]Flemming, *Akten*, 44, fol. 31v.
[45]Flemming, *Akten*, 44, fol. 31v–32r.
[46]Flemming, *Akten*, 44, fol. 31v.
[47]Flemming, *Akten*, 44, fol. 31v.
[48]Schwartz, *ACO* 4.1, p. 89, lines 24–25, #23; J. J. Overbeck, *S. Ephraemi Syri, Rabulae episcopi Edesseni, Balaei aliorumgue* (London: MacMillan, 1865) 225, lines 16–17.

deliberations against Theodore of Mopsuestia at the Council of Constantinople statements attributed to Theodore which suggest that all creatures will become immortal and immutable in the second state.[49] As Robert Devreese has shown, however, the statements about Theodore's teaching found in this Council—ruled by the Emperor Justinian—are to be treated with caution. Theodore's views were mingled, mangled, and mixed with a dose of Origenism.[50] Every indication is that Hiba, following Theodore, would have read the Scriptures literally, and would not have exempted sinners from punishment. Also like Theodore, Hiba, would have attempted to explain unusual words found in the Bible.

Number 4: Christ's Immortality

In Theodore of Mopsuestia's view of salvation history, Adam had been created immortal but, through his sin, had become mortal.[51] Christ's role was to change this. 'In the suffering of death, it was not God who suffered but He was with him . . . and he led him, through suffering, to perfection, making him immortal, impassible, incorruptible and completely unmoveable for the salvation of many'.[52] The statement of Hiba can be understood only in the light of a clear distinction between Christ's divine nature and Christ's human nature, so that it says that the human nature of Christ became immortal. If one insists on predicating all statements as referring to the Word of God, it is of course impossible

---

[49]Schwartz, *ACO* 4.1, p. 65, lines 8–28, ##67–69. See Origen, *On First Principles,* 3.6; trans. G. W. Butterworth (Gloucester, Massachusetts: Peter Smith, 1973).

[50]Devreese, *Essai,* 243–258.

[51]*On Romans 5:12-14:* PG 66.797. For a full collection of this commentary, see Karl Staab, *Pauluskommentare aus der griechischen Kirche: aus Katenenhandschriften gesammelt und herausgegeben* (2nd ed. Münster: Aschendorff, 1984). See Devreese, *Essai,* 98–99.

[52]Homily 8, 9. For the complete text, see Theodore, Bishop of Mopsuestia, *Commentary of Theodore of Mopsuestia on the Nicene Creed,* Woodbrooke Studies: Christian Documents, ed. and trans. with a critical apparatus by A. Mingana, vol. V (Cambridge: W. Heffer & Sons, 1932). See also Devreese, *Essai,* 117–118.

to say that the eternal Word of God 'became immortal'. Dioscorus, bishop of Alexandria, would—later in the proceedings of
the council—respond to this statement by saying, 'How was God
able to become what He was not?'[53] In his letter to Mari, Hiba
evidences a clear sense of the difference between the two natures
and yet their co-existence in the one Jesus Christ,[54] and in his
debate with the priest Samuel in the proceedings in Beirut, Hiba
reported how he had corrected Samuel in Edessa for not explicitly
distinguishing the two natures in his speech.[55] One finds it hard
to imagine, therefore, that Hiba would have made Statement 4
without any accompanying qualification which would ensure that
it referred to the human nature and not to the divine. Such care
to qualify would have been all the more necessary as the debate
between Cyril of Alexandria and Nestorius of Constantinople had
turned precisely on whether 'Christ' could be used of the Word
of God: Nestorius held that one could call Mary the 'bearer of
Christ' but not the 'bearer of God' *(theotokos)*. Would Hiba, carried
away in a sermon, have forgotten this important qualification? Or
had his adversaries taken a statement out of context?

Statement 3: Christ's Human Nature

The distinction between scriptural texts reflecting the human
nature and those reflecting the divine nature was well known
since the arian controversy of the fourth century CE. We noted
above how Cyril of Alexandria and Hiba's opponent, Samuel,
had an aversion to making such a distinction. The specific contrast between John 1:1 and Matthew 1:1 is found in a late and
anonymous collection of nestorian text excerpts.[56]

---

[53]Flemming, *Akten,* 56, fol. 39v.

[54]Flemming, *Akten,* 48; 52, fol. 34v, 36v.

[55]Schwartz, *ACO* 2.1.3, p. 28, #96.

[56]Louise Abramowski and Alan F. Goodman, *A Nestorian Collection of Christological Texts. Cambridge University Library Ms Oriental 1319* (Cambridge: Cambridge University Press, 1972) 1:117, lines 9–10 and 19–20; 2:67–68.

The adversaries of Hiba seem to have reached back to the earlier position of Cyril of Alexandria and his allies against Nestorius. After Nestorius preached against the application of the term 'Mother of God' to Mary in 429, a lawyer named Eusebius, later bishop of Dorylaeum, put up a poster in public which accused Nestorius of teaching, like Paul of Samosata, excommunicated for 'adoptionism', that a pre-existing human being had been adopted by the Word of God. He cleverly juxtaposed quotations from Paul and Nestorius in parallel columns to show that there was little difference between the two.[57] But the position of Hiba, as evidenced in the letter to Mari, cannot be so caricatured.

As for the comparison found in the proceedings between the honor given to the imperial garments and the honor given to the human Christ, Devreese suggests that Theodore of Mopsuestia had written, 'Christ was an image of God the Word, as an imperial image was adored by all'.[58] The comparison of imperial garments recurs in a collection of texts later ascribed to Nestorius.[59]

Number 2: The Foreknowledge of Christ

Theodore of Mopsuestia is held to have written in Book 14 of his treatise *On the Incarnation*:

> We say the same thing rightly about the lord that God the Word, knowing his virtue by fore-knowledge, benevolently wished to dwell [in him] right from the very beginning of his formation. He united him to Himself by intentional inclination, and was enveloping him with some greater grace, as the grace which is in him had to be divided among all humans. Wherefore, he was guarding for him a complete will for the good.[60]

---

[57]Schwartz, *ACO* 1.1.1, pp. 101–102.
[58]Devreese, *Essai*, 12 n. 2, taken from *On the Incarnation*, Bk 14.
[59]Abramowski, *Collection* I. 179, line 22; 180, line 22; II. 107.
[60]Schwartz, *ACO* 4.1, p. 64, #63. The Greek text is in PG 66. 989C.

The question of why Jesus became the dwelling-place of the
Word had a very long history. Origen, who believed passionately
in a just God, had argued that God at the beginning had made all
rational souls equal. The distinction between angels, devils, and
souls that dwelt in bodies resulted from the free choice of how
strongly each soul attached itself to God. The soul of Jesus clung
to God inseparably from the beginning, and so was chosen to be
the mediator between the Word of God and the flesh the Word
inhabited.[61] Origen's cosmology was not followed by many, and
particularly not by Theodore of Mopsuestia.[62]

To frame the question in this way—why was Jesus chosen?—was
already to suggest that Jesus the man was distinct from the Word,
that there were two independently acting subjects. Theodore, in
the continuation of the passage quoted above, stresses that the
human Jesus had free choice, and is a model of behavior for other
humans. But to talk of the Word having had 'fore-knowledge' of his
actions, as though the human Jesus could exist and act apart from
the indwelling Word, smacks of adoptionism, even if Theodore
speaks of the divine indwelling beginning at the very moment of
the formation of his human body. As the followers of Cyril might
say, the Word of God chose to become human, He did not choose
a human whom He could indwell. Here one comes to a major
difference in orientation between the followers of Cyril and those
of Theodore and Nestorius. The question for Cyril was: how does
the Word become human without ceasing to be divine? For Theodore and Nestorius the question was: how is this man Jesus Christ
divine in such a way that he remains human?[63] So, while Hiba
could not be accused of adoptionism as he insisted that there was
one son Jesus Christ, his use of the language of fore-knowledge
would have been abhorrent to supporters of Cyril.

[61] *On First Principles* 2.6.3; 2.9.7.

[62] See, for example, Elizabeth A. Clark, *The Origenist Controversy: The Cultural
Construction of an Early Christian Debate* (Princeton: Princeton University Press,
1992).

[63] See the treatment in Richard A. Norris, 'The Problem of Human Identity in
Patristic Christological Speculation', *Studia Patristica* 17/1 (1982) 147–159; J. J.
O'Keefe, 'Kenosis or Impassibility: Cyril of Alexandria and Theodore of Cyrus
on the Problem of Divine Pathos', *Studia Patristica* 32 (1997) 358–365.

Number 1: 'he is from my own nature'.

This alleged saying of Hiba is particularly fascinating as it exists
in three versions.

> 1. The first occurs in the second report of Flavius Chae-
> reas, when the priest Samuel retells the proceedings in
> Beirut and accuses Hiba of saying at Easter (448 CE): 'I do
> not envy Christ that he became God, for when/because
> he became, I became. For he is of my own nature'.

> 2. The second is found in the acts of the proceedings in
> Beirut, which were read at the Second Council of Ephe-
> sus. The priest Maras states that Hiba said: 'I do not envy
> Christ having become God. For inasmuch as he became,
> I also became'.

> 3. In the letter of the edessene clergy to the judges at the
> proceedings in Beirut, the clergy deny that they had ever
> heard Hiba say: 'I do not envy Christ having become God
> since I also, if I wish, become in accordance with him'.[64]

Both at Beirut and at Chalcedon[65] Hiba denied ever uttering
such a statement. Why would his accusers stress so strongly this
statement as heretical, and Hiba deny it so vehemently?

One must remember both the larger and the more immediate
contexts. As we noted above when discussing the question of di-
viding the statements found in the Gospels into those appropriate
to the divine nature and those appropriate to the human nature,
Cyril of Alexandria had used a phrase—which he thought came
from Athanasius of Alexandria but which in fact came from Apollinaris of Laodicea—that there was one incarnate nature of the

---

[64]Schwartz, *ACO* 2.1.3, p. 35, lines 7–8, #141: οὐ φθονῶ τῶι χριστῶι γε-
γονότι θεῶι, ἐπειδὴ καγώ, ἐι βούλομαι, γίνομαι κατ᾽ αὐτον; Schwartz, *ACO*
2.3.3, p. 43, lines 16–17, #141: *Non invideo Christo facto Deo, quoniam et ego, si
volo, possum fieri secundum illum.*

[65]Flemming, *Akten,* 40, fol. 29r; Schwartz, *ACO* 2.1.3, p. 27, ##83, 85.

Word of God.[66] For Apollinaris, this 'one incarnate nature' was not consubstantial with human nature, but something else. Jesus was 'the man from heaven'. As we also noted above, Cyril had reluctantly agreed to the notion of two natures. In a letter, Cyril insisted 'that the phraseology of the Formulary of Reunion, which seems to separate the natures but which Cyril takes to be the one Lord speaking both divinely and humanly, was necessary in order to allay Antiochene fears of Apollinarianism'.[67] In a series of works written after 438 CE, *Against Diodore and Theodore, Against the Synousiasts, On the Unity of Christ,* Cyril criticized the works of Diodore of Tarsus and Theodore of Mopsuestia.[68] By 447, after the death of Cyril, the monk Eutyches had, openly stated that there was one nature of the God incarnate, and had challenged the view that Christ was consubstantial with humans.[69] Eutyches would later, in 448, claim that there were two natures before the union, only one after it.[70]

The accusation that Hiba said that Christ is "of my own nature" would have put him in direct conflict with Eutyches and might even have made him suspect to Cyril's followers. If, as Hiba relates in the Council of Chalcedon,[71] one of the bishops presiding at the Beirut proceedings, Uranius of Himeria, had incited some of the edessene clergy to accuse Hiba of blasphemy to please Eutyches, one can see how the alleged statement of Hiba would have been a flash-point. Why was the sentence mentioned not by Maras in the proceedings at Beirut, but by Samuel in Edessa before Count Chaereas? The chronology may be a factor. In November 448, Eutyches had been deposed from his priestly status,

---

[66]The phrase of Apollinaris occurs in *Ad Julianum.* See the text in Hans Lietzmann, *Apollinaris von Laodicea und seine Schule* (Tübingen: Mohr, 1904) 248, frg. 151.

[67]Norman Russell, *Cyril of Alexandria* (London: Routledge, 2000) 56, referring to Letter 40.20; Schwartz, *ACO* 1.1.4, p. 29, lines 19–20.

[68]See L. Abramowski, 'Der Streit' (above, n. 9), 252–287.

[69]See R. Draguët, 'La Christologie d'Eutychès, d'après les Actes du Synode de Flavien, 448', *Byzantion* 6 (1931) 441–457; T. Camelot, 'De Nestorius à Eutychès', in A. Grillmeier and H. Bacht, *Das Konzil von Chalkedon; Geschichte und Gegenwart,* 3 vols. (Würzburg, 1953–1962) 1:213–242.

[70]Schwartz, *ACO* 2.2.1, p. 17, #145.

[71]Schwartz, *ACO* 2.1.3, p. 13, lines 25, 30–32, #4.

and he was still so when the proceedings took place in Beirut in February 449. Between the proceedings in Beirut and those in Edessa, on 30 March 449, however, the emperor Theodosius II had summoned a general council under the leadership of Dioscorus, bishop of Alexandria, to re-hear the case against Eutyches. Theodosius basically gerrymandered the council in favor of the one-nature party, as he forbade Theodoret of Cyrrhus to attend. Eutyches' theology was again respectable, and Samuel may have added the sentence more firmly to nail Hiba.

As for the sentence, 'inasmuch as He became, I also became, found in all three versions, the main difference lies in the causal clause. The wording found in the letter of the edessene clergy, 'since I also, if I wish, become in accordance with Him' is particularly troublesome, as it could be taken to mean that any human who energetically chose to obey God, could become God in the same way as Christ is. The conditional clause 'if I will' could, of course, simply be an exhortation to model oneself on the virtuous behavior of Jesus; even so, the whole clause does seem to relegate Christ to a state no different from that of other humans. The edessene clergy deny that they had ever heard Hiba utter such a statement.

Something similar may be said about the causal clause reported by Maras, 'inasmuch as he became, I also became'. There too, the conjunction 'insofar as', 'inasmuch as' hints at the possibility that other humans could become just as divine as Christ. Some Christians of the sixth century do seem to have believed that, in the final restoration of creation, all rational souls will be equal to Christ. They were known as ἴσοι τοῦ χριστοῦ/ἰσοχρίστοι. In the Chronicle of Michael the Syrian and the anonymous author of another chronicle, this view is said to have started with Theodore of Mopsuestia.[72]

In the letter sent by the armenian churches to Proclus, archbishop of Constantinople, Theodore is quoted as saying:

> The human Jesus is like all humans, having no difference
> from humans of the same species except for what grace

---

[72]Evagrius *HE* 4.38; PG 86:2780A. See Antoine Guillaumont, *Les 'Kephalaia Gnostica' d'Évagre le Pontique et l'histoire de l'Origénisme chez les Grecs et chez les Syriens* (Paris: Seuil, 1958) 149–150, 176–182.

gave him. However, the grace given did not change the nature.[73]

I say 'human' and I say what is connatural to me. If I say 'god', I say what is connatural to god. How are a human and a god one? Surely there is not one nature of a human and a god, of the master and the servant, of the maker and the made? A human is consubstantial to a human, but a god is consubstantial to a god. How, therefore, are God and a man able to be one through unity, the Saviour and the saved, he who was before the ages and he who appeared from Mary?[74]

Both these quotations are said to come from Book 7 of Theodore's *On the Incarnation*. Yet Theodore had also stressed the difference between the grace of the human Christ and that of other humans:

Whenever therefore [God] is said to indwell either in the apostles or in any righteous person, he makes the indwelling as taking pleasure in the righteous, as delighting himself appropriately in the virtuous. Of course, we say not that the indwelling happened in this way in [Christ]—for we would never be as insane as that—but *as in a son*. For so he took pleasure to indwell.

What is this *'as in a son'*? Indwelling in this way, he united the entire assumed to himself, and prepared him to partake with him all the honor which the same indwelling natural Son partakes, as to be counted as one person according to the union with him, and to share with him all rulership. He so accomplished everything in him, that the judgement and examination of the cosmos will be discharged by him at this coming, obviously with the understood difference between those characterizing traits which are according to nature.[75]

[73]Schwartz, *ACO* 4.1, p. 83, lines 21–23, #14.3; PG 66:969B.
[74]Schwartz, *ACO* 4.1, pp. 83, line 34; p. 84, line 3, #14.4; PG 66:969B–C.
[75]*On the Incarnation,* Book 7; PG 66:976B–C.

Hiba, in his letter to Mari, confessed the one son Jesus Christ. It is doubtful, therefore, particularly as he is a student of Theodore, that he could have uttered a statement which claimed a human being could become divine to the same extent as the humanity of Christ.

The causal clause in the syriac version, with the conjunction 'when/because', could, however, have been acceptable to Hiba. Athanasius of Alexandria, the revered opponent of Arius, had written: 'We all were liberated according to the kinship of the flesh and for the future we also were joined to the Word'.[76] The sentiment that the Word became human so that humans could become divine[77] was widely accepted. When commenting on Hebrews 1:1 in Bk 12 of *On the Incarnation,* Theodore of Mopsuestia had written:

> It is demonstrated, then, that [Paul] not only names [the human] 'son', distinguishing him from God the Word, but also joins him, according to the definition of sonship, to those who share in the sonship. Inasmuch as he shares the sonship by grace, not born naturally from the Father, yet he has this excellence beyond the rest, that he possesses the sonship by the union to him, which (possession) bestows a fuller share in the matter'.[78]

Here the connection between the grace given to Christ and that given to other humans is clear, while it is also differentiated.

The main clause of the sentence attributed to Hiba, and the one which he vigorously denied, is that Hiba does not envy Christ. Such a statement would have rung alarm bells after the nestorian controversy. For, as Neyrey and Rohrbaugh have noted in an article on Jn 3:30:

> *Who envies?* Basically peers envy peers, as Aristotle [*Rhetoric* 2.10.1] said: 'Envy is defined as a kind of distress at the apparent success of one's peers'. Cicero [*De oratore* 2.52.209] echoes this: 'People are especially envious of

---

[76]Athanasius, *Against the Arians,* 2.69; PG 26:293C.
[77]Athanasius, *Against the Arians,* 1.39; PG 26:91.
[78]PG 66:987A; Schwartz, *ACO* 4.1, p. 62, #57.

their equals, or of those once beneath them, when they feel themselves left behind and fret at the other's upward flight'. . . . Foster, in his excellent study of envy, declares that 'every society designates those of its members who are deemed eligible to compete with each other for desired goals', that is, 'conceptual equals'.[79]

To speak as if one could be envious of Christ was to put oneself on a par with Christ as if one could compete with him for the prize of being united to the Word. This would be tantamount to making Christ a mere human. Given Hiba's declaration in his letter to Mari, it is doubtful that he would have spoken in this way; given the witness of the sixty-six edessene clergy in their letter to the proceedings in Beirut—in which they declare that they had never heard him speak in such a way—as opposed to the five who appeared before the judges in Beirut; and given the vehemence of Hiba's denial, the evidence surely seems weighted in Hiba's favor.

THE CITY AGAINST HIBA

Hiba was not condemned at the proceedings in Beirut in February 449. The bishops Photius and Eustathius were satisfied that Hiba return to Edessa, anathematize Nestorius publicly, and work out some better way of administering finances. When he re-appeared in Edessa, however, riots broke out. When Count Chaereas came to investigate, he was met by a delegation of clergy, some of whom had just recently signed a letter to the bishops in Beirut stating that Hiba had not made the heretical statements of which he was accused. Now they approached Chaereas to ask that Hiba be deposed. What had intervened?

---

[79]Jerome Neyrey and Richard Rohrbaugh, ' "He Must Increase, I Must Decrease" (John 3:30): A Cultural and Social Interpretation', *CBQ* 63 (2001) 478. The work of Foster referred to is George M. Foster, 'The Anatomy of Envy: A Study in Symbolic Behavior', *Current Anthropology* 13 (1972) 165–202.

The clergy recognized that there had been rumors about mis-handling finances, but these had not caused them to want to depose Hiba. What had made them change their mind was Hiba's letter to Mari. How this letter, written fourteen to fifteen years previously, came to be produced in Beirut remains a mystery. Hiba did not introduce it, as he had to be shown the letter to identify it as his own. It seems as if some enemy of Hiba had found it and sent it to his accusers. Michael van Esbroeck has argued that Mari was 'archimandrite of the convent of *Akoimetoi* on the Asi-atic shore of the Bosphorus 15 miles north of Constantinople'.[80] Therefore, van Esbroeck suggested, the letter would have been known in Constantinople, as this nearby convent was opposed to Cyril's theology. What is in this letter that is so frightful? It was to become a bone of contention at the Council of Constantinople in 553 and was condemned. Yet, its orthodoxy was ably defended by Pelagius, a deacon of Rome and later bishop of Rome, who later devoted a whole book to the letter.[81] Pelagius showed how the letter had been acceptable to the Council of Chalcedon in 451. What then made it so offensive to the edessene clergy in 449?

The letter suggests that the twelve anathemas of Cyril of Alex-andria, written before the Formula of Reunion, smacked of the teaching of Apollinaris of Laodicea. Cyril was highly thought of as a defender of orthodoxy, and to attack him, as Hiba had done, suggested the non-orthodoxy of Hiba. Importantly, Cyril had been a friend and correspondent of the bishop before Hiba, Rabbula. As we know from the *Life of Rabbula* and from the accusations made before Chaereas in Edessa, Rabbula had had a sizeable following and was seen as a model bishop. For Hiba to label him a tyrant seems to have been what moved the clergy of Edessa against Hiba. Given that Rabbula in the *Life* is portrayed as devoted to help-ing the poor, Hiba's attack on Rabbula meshed with accusations of Hiba's financial mismanagement and self-enrichment to paint Hiba as the very antithesis of Rabbula.

[80]Michael van Esbroeck, 'Who is Mari, The Addressee of Ibas' Letter?', *JTS* ns 38 (1987) 129.

[81]Pelagius, *In defensione trium capitulorum,* ed. Robert Devreese (Vatican City: Bibliotheca Vaticana, 1932).

From 440 to 447, there had been no trace of any displeasure with Hiba's episcopacy or orthodoxy. Only when Eutyches seems to have interfered in the affairs of Edessa do we find the troubles starting. As the powerful followers of Cyril came more and more to influence the emperor Theodosius II, and when Dioscorus, Cyril's nephew and successor as bishop of Alexandria, was appointed to run the Second Council of Ephesus, more pressure was brought to bear against anyone who seemed to disagree with anything Cyril had written. Theodoret of Cyrrhus was placed under virtual town arrest and forbidden to attend the Council. From this we can surmise that the clergy of Edessa must have gone along with those of their number who worked to see Hiba removed. Once Theodosius II died and was replaced by another emperor who did not favor Eutyches or Dioscoros, Hiba was reinstated as bishop of Edessa, and the orthodoxy of his letter to Mari accepted. There were no riots on his return, and none during the remaining years of his episcopate. The case of Hiba illustrates how important imperial favor was in determining who or what is orthodox.

THE TEXT

The syriac text of the Second Council of Ephesus is found in one manuscript, BM Add 14,530. It was well edited by J. Flemming in 1917.[82] Besides Hoffman's german translation in the same edition, there is an english translation by S. G. F. Perry,[83] and a french translation by P. Martin.[84]

---

[82]Johannes Flemming, *Akten der ephesinischen Synode vom Jahre 449. Syrisch mit Georg Hoffmann's deutscher Übersetzung und seinen Anmerkungen* (Berlin: Weidmann, 1917).

[83]S. G. F. Perry, *The Second Synod of Ephesus together with certain extracts relating to it* (Dartford, Kent: Orient Press, 1881).

[84]P. Martin, *Actes du brigandage d'Ephèse* (Amiens, 1874).

ACTS OF THE SECOND COUNCIL AT EPHESUS IN 449 C.E.

RECORDS AGAINST HIBA, BISHOP OF EDESSA

T HE IMPERIAL CAESARS, THEODOSIUS AND VALENTINIAN, VICTO-
RIOUS AND GLORIOUS IN VICTORIES, EVER REVERED AUGUSTI,
TO DIOSCORUS.

Earlier, we commanded that Theodoret, Bishop of Cyrrhus, not come to the holy synod until that holy synod has transacted against him what it intended. For we have turned our back on him because he dared to make statements in opposition to what Cyril, of holy memory, former bishop of the great city of Alexandria, had written on behalf of the faith. However, it is possible that some of those who think along the lines of Nestorius might be concerned that by some means or other he might come to the holy synod. We therefore thought it necessary to make use of these imperial rescripts to your godly piety and by them inform your godly love and all the holy synod that we, adhering to the canons of the holy fathers,[1] give precedence and authority to your godly piety not only concerning Theodoret but also concerning whatever else might pertain to the holy synod now assembled.

---

[1] Each council promulgated canons, or regulations, on liturgical practices and disciplinary and judicial procedures. Here the reference may be to Canon 6 of the Council of Constantinople in 381 CE and to Canon 6 of the First Council of Ephesus in 431.

We rightly are convinced that the God-loving archbishop of Jerusalem, Juvenal, and the God-loving archbishop [of Caesarea] Thalasios and everyone who is likewise fervent and zealous and loves right doctrine are of the same mind as your holiness who, by the grace of God, is resplendent in venerable behavior and right belief. For we are indeed convinced that no freedom of speech should be given in the holy synod to those who dare to speak any addition or subtraction to those things that were decreed for the sake of the faith by the holy fathers in Nicea[2] and afterwards in Ephesus.[3] We also wish that they be subject to your judgement and for this reason we command that the holy synod now take place.

This decree was given on the sixth Ab [August],
on the eighth day before the Ides of August[4] at Constantinople.

THE IMPERIAL CAESARS THEODOSIUS AND VALENTINIAN, VICTORIOUS AND GLORIOUS IN VICTORIES, EVER REVERED AUGUSTI, TO THE HOLY SYNOD ASSEMBLED IN THE METROPOLIS EPHESUS.

Many reports were sent here from those in Edessa, a city of the province of Osrhoene, as well as the records made there, in which

---

[2] The Council of Nicea in 325 CE determined that the Son of God was *homoousios* or 'consubstantial' with, 'of the same nature' as God the Father.

[3] The First Council of Ephesus in 431 CE was convened to discuss the relationship of the divine and the human natures of Jesus.

[4] The Ides of August fall on the 13th, so eight days earlier would have been August 6th.

there are depositions from many honorable clerics, God-loving archimandrites, dignitaries and, one might almost say, from all the people of that city. They testify against Hiba, bishop of Edessa, on grounds of impiety and blasphemies. Now Your Holiness, after you read the things that happened and these testimonies, will agree that it is not proper to discount the testimonies of all these people: clerics, monks, dignitaries and lay persons. Therefore, because it is appropriate that you, through your holiness, should correct such a disgrace, you will save that city from such a blasphemy. You will appoint over it someone who is honorable in his actions and distinguished in the true faith. Under his control, anything similar to this and opposed to the orthodox faith will be forbidden. For if those who are placed at the head of metropolitan cities are orthodox, the rest will also necessarily follow their teaching. We had formerly ordered that the God-fearing Photius, bishop of the holy church of the metropolis Tyre, Eustathius, bishop of Beirut, and Uranius, bishop of Himeria, should be adjudicators of this case. We have also ordered Uranius to come to your holy synod so that he might inform your holiness in person about all these matters.

This decree was given on the fifth day before the Kalends of July,
which is the twenty-seventh day [of June], at Constantinople.[5]

---

[5]Following this decree is a list of those who took part at the Council of Ephesus. The proceedings pick up again at fol. 8r, Flemming, *Akten*, 12.

[John, priest of Alexandria and head notary, read:]

> The imperial Caesars Theodosius and Valentinian, victorious and glorious in victories, ever revered Augusti, to the holy synod in Ephesus. Many reports from those in Ephesus, a city of the province of Osrhoene, as well as the records [and the rest as just quoted].

John, the priest and head notary, said:

> Monks from the city of Edessa are standing outside and saying that they have brought imperial rescripts. What does your holiness ordain concerning them?

Eustathius, bishop of Ancyra in Galatia Prima, said:

> May the God-fearing bishops Photius, Eusthatius, and Uranius tell what they have seen concerning the affairs of Hiba, and what they have said. Then, seeing that the God-fearing priest and head notary John mentioned the imperial rescripts, let the God-loving monks enter so that the writings of the benevolent emperors given to them might be made known.

When those monks entered, John, the priest and head notary, read:

> The imperial Caesars Theodosius and Valentinian, victorious, ever revered Augusti, to Jacob.

> Your clemency is not unmindful in what a struggle the God-fearing priests[6] and archimandrites are occupied as they fight for the true faith in the eastern regions. They have turned away from certain bishops of those eastern regions who were infected with the impious opinion of Nestorius, while the faithful people were the protectors of the God-loving archimandrites. Therefore, because we desire that in every way the orthodox faith might shine forth, it rightly seemed to us about this affair that your

---

[6]The text reads ܪܟ.ܝ.ܩ = holy ones, but with Perry I would suggest one read ܪܟܝ.ܝܩ = priests.

reverence, splendid in purity of behavior and in the orthodox faith, should also come to the city of Ephesus in Asia
on the kalends of August. You should remain in the holy
synod which is appointed to gather there, and visit those
other holy fathers, bishops who are pleasing to God. This
decree was given on the thirteenth of Haziran, on the Ides
of June,[7] at Constantinople during the consulate of the
victorious Protogenes[8] and one yet to be made known'.

John, the priest and head notary, said:

A similarly worded benevolent letter was written to Abraham priest and archimandrite; also to Elijah, priest and archimandrite; to Pakidas, priest and archimandrite; to Isaac,
priest and archimandrite; to Eulogius, priest and archimandrite; to Habbib, deacon and archimandrite; to Abraham, deacon and archimandrite; to Ephræm, priest and
archimandrite; to Polychronius, archimandrite; to Benja-
min, archimandrite; and to Andrew, archimandrite.[9]

Dioscorus, bishop of Alexandria,[10] said:

Those God-loving archimandrites just mentioned should
be present, in accordance with the order of the beloved
emperors, at the matters which are to be investigated.
Now, according to the order of the God-loving Eusebios
the bishop, let the God-loving Photius, Eustathius, and
Uranius, bishops, say what took place in their presence
concerning Hiba.

---

[7]Haziran is the tenth syrian month, equivalent to June. In June, the Ides fall
on the 13th of June.

[8]See Martindale, *Prosopography,* 927–928.

[9]Often archimandrites were heads of monasteries. Some of the names occur
elsewhere among those who supported Hiba before the synod in Beirut. See
Schwartz, *ACO* 2.1.3, #141.

[10]Dioscorus succeeded Cyril as bishop of Alexandria and was bishop from
444–451 CE. He was deposed at the Council of Chalcedon in 451, and died
in 454.

The God-loving bishops Photius of Tyre, Eusebius of Beirut, and Uranius of Himeria said:

> There was brought forward against Hiba in our presence matters concerning the faith. Because witnesses were needed about this matter, and a long period of time had intervened, we ordered that those who are clerics of the city of Edessa should say under oath on the Gospels what they knew concerning the accusation brought against him concerning the faith. There was much agitation and many accusations in Edessa over this matter. These were made known to our merciful and benevolent emperor. Because we heard that the victorious emperor had received news of these events, and had received the testimonies of all those named in the records, as Your Holiness has just now heard, we request that the records be read. Now Daniel, bishop of Harran,[11] is accused of violence. Since we saw that he clearly was guilty, we desire that he be deposed, lest we be put to shame. He, however, saw what was best for him and he chose to send letters of resignation. Your Holiness has the authority to deal with him and determine whatever seems appropriate to you. We make known to Your Holiness that, after the lawsuit that we heard, we agreed not to have fellowship with Hiba.

Cyrus, bishop of Aphrodisias, said:

> If your reverence orders, let the affair of Hiba be examined first, and be brought to a close. If the holy assembly is willing, let it order that the records taken about him be read.

---

[11]Harran was a city a little to the south of Edessa. Daniel was a nephew of Hiba, and was accused of immorality and of taking the monies of the church for himself and his friends.

A

THE FIRST REPORT

John, priest and head notary, read the acclamations of the citizens.

After the consulate of the victorious Flavii Zenon[12] and Postumianus,[13] one day before the Ides of April, during the second Indiction,[14] all those who live in the metropolitan city of Edessa, together with the honorable archimandrites and monks, the women and men of that city, gathered together and went out to meet with the great and honored Chaereas, comes of the first rank and praeses of Osrhoene.[15] When he came and was present within the boundary [of the city] and entered the martyrium of the holy Zachaeus, all of them shouted out, 'One is God! Victory to the Romans! Our Lord, be merciful to us! Our lords are victorious at all times! May the victory of Theodosius[16] increase! May the victory of Augustus Theodosius increase! May the victory of Augustus Valentinian[17] multiply! May the victory of our lords multiply! May the victory of the friends of God increase! May the years of the orthodox be many! One God, victory to Theodosius! One God, victory to Valentinian! Many years for the prefects! Many years for Protogenes! Many years for the illustri! A golden statue for the prefects! May you be strengthened for the Augusti! May you be strengthened for the palace! Many years for Domnus! Many years for the friend of Christ!

[12]Zenon 6, in Martindale, *Prosopography,* 1199–1200.

[13]Postumianus 4, in Martindale, *Prosopography,* 901–902.

[14]In April, the Ides fall on the 12th of April, so the date is 12 April 449 CE. The indiction (Latin *indictio*) was an interval of fifteen years connected to taxation cycles.

[15]Both *comes* and *praeses* were titles used in the later Roman Empire. *Praeses* was a provincial governor, so Chaereas was governor of the province of Osrhoene. *Comes* literally means 'companion'; there were several ranks of this 'companionship' and a *comes* of the first rank belonged to the senatorial order.

[16]Theodosius 6, in Martindale, *Prosopography,* 1100.

[17]Valentinianus 4, in Martindale, *Prosopography,* 1138–1139.

Many years for the consul! Many years for the orthodox! One is God who preserves you! Many years for Zenon! Many years for the commander! A golden icon for the commander! You are the glory of commanders! You are the messenger of peace! The victors (i.e. Caesars) trust in you! May you be strengthened for the Roman Empire! May you be strengthened for the Augusti! A statue for the commander!

A golden icon for the Victor! Many years for Anatolius![18] Many years for the patricius! You are the father of the Augustus, our lords trust in you! One Anatolius for everything! The Trinity with the patricius! Many years for Theodosius!

Many years for the *Comes*! The whole city gives thanks to Theodosius! The whole city praises the *Comes*! Many years to Chaereas! Many years to the *Comes*! Many years to the Christians! You have come and everything rejoices! The Augusti rightly honor you. You are reckoned worthy by the Augusti. May you be strengthened for the palace!

Another bishop for the metropolis! No-one accepts Hiba! No-one accepts Nestorius! Let the faction of Nestorius be burnt up! Let what belongs to the church be restored to the church! Take Hiba away from the church! Let the church not suffer violence!

One God, Christ conquers! May Our Lord have mercy on us! Our brothers are one soul. In short, no-one accepts Hiba! In short, no-one accepts the Nestorian bishop!

Augustus Theodosius, have mercy on our city! No-one accepts a second Nestorius! No-one accepts one who fights against Christ! No-one accepts the enemy of Christ! No-one accepts the hater of Christ! No-one accepts the enemy of the orthodox! No-one accepts a Jew as bishop! An orthodox bishop for the metropolis! He who departs, let him depart!

We beseech you, announce it immediately! Let our lords learn these things! Let the commander learn these things!

Let the faction be quickly burnt up! Let the faction of Nestorius be quickly burnt up! Piroz[19] as auditor for the church! Piroz as steward for the church! To die for the sake of Christ is life!'

---

[18]Anatolius 10, in Martindale, *Prosopography,* 84–86.

[19]Piroz is mentioned in the accusations against Hiba and Daniel recorded in the Acts of the Council of Chalcedon in 451. Schwartz, *ACO* 2/1/3, #73.

On the day after the Ides, the fourteenth of Iyar, the second Indiction,[20] in the council chamber of lord Flavius, the great and honored Chaereas, *Comes* of the first rank and *praeses* of Osrhoene, honorable clerics, God-loving archimandrites, monks and sons of the covenant came and said certain words on record. There also came craftsmen and all those who dwell in Edessa the metropolis, and they asked to enter the chamber. They entered and cried out,

> May Our Lord have mercy on us! May our lords be victorious at all times! May the victory of Theodosius increase! Many years for our lords! Many years for the orthodox! May the victory of Valentinian increase! Many years for our lords! One God, victory for Theodosius! One God, victory to Valentinian! One God, victory to the Romans! Many years for the prefects! Many years for Protogenes!

> Golden icons for the prefects! Many years for Nomus![21] Many years for the orthodox! One God who protects you! Many years for Zenon the commander! Many years for Chrysaphius![22] Many years for Urbicius![23] Many years for Anatolius, *patricius!* May Anatolius be preserved for the Roman Empire! Many years for the senator! Many years for Theodosius *Comes!*[24] Many years for Chaereas! May you be preserved for the Augusti! No one accepts Hiba as bishop! No one accepts Nestorius! No one accepts Simonians! No one accepts the enemy of Christ! No one accepts whoever is jealous[25] of Christ! No one accepts the corrupter of orthodoxy! The conspirator with Nestorius to exile! No one accepts whoever has professed in writing the teaching of Nestorius! No one accepts the counsellor of Nestorius! The despoiler of the temple to exile! The associate of Nestorius

---

[20]The Ides being on 13th of April, the date here is 14 April 449. As the Babylonian Jewish month Iyyar normally falls in April/May, there seems to be some mistake here.

[21]See Martindale, *Prosopography,* 785–786.

[22]See Martindale, *Prosopography,* 295–296.

[23]See Martindale, *Prosopography,* 1188–1190.

[24]See Martindale, *Prosopography,* 1101 (Theodosius 11).

[25]The word used here, ܚܣܡ, is also found in the statement attributed to Hiba at fol. 30v.

to exile! Let him who adheres to Nestorius dwell in exile! Hiba has ravaged the church! He alone is guilty, he has plundered the church! His party seized the riches of the church! Let what belongs to the church be returned to the church! Let what belongs to the poor be returned to the poor! No-one accepts the harmer of orthodoxy! No-one accepts the enemy of the faith! No one accepts the Iscariot! A noose for Iscariot! Holy Rabbula, petition with us! Hiba has damaged your faith! Hiba has damaged the holy faith of the synod! Hiba has damaged the faith of Ephesus! Hiba has damaged the true faith of Cyril!

Merciful emperors, dismiss this one! Orthodox emperors, dismiss this one! Deliver your metropolis! Redeem your faithful handmaid! Another bishop for the metropolis! Many years for Dioscorus, head of the bishops! An orthodox bishop for the metropolis! May Alexandria, city of the orthodox be strengthened! Dagalaiphus[26] as bishop for the metropolis! Holy Rabbula, petition with us!

Hiba dissolved the worship of the church! Hiba took the riches of everyone! August Theodosius, have mercy on your own city! His faction seized the riches of the church! Our Lord, have mercy on us! Unbelieving and refusing to believe, go and follow Nestorius, your associate! An orthodox bishop for the church! No-one accepts an adversary of the right faith! No-one accepts a friend of Jews! No-one accepts an enemy of God! Carry off Hiba and redeem the world! The hater of Christ to the wild beasts! The faction of the polluted to the stadium![27] God's property is in their possession! Let our lords learn this! Let the prefects[28] learn this! Let the Master[29] learn this! Let the Senate learn this! Another bishop for the metropolis! An orthodox bishop for the metropolis!

---

[26]Dagalaiphus was a consul in 461 CE. See Fl. Dagalaiphus 2, in Martindale, *Prosopography,* 340–341.

[27]*Stadion.* This was the public arena where criminals were executed.

[28] ʹΥπαρχοι.

[29]Many important civil and military officials carried this title. For a discussion of the various officials, see A. H. M. Jones, *The Later Roman Empire 284–602* (Norman, Oklahoma: Oklahoma University Press, 1964) 368–377.

Hiba has ravaged Osrhoene! Hiba plundered many churches! Right now he is selling the riches of the church! We desire that this be declared immediately! In short, no one accepts Hiba! May Eusebius, his brother, be delivered to the council! No one accepts a false bishop! The party of Hiba to the stadium! Let the party of Hiba be burnt alive! Let he who departs depart at once! On our lords' life, make this known immediately! Let Eulogius the priest depart at once! Let the zealot depart at once! Hiba left nothing in Sarug! A warning to the rulers! One God, Christ conquers! Our Lord, be merciful to us! Another bishop for the metropolis! No one accepts Hiba! O, the boldness of that fornicator! August Theodosius, take control of your city! No one accepts an unbelieving bishop! In short, no-one accepts a nestorian bishop! Noble Zenon, carry this one off! Take away oppression from the city! Many years to the consuls! Many years to the commander! Let a christian city not endure oppression! Where are these possessions? Daniel and Challoa to the brazier![30] The city kept closed because of Hiba! Hiba ravaged the city! It is not true, O *comes,* that no-one opens. No-one opens because of Hiba! Unless an orthodox bishop has come, no-one opens! The writings of Nestorius were found by Hiba! Who is the deceitful bishop? What bishop makes forged reports? Hiba voids the order of our lords! Let Hiba receive the punishment of Nestorius! Let the orthodox speak freely! Hiba drove away the saints! Hiba received the Nestorians! Take away coercion from the church! Another bishop for the metropolis! An orthodox bishop for the metropolis! All the people request this! All the city cries this out! For fourteen years Hiba has led astray this christian city, Edessa, the christian city blessed by God. One Hiba, one Simon![31] Musarius, the sorcerer[32] waxed strong, Hiba waxed strong!

---

[30] ܬܐܘܡܠܐ = θυμέλη. The Greek has the meaning 'hearth, altar' and, from being applied to the altar to Dionysos in the theatre, came to be used for a theatre, or stage. Is the acclamation to have Daniel, a bishop, and his alleged mistress Challoa burnt, or sent to the disgraceful status of stage players? Or both?

[31] The magician in Acts 8:9-24.

[32] Perry, Martin (with reservations), and Flemming take this as a proper name, Musarios. Perry suggests it is a mistake for 'Samaritan'. The syntax of the sen-

Take your companion away! Holy Rabbula, petition with us!
An orthodox bishop for the metropolis! No-one accepts
Hiba! Let his name be stricken from the church register! The
holy Rabbula cast Hiba into exile! Let Hiba go to the mines!
We petition, we do not command. We are doing all this for
the sake of Christ.

B

THE SECOND REPORT

Greetings from Flavius Chaereas to the great and praiseworthy Flavians, Florentius Romanus Protogenes for the second time and consul
ordinarius, Albinus and Salomo, prefects.[33]

Given the attitude of the city of Edessa towards its honorable
bishop, Hiba, and that so many were crying out and saying that he
agreed with Nestorius and that they do not accept him in their city;
given also the many disturbances and uprisings [the city] endured
because of this, I thought it hazardous that these events be hidden
from your high authority and I earlier made this known to your
exalted throne, lords noble and praiseworthy in every way, because
I am convinced even now that this affair could be hazardous unless
we inform Your Eminence about these events. Now I pass over in
silence how and by whom these disturbances and uprisings came
about. However, I will relate briefly what occurred after the letters
of our feeble self to your high and exalted throne.

All the clergy of the holy catholic church of Edessa, the metropolis,
together with the leaders and the foremost of those who undertake

---

tence plus the plural personal pronoun, 'your companion', suggests, however,
someone else besides Simon.

[33]Albinus 10, in Martindale, *Prosopography,* 53; Salomo, in Martindale, *Prosopography,* 973. Martindale suggests (973) that Protogenes was praetorian prefect
for the East, Albinus for Italy, and Salomo for Illyricum.

the monastic way of life as well as the learned, assembled and approached my feeble self. They petitioned me about a written petition. This was a vote by them and by others holding authority, by those who rank below these,[34] and by workers (as their signatures placed show, some work in agriculture and others in crafts). These made the petition, and requested that our feeble self accept it from them, and bring it to the knowledge of your praiseworthy selves. However, I was refusing this petition, so as not to vex the hearing of Your Eminence. Then, because they overpowered me with oaths which I could not cancel, I thought it presumptuous to treat with contempt the unanimous petition of the whole city and not be persuaded by the fearsome oaths, especially since they mentioned our victorious lords. Because of this, I bring forward these written reports. I also joined to them their written petition with the action surrounding it.

We pray for many years, that whatever you command be done, and that you be well and useful to God, exalted and always praiseworthy lords.

A copy of the acts which took place in Edessa after the consulate of Flavius Zenon[35] and Flavius Postumianus[36] in the presence of Asterius, Patroinus, Micallus and other priests, Sambatius, Sabas and other deacons, Callistratus, Euphorus and other sub-deacons of the holy church of Edessa, Elijah, Iamblichus and other monks, as well as certain magistrates, palace officials and others.

The honorable Micallus, priest of the holy church of the city Edessa, said:

> We carry a petition from those who dwell in the city, which contains the signatures of us clerics. In order that the tumults which have come upon the city and upon the holy church because of this affair be calmed, we entreat your excellent eminence that you order that [the petition] be received and read and placed in the acts and that you will send its contents to our exalted and praiseworthy lords the prefects,

[34]Segal (*Edessa*, 126) suggests two levels of administration in Edessa: a select inner committee, and the regular councillors. Here, those holding authority would belong to the first group, those ranking below them to the second.

[35]Fl. Zenon 6, in Martindale, *Prosopography*, 1199–1200.

[36]Rufius Praetextatus Postumianus 4, in Martindale, *Prosopography*, 901–902.

to the *comes* and Master of the divine offices, to the greatly praised commander and ex-consul, Zenon.

Flavius Thomas Iulianus Chaereas, exalted and praised **Comes** of the first rank and judge, said:

Let the petition, given by honorable and God-loving men, be received and read.

[The notary] read:

To Your Eminence from the distinguished citizens, clerics, archimandrites, monks, craftsmen and from all the city of Edessa together. From the very beginning our city, by the grace of God, excelled in faith: First, because of the blessing with which he, who created heaven and earth, blessed it as he willed in his mercy and consented to become a human for the sake of our redemption and the life of us humans; secondly, because [the city] was esteemed worthy that [in it] were placed the bones of the apostle Thomas, he who first proclaimed our Savior to be the Lord God.[37] It is our custom to love and honor our orthodox bishops and to reverence [them] as benefactors. This has been our behavior till now. As regards Hiba the bishop, although he was often vilified concerning the administration of the resources of gold of the holy church and, in sum, other matters, even so we continued to honor him until he was vilified and accused about the correct faith.

When we understood the truth from what he had written to the Persians, things which he was not able to deny, on this account we did not allow ourselves to accept him because we are anxious to protect the faith which was ours from of old. For those things written by him did no small harm also in the land of the Persians, and through all these it was known that he is a heretic. Therefore, because of this, he ought of his own free-will to renounce the episcopate, and be loathe with forceful violence to enter our city so as to teach us another faith besides the true one. Because of this, we petition Your Eminence to write to him so that

[37]Jn 20:28.

he not be occupied to enter our city until an order is sent
from our benevolent emperors. We further petition that
you inform the exalted and praiseworthy prefects and the
praiseworthy and exalted Magistros of these same events
so that, when they learn, through their authority the serene
and Christ-loving emperors might order that what happened
in Beirut be brought and read before your mercifulness, and
you might know how wickedly and incorrectly Bishop Hiba
thinks. Further, we petition Your Eminence that you go up
and inform also the exalted and powerful commander and
ex-consul, Zenon, so that he not be commandeered by Hiba.
For he [Hiba] is prepared to take for his own purposes the
army of the Romans, and attack us with force. We think that
this great authority, when he learns from your splendor, will
not be commandeered by Hiba, and his eminence will not
agree to provide a troop of Roman [soldiers] against the
orthodox who honor and walk according to the faith of
our benevolent lords, the emperors. For his praiseworthi-
ness is anxious to establish, set firmly and put into action
in every respect what our merciful lords commanded. For
it has come to the attention of all us orthodox that a new
edict has been decreed by their mercifulness which removes
from the priesthood Irenaeus, formerly bishop of Tyre. We
petition that all these things be made known to the God-
loving arch-bishop: In the judgement that took place in Beirut,
when his speeches were brought to light—those which he
denied were his—, [the bishop of Antioch] disallowed the
witnesses who testified concerning this, because they went
on the journey with his accusers. So we petition that every
one of those who are here and know well by his perverse
speeches how he preached against the correct faith might
come and witness in writing what they heard him preach
against the faith. Because we see all this wrong faith of Bishop
Hiba, we are compelled to manifest zeal for our faith, to extol
the benevolent lords of the earth and petition that these
very things be made known to those renowned majestic
authorities as we honor order everywhere and above all
are diligent for orthodoxy. We petition Your Eminence, as we
swear many oaths by the omnipotent God and by his Christ

and by the Holy Spirit and by the victory of the merciful lords of the earth, Flavius Theodosius and Flavius Valentinian, Augusti for ever, that you receive this petition from us and that you send it and make it known to the exalted authorities mentioned above.

Then [follow] the signatures of the whole city. I, Flavius Theodosius,[38] was present at what took place: All the clerics, archimandrites, monks, sons of the covenant, dignitaries, councillors,[39] Romans, students from Armenia, Persia and Syria, craftspeople and the whole city signed. Everyone wrote in his own hand and agreed about what had happened and with the presentation of the petition.

The shouting lasted three or four days, as all the people of the city shouted: The clergy with the priests, deacons, sub-deacons and lectors, holy monks, all the deaconesses and daughters of the covenant, Romans and women and children with all the rest of the city [shouted]:

Our Lord, be merciful to us! One God, Christ conquers! Our lords be always victorious! May the victory of Theodosius increase! May the victory of Valentinian increase! May the victory of the Christ-lovers increase! This city belongs to the Augusti! This city belongs to Christians! Edessa, city of the orthodox! Many years for the prefects! Many years to Nomus! Many years to the *patricius*![40] Many years to Zenon! Many years to the commander! Many years to Urbicius, *praepositus*![41] Many years to Chrysaphius![42] Many years to Anatolius![43] May the court of the orthodox be strengthened! May our lords be conquering at all times! No one accepts Hiba the Nestorian! He parts asunder the worship of the

---

[38]Theodosius 11, in Martindale, *Prosopography,* 1101.

[39]See n.15 for the distinction between dignitaries, i.e. those holding authority, and councillors.

[40]Nomus 1, in Martindale, *Prosopography,* 785–786. Nomus became a *patricius* in 448.

[41]Urbicius 1, in Martindale, *Prosopography,* 1188–1190.

[42]Martindale, *Prosopography,* 295–297.

[43]Fl. Anatolius 10, in Martindale, *Prosopography,* 84–86.

Church! No one communicates on the holy day! Let our
lords learn these things! Let the orthodox emperors learn
these things! Take away the one and deliver the city![44] He
sold the holy Thomas! He plundered the holy church! He
gave the money of the poor to his own party! All the people
ask, 'Let Hiba be thrown to the stadion! The Nestorian Hiba
to exile!' The whole city asks, 'Let the bones of John, who
appointed him, be cast out![45] For thirteen years he has led
us astray! Hiba to exile! This city belongs to the Augusti!
Hiba was strengthened, Simon[46] was strengthened! Musarius,
the magician, was strengthened, Hiba was strengthened!
Take away your associate! He stifled the poor, he pillaged
the church! He set apart the holy vessels! He used some
of the holy vessels for his own service! Christ-loving emperors, dismiss him! Benevolent emperors, let this one go
into exile!' All the people ask for this. Benevolent emperors,
have mercy on the city! This city belongs to believers! He
corrupted the writings of the orthodox Cyril! He corrupted
the correct teaching of the holy Rabbula! He corrupted the
correct teaching of the three hundred and eighteen! Take
away one and redeem the city! This is a city of Christians!
May the victory of Theodosius increase! May the victory
of Valentinian increase! May the victory of the orthodox
increase! Let the party of the Christians increase! Merciful
emperors, have mercy on us! Hiba to exile! Hiba to the
mines! Hiba the Nestorian to exile! Holy Thomas, pray with
us! Through your help, may holy Rabbula be remembered!
Through your help, may holy Cyril be remembered! These
established orthodoxy! Hiba and Nestorius have corrupted
it! They have corrupted the synod at Ephesus! The writings
of Nestorius were found at Hiba's place! The writings of
Theodore were found at Hiba's place! He transgressed your
edict! The whole city petitions this! All the people earnestly
entreat this! Erase him from the diptychs! Another bishop
for the metropolis! We do not accept him! No one accepts

[44]Cf. the slaying of Sheba in 2 Sam 20:21-22; and the saying in Jn 11:50.
[45]Bishop of Antioch.
[46]The magician in Acts 8:9-24.

the magician! No one accepts the charioteer! No one accepts a charioteer as bishop! He assumed fine linen for his personal attire at the church of Bar Laha! Abraham made him an athletic enclosure! The holy Eliades as bishop for the city! Flavian as bishop for the city! Daglaiphus as bishop for the city! Grant one of these three to the city! They are orthodox! The whole city petitions this!

Hiba to the mines! Hiba to exile! No one accepts such a bishop! An orthodox bishop for the metropolis! Those who plead on Hiba's behalf to exile! Basil the arch-deacon to exile! Abraham, the hospital administrator, to exile! Isaac and Cajunas, the corrupted lictors and sub-deacons, to exile! Notarius, Hypatius and Theodosius, sub-deacons, to exile! Maron the deacon to exile! The writings of Nestorius were found at his place. Bishop Hiba knew about this! Abba the priest, a Nestorian, to exile! He is the supporter of evil! The Persians Babai, Barsauma and Balash to exile! These are the cause of evil! Let our lords learn this! Holy Rabbula, send Hiba away! Holy Rabbula, petition with us! Our lords be always victorious! Our Lord, be merciful to us!

The *Comes* said:

It would be presumptuous and dangerous for us to frequently importune the praiseworthy and exalted authorities about these same things. For you yourselves know that yesterday I consented to your request and I made reports, one to the exalted and lofty throne and one to the praiseworthy Master. So I have not failed to already make known these affairs of yours to the praiseworthy and powerful authorities. How then do you ask, as if you forgot what was done yesterday, that I do today things so similar and alike?

Micallus the priest said:

The charge of the tribunal is right, and we praise in every way Your Eminence. However, seeing that a few days have passed by—for these reports were sent yesterday—today we present this petition which has been read, and we petition and swear copious oaths by omnipotent God and his Christ and his Holy Spirit and the victory of our powerful lords, the Flavians Theodosius and Valentinian, Augusti for ever, that this petition be made known to the exalted authorities so that the tumult which grips the city and the holy church and what happens to us every day because of what was recounted above might cease.

The *Comes* said: 'Have you presented the oath, which you have just sworn, at the desire of the entire group of honorable people here present?'

Micallus the priest said: 'At the desire of all the honorable priests, deacons, and of all the clergy and monks have I presented this petition and the oath which I swore. Therefore, I request that those standing here will say that we came to this tribunal for this purpose'.

The *Comes* said: 'Let everyone say whatever he wishes concerning what was said by the honorable and eloquent priest'.

Asterius the priest said: 'The honorable priest Micallus presented the petition at my desire, and I swear the same oath to Your Eminence'.

Patroinus the priest said: 'I also present the oath to Your Eminence. Also, the honorable priest Micallus presented the petition at my desire'.

Eulogius the priest said: 'At my desire, the honorable Micallus presented the petition, and I present the same oath'.

Ursicinus the priest said: 'At my desire, the honorable priest Micallus presented the report and the oath to Your Eminence, and I myself present the same'.

Zeoras the priest said: 'I am presenting the oath to Your Eminence. Also, the honorable priest Micallus offered the petition and oath at my desire'.

Jacob the priest said: 'The honorable priest Micallus presented the petition and oath at my desire, and I also am presenting the same oath to Your Eminence'.

Eulogius the priest said: 'The honorable priest Micallus presented the petition and the oath at the desire of the group'.

Samuel the priest said: 'I also am presenting the oath to Your Eminence. Also, the honorable priest Micallus presented the petition and the oath at my desire'.

Bassus the priest said: 'The honorable priest Micallus presented the petition and the oath at our desire, and I also am presenting the oath to Your Eminence'.

The deacon Sambatius said: 'The honorable Micallus presented at our desire the petition and the oath. I also am presenting the oath to your authority'.

Maras the deacon said: 'The honorable Micallus presented the petition and the oath at our desire to Your Eminence. I also am presenting the oath'.

John the deacon said: 'At the desire of us all, the honorable Micallus presented the petition and the oath to Your Eminence, and I also am presenting the oath'.

Sabas the deacon said: 'I am presenting the oath to Your Eminence, and the honorable Micallus presented the petition and the oath at our desire'.

Patricius the deacon said: 'By communal desire, the petition and the oath were presented to Your Eminence by the honorable Micallus, and I myself am presenting the oath'.

Cyrus the deacon said: 'The honorable Micallus presented the petition and the oath at my own desire. I also am presenting the oath'.

Abraham the deacon said: 'I also am presenting the oath to Your Eminence. Also, at our common desire, the honorable Micallus presented the petition and the oath'.

Hypatius the deacon said: 'The honorable Micallus presented the petition and the oath at our common desire, and I also am presenting the oath'.

Eusebius the deacon said: 'The honorable Micallus presented the petition and the oath at our desire. I also am presenting the oath'.

Paul the deacon said: 'The honorable Micallus presented the petition and the oath at the desire of all of us, and I also am presenting the oath'.

Romanus the deacon said: 'At the desire of us all, the report and the oath were presented by the honorable Micallus, and I also am presenting the oath to Your Eminence'.

Cyrus the deacon said: 'I also am presenting the oath to Your Eminence, and the honorable Micallus presented the report and the oath at the desire of us all'.

Maron the deacon said: 'The honorable Micallus presented the report and the oath at the communal desire, and I also am presenting the oath'.

Thomas the deacon said: 'I also am presenting the oath to Your Eminence. For the honorable Micallus presented the petition and the oath at our desire'.

Lucian the deacon said: 'I am presenting the oath to Your Eminence, for at our desire the honorable Micallus presented the report and the oath to Your Eminence'.

Abraham the deacon said: 'The honorable Micallus presented the petition and the oath at our desire, and I also am presenting the oath to your authority'.

Paul the deacon said: 'At our desire, the petition and the oath were presented by the honorable Micallus, and I also am presenting the oath to Your Eminence'.

Maras the deacon said: 'At our common desire, the honorable Micallus presented the petition and the oath to Your Eminence'.

Euphrodanius the deacon said: 'I also am presenting the oath to Your Eminence. At our desire, the oath was presented to Your Eminence by the honorable Micallus'.

Sabas the deacon said: 'I also am presenting the oath to your authority, for at our desire were said those things said by the honorable Micallus'.

Callistratus the sub-deacon: 'I also am presenting the petition and the oath to Your Eminence'.

Euphorus the sub-deacon: 'I am presenting the petition and the oath to Your Eminence'.

Antoninus the sub-deacon: 'I am presenting the petition and the oath to Your Eminence'.

Maras the sub-deacon: 'I also am reporting these things and presenting the oath'.

Elijah the sub-deacon: 'I am presenting the petition and the oath to Your Eminence'.

Maras the sub-deacon: 'I am presenting the petition and the oath to Your Eminence'.

Eusebius the sub-deacon: 'As I report these things, I present the oath'.

Thomas the sub-deacon: 'I also am presenting the petition and the oath'.

Pakidas the sub-deacon: 'I also am presenting the petition'.

Elijah the monk: 'At our desire, the honorable Micallus presented the petition and the oath to Your Eminence, and we also are presenting the petition and the oath'.

Iamblichus the monk: 'We also are presenting the petition to Your Eminence. For the honorable Micallus presented the oath and the petition at our desire'.

Habbib the monk: 'At our desire, the petition and the oath were presented by the honorable Micallus. I also am presenting the oath'.

Dios the monk: 'I am presenting the oath to Your Eminence, as I report that, at our desire, the honorable Micallus presented the report and the oath'.

Abraham the monk: 'At our desire, Micallus presented the petition and the oath, and I also am presenting the oath'.

Euphorus the monk: 'I also am presenting the report and the oath to Your Eminence'.

Simon the monk: 'I also am saying these things as I present the oath which was spoken'.

Elijah the monk: 'I also am presenting the report and the oath to Your Eminence'.

Asterius the monk: 'The same for me, as I present the awesome oath'.

Abraham the monk: 'I also am presenting the report and the oath to Your Eminence'.

Andrew the monk: 'I also petition the same, as I present the awesome oath'.

Flavius Thomas Julianus Chaereas, *Comes* of the first rank, said: 'Even though I had not been willing to accept your petitions, the awesome oath given by you, in part written, in part unwritten, compels me [to do so]. The oath mentions the Trinity equal in essence and the redemption and the victory of the lords of the earth. Because of this, I will now send and make known these things in your petition to the crowned and praiseworthy hearing'.

C

THE THIRD REPORT

To the eminent and praiseworthy Flavius Martialis,[47] *Comes* and Master of divine offices, greetings from Flavius Chaereas.

The power of our gloriously victorious and undefeated emperors, reverence for you and the diligence of my humble self have prevented Edessa the metropolis from falling from the rank of cities. For an evil spirit seized it like a fire, as I formerly made known to Your Eminence by a notification sent from our humble self. At that time, [it was prevented] as I said, but now nothing will extinguish this [flame] except your eminent and powerful name. For there is no one from any rank[48] within [the city] who stops crying out that it is impossible

[47]Martindale, *Prosopography,* 729.

[48]The word printed in Flemming, ܚܩܘܡ, makes no sense. In a private

for this agitation to cease until you, when you are informed, effect an end to this affair.

Although I was reluctant to write and disturb Your Eminence, it seemed to me that the only remedy and healing for the evils that have come upon this city was to bring what had happened to your attention. I set down accurately how and from where the events of this uprising were set in motion, and I sent a report which gives you what you should know. After the city had regained order from this [first flame], and was at peace and doing what was customary, only a few days had passed before an evil demon took it upon himself to stir up what had previously been extinguished. [This demon] will destroy everything if you and the orders expected from you cannot again extinguish the fire. The evil from the outbursts of those crafty ones will not be checked unless you again, when you are informed, apply a remedy to them. All these things and those which went beyond what I had previously made known to your exalted throne suffice concerning the hatred and the great hostility towards the honorable Hiba, whose episcopate they disavow and they refuse to be governed by him, and how all those who live in that city will go even into the fire, as they do not neglect to say or to do anything evil if only his name is mentioned. For I do not think it would be without danger to trouble your hearing, wise in everything, with anything extra, as the action, which took place and is herein set down below, is able to inform you clearly about everything that was set in motion by this affair. Exalted lords and praiseworthy in every way, I frequently pray to God that you, my exalted and praiseworthy lords, be well always, my victorious lords and helpers of the commonweal.

A copy of the acts which were made in Edessa in the presence of the dignitaries of the city, among them *Comes* Theodosius, of the above named clergy of the church of Edessa, and of the monks as well as the rest.

The same *Comes* Theodosius said:

> So that not even one tumult happen in the metropolis, I have been forced to avail myself of this report. For, when

---

communication, Sebastian Brock suggested that one should read ܡܩܘܡ̈ܐ = conditions, states, ranks, stations.

all the city gathered together in the holy church on the previous day, i.e. holy Sunday, they all asked that these accusations against bishop Hiba be declared. When the liturgy ceased, Your Eminence was forced to go to the holy church to quench the whole tumult. I also was forced to come so that by every means the city might be at peace. All those gathered together were barely persuaded to be silent when Your Eminence promised, 'I myself will come tomorrow for an enquiry into the account'.

I, as well as Your Eminence, also promised them [that I would come] so that the agitation might cease. Now, because matters concerning the city are in confusion—for Your Eminence sees that we are not allowed to dwell in peace or to remain in our homes—and because moreover I gave heed to what had formerly been ordered by the eminently great and powerful commander of the *Oriens* and ex-consul who, being concerned for the tranquillity of the city, ordered that all tumult should cease—I was forced by reason of the commotions presently existing to present the report to Your Excellent Eminence, who is able, as I think, to still the existing commotions. I have been led to this report because of the opinion of the community of all the clerics, archimandrites, covenanters, councillors, and other owners here present. In this report, I petition Your Eminence to put a stop to the turbulence of the people, and order that the existing tumults finish. For these happened because an accusation was made against bishop Hiba in the city of Beirut, and the multitude was told that he was outside the true faith, that he said many blasphemous things, and that he did many things abhorrent to the laws and against the Christian faith.

Therefore, I petition Your Eminence that, in order that the evils cease, those who were his accusers and who are now here might be constrained to say what are those things which have been done, what are the accusations against him, and under what counts he has been indicted. For, since I was petitioned by the dignitaries, the free-born councillors, by the honorable clergy and archimandrites, and by the craftsmen here present, and since I was readily assiduous to stay the confusion, which is on account of the faith, and which occurs every day and of which all are guilty, I presented this report and I petition that all of them say whether this took place in this way.

Flavius Thomas Julian Chaereas, *Comes,* said:

Now that you have heard what was said by the eminent and praiseworthy *Comes* Theodosius, let those here present—illustrious noblemen, God-loving priests, free-born councillors of the metropolis, and honorable monks—also make known, if they wish, their opinion by deposition.

Eulogius, *Comes,* said:

Just as he said, the praiseworthy *Comes* Theodosius, splendid in his eminence, presented the report on the counsel of us city nobles, clerics, monks, and those who dwell in the city.

Faustinus *magistrianus*[49] said:

I also acknowledge that, at my own desire and that of the whole city, *Comes* Theodosius, praiseworthy and splendid in his eminence, presented the report.

Theodorus *magistrianus*[50] said:

At my desire and that of all here present, *Comes* Theodosius, praiseworthy and splendid in his eminence, presented the report.

The honorable Micallus, the priest, said:

All of us petitioned the splendidly eminent and praiseworthy *Comes* Theodosius to petition these things to Your Eminence, and we are grateful that he consented to our petition.

Rodon, Zeoras, Isaac, Patroinus and the rest of the honorable priests said:

All of us petitioned the splendidly eminent and praiseworthy *Comes* Theodosius to present this report to Your Eminence on our behalf.

[49]Faustinus 3, in Martindale, *Prosopography,* 450.
[50]Theodorus 23, in Martindale, *Prosopography,* 1089.

Abraham, Martyrius, Lucian, Sambatius and the rest of the honorable deacons said:

> All of us also petitioned the splendidly eminent and praiseworthy *Comes* Theodosius to present this report to Your Eminence on our behalf.

John, Callistratus, Maras, Thomas, Eulogius and the rest of the sub-deacons said:

> The splendidly eminent and praiseworthy *Comes* Theodosius was petitioned by all of us to present this report to Your Eminence.

Iamblichus, Elijah, Dios, Abraham, Ephræm and the rest of the honorable monks said:

> The splendidly eminent and praiseworthy *Comes* Theodosius presented this report to your mercifulness because he was petitioned by us.

Constantine, John, Sergius and the rest of the covenanters said:

> The splendidly eminent and praiseworthy *Comes* Theodosius, because petitioned by us, presented the report to Your Eminence.

Constantius said:

> I also witness that, at the desire of all the city, the splendidly eminent and praiseworthy *Comes* Theodosius presented this report to Your Eminence.

Bias said:

> We petitioned the splendidly eminent and praiseworthy *Comes* Theodosius to present this report on our behalf.

Gainas said:

> I with my associates and all the city also petitioned the splendidly eminent and praiseworthy *Comes* Theodosius to present the report to Your Eminence.

Asclepius said:

> When the splendidly eminent and praiseworthy *Comes* Theodosius was petitioned by the whole city together and by the magistrates, he presented the report to your mercifulness'.

Andreas said:

> When the splendidly eminent and praiseworthy *Comes* Theodosius was petitioned by us and by everybody, he presented on our behalf the report to your authority.

Eusebius said:

> It was just as my associates have reported. For, when the splendidly eminent and praiseworthy *Comes* Theodosius was petitioned by everyone, he presented the report to Your Eminence.

Aurelianus the *princeps* said: 'I also report this'.

Abgar the barrister, said:

> The splendidly eminent and praiseworthy *Comes* Theodosius accepted our petition. As his eminence performed the action worthy of him, he presented the report to Your Eminence.

Demosthenes said:

> It is just as the noble councillors reported. For the splendidly eminent and praiseworthy *Comes* Theodosius presented the report to Your Eminence at the urging of everyone together.

Palladius said:

> What my associates said is true. For by the petition which was presented to the splendidly eminent and praiseworthy *Comes* Theodosius, he was persuaded to present the report to Your Eminence who upholds the laws.

The judge said:

> In my opinion, it is appropriate that Your Eminence make known in your deposition the names of those honorable

priests who also took part in the presentation and in the accusation.

Comes Theodosius said: 'They are the honorable priests, Samuel, Maras and Cyrus'.

The judge said:

> Now that these have heard what was said by the splendidly eminent and praiseworthy *Comes* Theodosius, let the honorable members of the God-fearing clergy say of their own will what they seek.

The honorable priest Samuel said:

> Far superior to, and more trustworthy than, our deposition is the witness of someone who pronounced judgement on the affair in accordance with the order of the merciful and Christ-loving emperors. Now this is the God-fearing Uranius. He, however, is not now here. Doubtless for the sake of the same cause he was forced to go and tell our lords what had happened. Also, one of us, the honorable Eulogius, is likewise missing because of the same matter. So, then, three are coming here, of whom I am one. I am saying all of this under deposition. After suffering much everywhere and enduring stratagems because of Hiba the bishop, his constant molestation and the gold that he had lavished everywhere to condemn the truth, we were hardly deemed worthy for what were sought on approaching the merciful emperors so that judges be assigned to us. Their names are: The God-fearing Photius, bishop of Tyre, Eustathius, bishop of Beirut, and the holy Uranius, bishop of Himeria, of whom I made mention a little earlier. When the affair was discussed before them in written form, they resolved certain points as seemed good to them. Records on the affair were kept by them, which we frequently requested that we might publish. I do not know why they did not allow us to make them public. If we are again required to take up the argument and speak before your splendid eminence about the disorder which still emanates from the city which has suffered over the events—for everyone ought to be grieved—we will speak. For these are

not minor matters which were brought forward by us. All
the clergy know the greater part of them and, so I think, will
witness that we report truthfully.

At first, acting as required and submitting to the canons, in
the great city of Antioch we approached the arch-bishop of
that city, the pious Domnus, and gave him the specific main
points. When he learnt these things accurately and knew that
each one of them would bring punishment on the sinner,
he cast us out capriciously. Afterwards, as we could not appeal his negligence, we were forced to go and report these
things to the imperial city and to the synod of the western
region, i.e. to the pious archbishop Flavian. [We also went]
to our merciful emperor. We discussed not just what had
been brought forward in Antioch and had been given by us
in writing, but also questions of faith. Now, if your splendid
eminence orders, we will provide these main points; we
cannot repeat everything before you now but [will provide
them] separately to the attendants. So the trial about the
faith occurred in this way, with our bringing forward and
stating that, in the banqueting-hall of the bishop's palace,
while the festival gifts were being given—for it was the custom every year that, as the gifts were given by him to the
honorable clergy, he would preach and then distribute the
gifts—he said in the presence of many, 'I do not envy Christ
that he became God, for when he became, I became. For
he is of my own nature.[51]

Many from the clergy, if they fear God, know that I immediately charged him, and that, from that time till now, I
took nothing from the church and I did not communicate
with him because I recognized his blasphemy. Likewise, [they
know] that I was ready to stand up and make a tumult at
that very moment, but those sitting near me did not let me

[51] The Greek text, as found in the Acts of the Council of Chalcedon (Schwartz,
ACO 2.1.3, p. 27, #81), is: οὐ φθονῶ τῶι χριστῶι γενομένωι θεῶι· ἐφ ὅσον
γὰρ αὐτος ἐγένετο, κἀγὼ ἐγενόμην. The latin text (Schwartz, *Prosopography*,
2.3.3, p. 33, #81) is: *non invideo Christo facto Deo; in quantum enim ipse factus est,
et ego factus sum.* These accusations are denied by Hiba (Schwartz, *ACO* 2.1.3,
p. 27, #83; 2.3.3, p. 33, #83).

because, they said, 'A tumult will erupt'. After I went away, they questioned me and I told them and made them remember that he had so spoken. He denied this before the judges who were appointed, and he anathematized himself: 'If I said [this], may I be accursed and alien to the episcopacy'.

Aware of this and wanting to manipulate matters so that he could reject these [witnesses], he said that they were under suspension by him and not admissible by the law. When we retorted, 'If you made these excommunicate for some other reason, you spoke well. But if [you made them excommunicate] because of this very affair so that they could not testify—just as you made us excommunicate because of our accusation so that we could not accuse—they ought to be admitted. So say that they ought not to be admitted because of some other reason and that they have a transgression prior to this affair.

He could not find another reason except this one alone. So he slandered them by saying, 'They were with you in Constantinople'. The judges—whether because they were bestowing a favor on him or not, I cannot say—were still not persuaded to admit them as the sole [witnesses] but they disregarded them by saying, 'Others must come'.

Then it happened by the will of God that the honorable Eulogius, a worthy son to the good memory of Hypatius, came that very evening, as well as the pious priest, Jacob. On the next day, we took them and hastened to bring them and have them stand up and declare. But again, [the judges] did not even agree to admit them for they said: 'Others must be summoned'. We spoke a great deal about this, and this is also in the acts of the records.

My own words are there: 'We suffer violence. The laws do not reject five [witnesses]. Accept the first group, or these, or all of us together'. Because this did not please them, the affair remains in this neglected state on this main point. Now, because it is right that those who did not make their depositions there, might at least here and now declare them in writing, I petition Your Splendid Eminence that those who

were with us in Beirut and all those who know about this
main point might speak what they know about the affair.

The judge said:

> The reliability of the acts declare what was said\ in Beirut by
> the God-fearing priest Samuel. But let these other honorable
> priests say what they have to say, if they wish.

The honorable Maras, a priest, said: 'It was so. For it was debated
about the same main point, and we petition that those who know
might speak'.

The honorable priest Cyrus spoke in this way: 'Let those who know
about this main point speak what they are acquainted with for the
reliability of the acts'.

The judge said: 'Let everyone of those present in the city of Beirut or
in Tyre, when there was an inquiry there, speak unhindered whatever
he knows, if he wishes'.

The honorable Eulogius, priest, said:

> In my own presence with my fellow clergy inside the bishop's
> residence, Hiba said, 'I do not envy Christ that he became
> God. For he became, I became. For he is from my own
> nature'. I was prepared, when I went to Beirut, to testify the
> same, if summoned.

The honorable Maras, deacon, said:

> When I was with the honorable fellow clergy in the bishop's
> residence, Hiba the bishop said as he preached, 'I do not
> envy Christ that he became God. For he became, I became.
> For he is from my own nature'. I testify before God and
> humankind. I was prepared to testify so in Beirut when I
> was there, if summoned. So I heard that he preached that
> God the Word had known in his fore-knowledge that Christ
> would be justified from his deeds and, because of this, he
> dwelt in him.

The honorable deacon David said:

> In my presence, Hiba the bishop said as he preached, 'I do
> not envy Christ that he became God. For he became, I

became, for he is from my own nature'. If I had been summoned while I was in Beirut, I would not have declined to testify to this.

The honorable priest Samuel said:

Some of those who were in Beirut are now far away, namely Saba and Jacob. However, there are others from the pious clergy who know as well as them about this affair, and I petition them to say on the record what they know as they give an oath.

The judge said: 'Let it be so from anyone who knows what pertains to this narrative, if he wishes'.

The honorable priest Samuel said:

I petition first of all that the honorable priest Leontius might state, as we were sitting near each other, if straightaway I charged him [Hiba] and, in the episcopal residence, I was ready to stand up and I was not allowed to by him. After we went down, when questioned I said all these things, as he knows.

The honorable priest Leontius said:

What the honorable priest Samuel said, he said in truth. I was present when what is in the depositions by my colleagues was said by Hiba, 'I do not envy Christ that he became God. For he became, I became. For he is of my nature'.

The honorable Bassus said:

I was present with my honorable colleagues of the clergy and I heard Hiba say, 'I do not envy Christ that he became God. For he is honored, I am honored. For he is of my own nature'.

Eulogius the deacon said:

I was present and heard Hiba say, 'I do not envy Christ that he became God. For what he became, I became. For he is of my own nature'.

The priest Ursicinus said:

> I heard Hiba say in a sermon in the church that John the Evangelist said, 'In the beginning was the Word', but the Evangelist Matthew said, 'The book of the birth of Jesus the Christ, son of Abraham, son of David'. In explaining, he said, 'Is not this one, and this another?' On Easter of last year as he preached on the throne, he again said, 'Today Christ became immortal'. Again, as he spoke with Theodotus, a senator splendid in his eminence, he said about Gehenna, 'That is a threat written [to cause] fear'. I know these things, and I heard them from him.

The honorable deacon Sabas said: 'I also heard Hiba saying on Easter day, "Today Christ became immortal"'.

The honorable priest Barsauma said:

> I heard Hiba say on Easter day, 'Today Christ became immortal'. He also said this: 'We ought wisely to think separately about God and about human: One is assumed by grace, the other assumes by grace'.

The deacon Lucian said:

> I heard Hiba say, 'The name "Gehenna" possesses only the sense of a threat'. I know that he also had writings of the wicked Nestorius, whose name is expunged.

Arsenius the priest said:

> I heard Hiba preaching to the people in the church, 'The Jews should not boast because it is an ordinary human being that they crucified'.

Abraham the deacon said:

> I also heard Hiba say, 'The Jews should not boast, because they did not crucify God but the mere human'.

John, a covenanter, said:

> I heard Hiba preaching in the church and he said, 'One is he who died, another he who is in heaven. One is he who is without beginning, another he who is subject to a beginning.

One is he who is from the Father, another he who is from the virgin'. He also said, 'If God died, who restored Him to life?'

The honorable priest Maras said to Constantine: "By the God whom you worship and by the Holy Trinity, what did you hear Hiba say as he preached?'

Constantine said:

> Because it is necessary for me on account of the oath which the honorable Samuel summoned, I will say what I am aware of. God, the Lord of Truth, knows—and, moreover, those present who heard can testify for me—that many times I heard him speaking and saying, 'As when the purple garments are dishonored, the dishonor runs to the emperor, so the suffering runs to God'. Many times I left and went outside. I am confirmed by many witnesses of the city over this.

Theodorus spoke about the teaching:

> When Hiba was speaking in his own banqueting-hall, and something was said about the resurrection of our Lord Christ he said, 'His body before the resurrection was not what was after the resurrection'. When I responded to this, 'How did the holy apostle Thomas, when he doubted, at his command touch his side and see those places where the nails were fastened and hear our Lord say, "Be believing and not unbelieving"'. Then Hiba responded, 'This was an apparition'. Dumbfounded by what was said, I went out to several of the monks, and said to them what had been spoken by Bishop Hiba. They said that whoever says this is accursed.

Sergius, a covenanter, said:

> Hiba was always making a division between the divinity and the humanity, and I often truly complained a great deal about this on the *bema*[52] [of the church].

---

[52]The *bema* was a raised platform in the nave of the church from where scripture readings, sermons and blessings would be given. See Erich Renhart, *Das syrische Bema: liturgisch-archäologische Untersuchungen,* Grazer Theologische Studien 20 (Graz: im Eigenverlag des Instituts für Ökumenische Theologie und Patrologie an der Universität Graz, 1995).

Jacob, a monk, said:

> I heard Hiba say, 'Let the Jews not boast as if they hanged God. They crucified a human'.

Sergius, a covenanter, said:

> On the Thursday of Holy Week, Hiba said during the night, 'Let the Jews not boast that they crucified God. They did not crucify God'.

Abraham said:

> I heard Hiba say, 'Let the Jews not boast that they crucified God, for they crucified a human'.

John, a covenanter, said:

> As he was coming out from the baptistery in the evening,[53] I heard Hiba say, 'Today Christ has become immortal'.

Constantine, a covenanter, said:

> I also heard Hiba, as he returned from the baptistery in the evening, say, 'Today Christ became immortal'. Another day, as he was preaching, he said, 'One is he who is from the Father, another he who is from the virgin'. And, 'as purple garments to the emperor, so is the body of Christ'.

The honorable Samuel said:

> I heard Hiba say, 'As an emperor is dishonored by way of his purple garments, so God the Word is dishonored by way of his body'.

Theodosius, the *Comes,* said:

> Your excellent Eminence has learnt what are the depositions against Hiba who was bishop of this metropolis from the individual depositions. That the city which has been so disturbed might be at ease, I petition Your Eminence and I adjure you by the Holy Trinity, by the benevolence and victory of our lords of the world, and by our lord Theodosius whom the Son, so that He bring joy to us, pronounces acceptable:

---

[53] This would be at Easter time.

Let these be sent to the excellent eminence, the Master of Divine Offices, so that, through his excellent eminence, the victorious and divine crown might learn; to the praise-worthy and well-blessed governors; and to the powerful general of the two armies, the ex-consul. May the following also learn through the letters of Your Eminence: The holy archbishops of flourishing Constantinople and Alexandria; Domnus, the honorable archbishop of Antioch; Juvenal, the holy bishop of Jerusalem; Eustathius and Photius, the holy bishops of Tyre and Beirut, who were the judges of this affair.

I also petition that a copy of the letter in Syriac, which is said to have been from Hiba to the Persian Mari, be read before the honorable clerics and all those present, and be placed in the acts. For I reported these when I was petitioned by the honorable clerics, monks, and all the citizens, as the depositions from them show.

The judge said:

As for whatever declarations were made in the court-house, we will report everything previously discussed to the exalted and higher authorities in accordance with the meaning of the instruction which was presented to the court-house, as well as the fearsome oath made after the declarations concerning the above-mentioned account. What is appropriate is being written to these God-loving bishops whom the praiseworthy Theodosius mentioned. Now, let the writing which the praiseworthy man mentioned be admitted according to rule and read.

A Translation of the Letter Written by the Honorable Hiba to Mari the Persian[54]

After the introduction:

In brief, then, we take pains to make known to your clear intelligence—which grasps many things through few—what happened a little while ago and even now. We know that,

---

[54]The Greek text is found in Schwartz, *ACO* 2.1.3, pp. 32–34, #138. The Latin at *ACO* 2.3.3, pp. 39–43, #138.

when we write these things to your godly piety, what we say is, through your diligence, comprehensible to all who are there that the writings given by God have not received even a single alteration. So I start the account with those events with which you are cognizant. Since your Godly Piety was here, a contention arose between these two men, Nestorius and Cyril. They composed against each other hurtful words which offended those who heard them. For Nestorius said in his discourses, as your Godly Piety knows, 'the blessed Mary is not the mother of God', so that many thought that he belongs to the heresy of Paul of Samosata, who said that Christ is a mere man. Then Cyril, as he desired to reject the words of Nestorius, was found to fall[55] into the teaching of Apollinaris. For, like him, [Cyril] wrote that God the Word became a human so that there was no distinction between the temple and him who dwells in it. For he wrote twelve chapters, with which I think your Godly Piety is acquainted, 'there is one nature of the divinity and of the humanity of our Lord Jesus Christ'. One ought not, as he says, distinguish the expressions which either Our Lord said about himself or the evangelists said about him. How full of impiety these words are Your Holiness knows before we speak. For how is it possible that this *In the beginning was the Word*[56] can be understood about the temple that was born by Mary? Or that this *You made him a little less than the angels*[57] be said about the divinity of the Only-begotten? For the Church, as your Godly Piety[58] learned from the beginning—and it is confirmed by the words of the blessed fathers by divine teaching—speaks in this way: 'Two natures, one power, one person',[59] that is, the one son, the Lord Jesus Christ. Because of this contention, the victorious and merciful emperors commanded the archbishops to gather at the city of Ephesus that, before all of them, the discourses of Nestorius and Cyril might be adjudicated. Before all the bishops commanded to gather came to Ephesus, Cyril ar-

---

[55]The Greek text adds ὤλισθεν: It reads 'slipped and was found to fall'.
[56]Jn 1:1.
[57]Heb 2:7.
[58]The Greek adds: ἐπίσταται, 'knows'.
[59]πρόσωπον, ܩܢܘܡܐ.

rived early and he seized the hearing of all beforehand by a drug which blinded the eyes of the wise. He found a pretext in the hatred towards Nestorius and, before the God-loving archbishop John came to the synod, they dismissed Nestorius from the episcopate, although a trial and investigation had not taken place. Then, two days after his deposition, we arrived in Ephesus. We learnt that, during the deposition effected by them, they had affirmed the twelve chapters written by Cyril, which are opposed to the true faith. They ratified and approved them as if they were approving something of the true faith. Then, all the bishops from the east deposed Cyril, and determined excommunication for all those other bishops who approved the chapters.

After this irregularity, everyone returned to his own city. Nestorius, however, as he was hated by his own city and by the nobles in it, was not able to return there. The eastern synod did not remain in communion with the bishops who were in communion with Cyril. Because of this, there was great animosity between them: Bishops were contentious towards bishops, and peoples towards peoples. What was written [in Scripture] was fulfilled in deed: *The enemies of a man will be of his household.*[60] Because of this, great abuse against us came from the pagans and heretics. For no one dared to go from city to city or from district to district, but everyone was persecuting his neighbor as an enemy. Then many, in whom *there was no fear of God before their eyes,*[61] strove to bring about in deed the enmity which they felt and had hidden in their hearts, on the pretext [that they were acting out] of zeal on behalf of the Church. One of them is the tyrant of our metropolis, who also is not unknown to you. On the pretext [of acting on behalf] of the faith, he takes vengeance not only on those who are alive, but also on those who have earlier departed to the Lord. One of these was the blessed Theodore, preacher of the truth and teacher of the faith.[62] [Theodore] not only subdued the heretics by the

[60]Mt 10:36.
[61]Ps 36:1.
[62]Theodore of Mopsuestia.

true faith while alive, but also after his death left behind in
his writings spiritual weapons to the children of the Church.
This [tyrant], who is presumptuous in everything, dared to
anathematize such a one openly in the church, someone[63]
who through zeal for God not only changed his city from
error to truth, but also by his teaching instructed churches
far distant. A great search was made everywhere for his
books, not because they were alien to the true faith—for
while he [Theodore] was alive he [Rabbula] constantly glorified him and was studying his writings—but because of
the enmity which he [Rabbula] had towards him [Theo-
dore], [an enmity] which had secretly seized him because
he [Theodore] had rebuked him openly in the synod. After
these unfortunate events had taken place between them
and *everyone walked as he willed*—as it is written[64]—our
God—worshiped be He who at all times in his mercifulness
is solicitous for his holy Church–so aroused the heart of
our pious[65] emperor that he sent a great and famous man
from his palace to force the holy and God-loving bishop of
the east, Mar John, to be reconciled with Cyril, for he had
expelled [Cyril] from the episcopate. After he received the
documents of the emperor, [John] sent the venerable, God-
loving Paul, bishop of Emesa, with letters to Alexandria. He
sent through him the true creed, and he instructed him that,
if Cyril approved this creed and anathematized both those
who said that the divinity suffered and those who said that
there was one nature of the divinity and of the humanity,
he would hold him in communion. Thus willed the Lord, He
who is always solicitous of His holy Church redeemed by
His blood. He softened the heart of the Egyptian[66] so that
without any trouble or difficulty he agreed[67] and accepted
the creed. He anathematized all those who are outside this

[63]The Greek text adds: 'as your piety, who has met him, knows and is persuaded by his writings' (Schwartz, *ACO* 2.1.3, p. 33, lines 31–32).

[64]Acts 14:16. Cf. Jdgs 17:6; 21:25.

[65]The Greek text adds: 'and victorious' (Schwartz, *ACO* 2.1.3, p. 34, line 4).

[66]This may echo Is 19:1.

[67]'Without any trouble or difficulty he agreed' is not in the Greek (Schwartz,
ACO 2.1.3, p. 34, line 13).

faith. When [the two bishops] held each other in communion, the contention was lifted from their midst and there was peace in the Church.

Thenceforward there was no division in [the Church], but peace as formerly. What are the words which were written by the God-loving archbishop and what answer did he receive from Cyril? I have joined these letters to the one to your Godly Piety. I sent them so that, when you read them, you will know and declare to all those brethren who love peace that the contention has ceased. The wall of enmity is breached, and those who were so intemperately lifted themselves up against the living and the dead are in disgrace, because they apologize for their wrongdoing and they teach what is the opposite of their former teaching. For no one dares to say, 'There is one nature of the divinity and of the humanity', but they confess that the temple and he who dwells in it is the one son, Jesus Christ.

So I have written these things to your Godly Piety out of the great love I have towards you. For I know that Your Holiness trains yourself night and day in the divine teaching, in order to benefit many.

The judge said:

This writing just read, as you also know, is a copy of the letter. For the deposition of the praiseworthy man acknowledges this. How then can this copy be admitted in place of the original and placed in the acts so that it may be made known to the above named God-loving bishops?

The priest Samuel said:

This copy of the letter appeared in the accusation that was against Hiba who was accused by us. He acknowledged it, and this is in the genuine acts which took place in the city of Beirut before those judges appointed to us by the grant and order of the emperor, one of whom is the honorable bishop Uranius. He testified and does still testify that this letter was acknowledged by [Hiba] as his own. Others are here who were there at that time and who know that it was manifestly read as his own. I petition that they make depositions.

The judge said:

Let those who are acquainted with this matter, instruct [us] whether, when the investigation was set in motion in the city of Beirut before the God-loving bishops appointed judges by divine commands, a copy of the letter just read appeared before the same pious bishops and was acknowledged by the honorable Hiba that it was from the original sent by him, as the honorable Samuel stated.

Maras, a deacon, said:

I was present and Hiba acknowledged in my presence that this letter was his. He said, 'So I acknowledge and so I believe till today. Even if the emperor were to command that I be slain and done away with, so do I believe'.

The priest Eulogius said:

In the city of Beirut, I heard from the honorable bishop Uranius that Hiba acknowledged that it was his and that the copy mentioned was from his own letter and so he believes.

The deacon David said:

I also heard the holy bishop Uranius in the city of Beirut say, 'Hiba acknowledged that the letter was his, and so he acknowledges and so he believes'. He said, 'If I were to be killed and if the emperor were to command that I die, so I believe and I do not believe otherwise'.

Asterius, the priest, said:

I heard Hiba say, 'This is a copy of my original letter which was shown and read before the judge in Beirut'.

The deacon Eusebius said:

> I heard Hiba say, 'They showed a copy of my letter. As soon as they began to read, I said, "This is my letter"'.

Eulogius, the priest, said:

> I was not inside, but outside I heard Hiba [say], 'The copy of the letter which was read is mine'.

The priest Bassus said:

> Hiba wrote a letter here [which stated], 'Enemies and accusers made public a letter which I wrote some years earlier to the Persian Mari. They began to read it, and, as soon as they began to read, I recognized a copy of the letter which I had written'. All the clergy know this.

Eusebius, the deacon, said:

> Maron the deacon read to us the letter of Hiba which acknowledges, 'My enemies and accusers made public a copy of the letter which I wrote to the Persian Mari'. So Hiba himself acknowledged in Beirut that the letter was his.

Flavius Thomas Julian Chaereas, *Comes* of the first rank and judge, said:

> What the honorable clergy said in deposition about the copy of the letter are also known. As regards what was done today according to the instructions of the praiseworthy *Comes* Theodosius, that is, what was presented and made public on behalf of the whole community, they will be made known to the renowned, great and exalted authorities. We will write what is appropriate to the God-loving bishops mentioned, because we are not able to neglect such fearsome oaths as these.

When [all these documents] were read in Ephesus, the holy synod said:

> These pollute our hearing! Always a memorial to Cyril for the sake of archbishop Dioscorus! Cyril is immortal! Let Alexandria be confirmed as a city of the orthodox!

The holy synod said: 'These actions are true, a crown of the whole synod'.[68]

The holy synod said:

> These pollute our hearing! They are appropriate for pagans! Spare our hearing! Let them not be spoken! Spare our hearing! Spare our souls! Spare the orthodox! Let Hiba be burnt in the middle of the city! Let Hiba be burnt in the middle of Antioch! Let Hiba be burnt for the correction of others! Not even the evil spirits said these things! Not even the Pharisees said these things! Not even the Jews said these things! This is a saying of pagans! This is a saying of Satan! This is a saying of atheists! The demons acknowledged Christ as God! Hiba does not acknowledge him! The demons are more respectful than Hiba! The evil spirits acknowledged Christ as Son of God![69] Satan is more respectful than Hiba, the tempter is more respectful than Hiba! Hiba is the shame of all the earth! Let Hiba be burnt as well as those who agree with him! Let Hiba be burnt as well as those appointed by him! Whoever does not hate Hiba is an evil spirit! Whoever loves Hiba is a satan! Whoever does not hate Hiba is not orthodox! Whoever loves Hiba is Nestorian! Whoever does not set Hiba on fire is not orthodox! Satan is no match compared to the blasphemy of Hiba! We beseech the emperors, 'Kill Hiba!' We beseech the emperors, 'Let Hiba be burnt alive! Let this happen for the correction of heretics! Let Hiba be burnt in Antioch! Burn one and save many! Let Nestorius and Hiba be burnt together! Let Nestorius and Hiba be burnt

[68]That is, Dioscorus.
[69]See Mt 8:29.

in the middle of Antioch! Exile is of no use! Exile harms the city! Let Nestorius and Hiba be burnt together! Exile does nothing at all to them! Let Nestorius and Hiba be burnt together! Let Satan and his son be burnt together!' Patriarch, help the orthodox! Get rid of all these! Let no remnant from Pharaoh remain![70]

Dioscorus, bishop of Alexandria, said:

It is not clear what this evil spirit said. For he said, 'I do not envy Christ that he became God'. How was God able to become what He is not?

The holy synod said:

Many years to the patriarchs! Dioscorus and Cyril have ratified the faith of the fathers! Many years to the patriarchs! Many years to the orthodox!

Dioscorus, bishop of Alexandria, said:

You have not shouted this out by yourselves, but the Holy Spirit proclaimed [it] through you, and Christ, who is persecuted by him [Hiba].

The holy synod said: 'The whole world recognizes your faith. Dioscorus is unique in the world'.

When Eulogius, a priest of Edessa, entered and reported a certain event that had taken place in Antioch, the holy synod shouted out: 'We petition that what is said be put on record. They concern the faith. Let them be said on record! Let what is against Christ be said on record!'

Dioscorus, bishop of Alexandria, said: 'Is it your pleasure that what was said be placed on record or not?'

The holy synod said:

All of us petition this: Let them be said on record! We ask that what he said be on record. Let what concerns

---

[70]See Ex 14:28, where the Israelites escape the forces of Egypt, but the forces of Pharaoh are destroyed.

the faith be on record! Let them be placed on record!
Let them be made known to the emperor! Let them be
made known to the merciful emperor! Let them be made
known to the orthodox emperor! Let it be said on record:
The faith is in danger! We orthodox petition that these
be said on record! Let it be said on record: Christ is insulted! Cast the heretic outside! Send the heretic outside!
Cast outside those against Christ! You have received the
authority: Send the heretic away!

Dioscorus, bishop of Alexandria, said:

> Let the synod be calm. For it is written: *Let the words
> of the wise be heard in quiet.*[71] Let us not be violent. Let
> us not give a pretext to the heretics. I know what your
> God-loving fervor is. The bishops, the clergy, and the
> lay-people are permitted to speak on behalf of the faith,
> but keep it orderly.

Eulogius, priest of Edessa, said:

> All of us who dwell in the city were in great distress
> because many wicked things happened and were done
> by the honorable bishop Hiba in the church of Edessa
> concerning the faith and other matters of the Church:
> The plunder of the sanctuary, and all the rest. We did not
> know whom to approach about this. We thought it right
> to approach the holy archbishop Domnus, and we laid
> down certain main points. But we were advised by certain
> orthodox people, who live in the city of Antioch, not to
> bring forward anything about the faith before him who
> held the throne of Antioch. For they said, 'The just claims
> over the sacrilege and the rest will be especially weakened
> if you do this'. Because we thought and knew that these
> main points of the sacrilege sufficed to deliver our city
> from Hiba, we thought that we would bring forward
> nothing concerning the faith. So subsequently, when a

[71]Qo 9:17.

merciful and believing edict was decreed in the great city
of Antioch, on a Sunday we went to the assembly as usual
and asked if we could assemble in the church. We found
many people there, among whom were mingled certain
lectors from the clergy of Antioch, as well as some of
those called *lecticarii*.[72] While the holy archbishop Domnus presided, the honorable bishop Theodoret being also
present, we encountered a great shout, like this: 'Send
away the edicts! No one is a believer by edicts!'

When we perceived this, we did not again dare to speak
or say there anything about the faith, but we only brought
forward for discussion five main points, one of which was
sacrilege. We made public before the God-fearing archbishop Domnus that Hiba had melted down consecrated
vessels up to two hundred pounds of silver. Although
he announced in the church of the metropolis Edessa
'Whoever wishes to offer for the ransom of captives and
to participate in this, does well', we showed that even
from this donation he borrowed about five hundred
pounds. Again, he took from the treasurer two bags and
one bundle which amounted—according to what the
treasurer said—to six thousand *dinars*. He said that he
had sent all of these and ransomed captives, although we
showed that he did not send even a thousand *darics*. He
acknowledged that this was so, and he was discovered
to have lied under oath. [After we had done this], we
petitioned that Hiba receive punishment. We could not
find anyone to respond to us about this, but in every way
bishop Domnus stood steadfastly by him. For, he said, 'It
was in his power so to manage'.

When we pointed to the holy canons and petitioned for
two days that they be read and that he decree according
to the will of the canons, we were not counted worthy
of an answer. So we made the following deposition:

[72]I.e. litter-bearers.

If it please you that: holy vessels were melted down; that one thousand, five hundred dinars, which were collected from the yield of widows and orphans[73] and women who raised it by themselves, so that sometimes fifty, sometimes a hundred lumi were offered; that two thousand dinars were taken from the treasurer. However, [these sums] were not sent for the ransom of captives except only one thousand dinars—although those captured were monks and nuns: the monks were forced to serve idols, or what is worshiped by uncivilized Arabs, the nuns [were forced] to become prostitutes, and be present in the market places (for this is the custom of the barbarians); that Hiba received the value (of the above-mentioned) and kept it at the house of his brother, Eusebius, judge about this whatever you think (is right).

When this deposition was made by me and we were not considered worthy to receive an answer, two of us, who became frightened at seeing the molestations and the stratagems against us and went to the merciful emperor, were deposed in their absence. We two—who remained and raised the accusation and made public the five main points—we were excommunicated. We were saved from these things by your prayers, after that matter of faith appeared before the holy bishops Photius, Eustathius, and Uranius. After we left there, we went to the synod in Constantinople and said the same things against Hiba. Then we approached the merciful emperor who, merciful upon our wretchedness, asked us, 'Why did you not bring forward before Domnus, archbishop of Antioch, this main point about the faith?' Although we kept silent and did not wish to skip from one cause to another—for we had set ourselves against Hiba—we were compelled in the presence of the whole palace in the apostolic church of holy John[74] to say, 'We are suspicious of him [Domnus]'. So [the emperor] said: 'What is this cause of suspicion?'

[73]See the *Life of Rabbula*, where Rabbula is said to have set aside certain acreage for the sustenance of widows and orphans.

[74]This would seem to refer to the church built by Theodosius the Great to honor the head of John the Baptist. See Sozomen, *Ecclesiastical History* 7.21.

We were forced to say—for how can one lie before such a lord of this world who is established by orthodoxy?— 'When archbishop Domnus presided in the church and the command of your mercifulness against the Nestorians and Irenaeus, who was bishop of the city of Tyre, was proclaimed, we entered the church and we heard certain people scream out, "Take the edicts away! No one is a believer from edicts!" We did not see anyone who rebuked them, but rather, through their silence, they were in agreement'. Because of this, as he was merciful to us, [the emperor] sent us to the aforementioned holy bishops, Photius, Eustathius, and Uranius, and those events took place which were read before your holy synod.

Dioscorus, bishop of Alexandria, said:

Hiba, who made himself alien to the dignity of the episcopate by what he dared so wickedly to do, who lawlessly uttered words against our Saviour and, as if by his own part, would undo the mystery of the economy, he who from above received a sentence in this world and in the one to come because he showed that he is not worthy of the mercifulness of God, we also, because in everything we are in accord with the will of the fear of God, have passed sentence that he be alien to the dignity of the episcopate and to the fellowship of the laity. For it is not right that he, who denied the mysteries of Christ and trampled [them] under foot by his word, partake of the Eucharist or be deemed worthy of the mystical blessing. So I consider it fitting that, along with the canonical decision of deposition that he received, all the gold of the Church be reclaimed so that he may not obtain support for his ungodliness.

Juvenal, bishop of Jerusalem, said:

Hiba, from what was read, appeared to speak most impiously about Our Lord Jesus Christ. Because of this, the Lord Christ takes away his priesthood and places him alien to every rank of the priesthood and even to the communication of the laity. Because we now follow the will of our Savior Jesus Christ, we cast him out and decree that he be alien to every dignity of the priesthood, and, along with this, from the communion of the laity. It is right that he also bring the gold of the Church so that the holy Church may be preserved unharmed and the impious one not enjoy the gold entrusted to God.

Thalassius, bishop of Caesarea in Cappadocia Prima, said:

Those who blaspheme against the Son of God are not worthy of the goods promised by Him. For they make themselves aliens to the mercifulness through their blasphemy against Him. So, because Hiba was lifted up against the belief of the human community and dared to instigate blasphemous speech against our Saviour Jesus Christ—as we know from what was read—he has made himself alien to the priesthood and to the rank of the episcopate and to the communion with the laity.

Stephen, bishop of Ephesus, said:

The blasphemy of Hiba, who is in every way impious, exceeds everything in effrontery against God and our Saviour Jesus Christ. Because of this, in my humble judgement, let him be alien to the episcopate and to the communion of the pure mysteries and to the whole ecclesiastical membership. For there is no defense, either here or in the world to come, because he dared speak so profanely. Let the possessions of the Church be reclaimed, for it is not right that he, who has been shown to be in every way impious, enjoy what has been consecrated to God.

Eusebius, bishop of Ancyra in Galatia, said:

May Hiba, deviser of foul blasphemies for the adversary, produce in gehenna a judgement equal to his presumptuousness. Before his bodily death, may Christ—blasphemed by him—alienate him not only from the priesthood but also from the calling of Christians. Further, may what rightly belongs to the holy Church be reclaimed from Hiba. It is proper that the enemy of the fear of God not revel in the gold of the poor.

Eustathius, bishop of Beirut, said:

Hiba has shown that he has joined himself to Nestorius, if he had not done so formerly,[75] and become a teacher of that impious heresy. He dared to go beyond him in impiety so that it is just, as Your Blessedness thinks, that he, who alienated himself by his speech, be deposed from the rank of the dignity of the priesthood. Let him be prohibited from the communion of the pure mysteries, because he denied the remedy of the mercifulness of God, and let all the gold of the Church be reclaimed, in accordance with your judgement.

Cyrus, bishop of Aphrodosias in Caria, said:

Justly and canonically has Hiba been cast out in complete deposition by this great ecumenical synod. He sharpened his polluted tongue against orthodoxy, so that he caused many to stumble and made them err by his wicked and polluted teaching, which originated with Satan. Therefore, let him be cast out both from contact with the laity on whose account he should present the gold of the church to the holy church.

Diogenes, bishop of Cyzicus, said:

From the acts which were just read to this great and holy synod about Hiba, we know that he thought and wrote what is alien to the statements of the fathers. Because of this, I also, following the example of the holy fathers, determine that he be alien to the dignity of the episcopacy and to the communion of the pure mysteries. Besides this, he should present the gold of the church, which he took tyrannically, to the holy church.

---

[75]Flemming puts a question mark after his reading of ܐܠܕ, and, in a footnote, refers to a reading by Martin (*Actes du Brigandage,* 70) of ܐܠܕܐ. I have accepted Martin's reading.

John, bishop of Armenia Prima, said:

> It is just that those who speak wrongly against the Most
> High should go down to sheol. For catastrophe follows
> when a human blasphemously exalts himself to what is
> not fitting. So Hiba, who first became sick with blas-
> phemy in the rank of the presbyterate, brought this [blas-
> phemy] out into the open when firmly established in the
> high-priesthood, so that he not only filled the church en-
> trusted [to him] with impiety, but also, through his speech,
> quarreling with God, like a fire he devoured [churches]
> as far away as the land of the Persians. Therefore, let him
> be made alien to the priesthood and the communion of
> Christians. For it is not right that he, who has been un-
> masked by those blasphemies read from the acts and by
> his own words, should again with his heresy infect like a
> disease the flock entrusted [to him]. Let us also pronounce
> judgement over the sacrilege, for it is not becoming that
> what were once offered correctly should become an oc-
> casion for impiety and be illegally used according to the
> defrauder's desire.

Basil, bishop of Seleucia in Isauria, said:

> The utterances of the impious Hiba are alien to, and war
> against, the church, and come closer to the vain errors
> of paganism. For with the pagans, certain people, makers
> of fables, turned things around and fashioned God from
> humans. We, however, do not worship a temporal God,
> but we worship the Only-Begotten, consubstantial to
> the Father, God the Word, our Lord Jesus Christ,[76] who,
> because of his mercifulness towards us, became human as
> he willed. So Hiba has no need of our speech by which to

[76]The text of Flemming is here confused. Literally: 'we worship the Only-
Begotten Jesus Christ, who, because of his mercifulness, but we worship the
Only-Begotten, consubstantial to the Father, God the Word, our Lord Jesus
Christ who, because of his mercifulness . . . '. The writer of the manuscript
may have made an error through homoiteleuton, but quickly corrected himself
without erasing his previous writing.

be excommunicated, for he cut himself off from the limbs of the church through so great a blasphemy. Nevertheless, we also depose him by what justly proceeds from our mouth. We stone him with stones, and we expel him from all governance of the priesthood and the communion of the laity. Furthermore, we consider it proper that, because he despoiled the church of gold and he desired to despoil our Lord Jesus Christ of glory, he not enjoy those things he presumptuously despoiled from the sanctuary, but that he hand over to the church its gold.

John, bishop of Rhodes, said:

From the acts just now read, Hiba has shown himself to be alien to the priesthood. Therefore I also determine that he be without the dignity of the episcopate and of participation in the mysteries. Also, he is bound to hand over the gold of the church, so that there be to him no harvest from impiety.

Photius, bishop of Tyre, said:

Even earlier the choice of the harmful belief of Hiba, who became bishop of Edessa, was rejected by me. Now more than ever, because of what was just read before Your Blessedness, he has been shown to be guilty and alien to the ecclesiastical throne. For those who share the views of the devil and are caught up in the heresy of Nestorius are cut off from all excuse in that they are fighting against the very redemption. Therefore, I also agree to what was determined by your piety, as I reckon him alien to all the dignity of the priesthood and to the communion of the laity. Moreover, let the accounting of the gold of the church be protected in accordance with your holy judgement.

Florentinus, bishop of Lydda, said:

Let Hiba, rich in faults and flourishing in impiety but poor in conscience towards God and a true Iscariot by

his theft of consecrated vessels and by the betrayal of his
companions, be stripped of the dignity of the priesthood.
Let him, in whose mouth impiety was like a wicked servant because he was plotting hatred against God, be cut
off from all this body of the priesthood inasmuch as he
dared to tear asunder the church of God by the impiety
of his tongue. Let him give an accounting of the gold of
the church which he robbed, because it is lawful that he,
who received offerings in the semblance of virtue and
then diligently used them to act wickedly, should give an
account without harm to the church.

Marinus, bishop of Synnada, said:

Hiba, who was shown by what was read to be full of impiety, by the grace of God let him be separated from the
dignity of the priesthood and let him cease from communion of the holy mysteries. As he submits to the verdict
of sacrilege, let him return the gold of the church which
he wickedly plundered.

Constantine, bishop of Bosra, said:

Through everything that was read, the blasphemy and
impiety of him who formerly was bishop of the city of
Edessa is demonstrated. Your holy and great synod has
imposed on him an upright judgement, as it alienated
him from all the ministry of the priesthood and the dignity of the episcopate. I concur with what was rightly
decreed by Your Holiness and I reckon him alien to all
the ministry of the priesthood and to the dignity of the
episcopate and to the communion of the holy mysteries.
As for the gold, I also impose on him the sentence which
Your Holiness determined.

Acacius, bishop of Ariartha and who also represented Constantine,
bishop of Melitene, said:

Let Hiba, who so sharpened his pitiless and polluted
tongue against our Lord Jesus Christ, decree on himself

his fall from the priesthood and from the communion of
the holy mysteries. Along with the punishments on him,
let the gold of the poor also be reclaimed, so that it may
be given to those for whom indeed it was given.

Atticus, bishop of Nicopolis in Old Epirus, said:

> It sufficed from those blasphemies against our Lord Jesus
> Christ with which he was full that he receive an ap-
> propriate sentence. Yet because he denied our Lord Jesus
> Christ, we, following the just sentence decreed by our
> holy fathers, determine that he be outside all stewardship
> of the priesthood and the communion of the laity. [We
> also determine] that he be compelled, in accordance with
> your canonical sentence, to replace the gold of the poor
> which he seized.

Nunechius, bishop of Laodicea in Trimatria [Phrygia], said:

> No human understanding can find a punishment ad-
> equate to the impiety of Hiba. However, because it is
> fitting [that he be punished]—even if [the punishment]
> is small in comparison to the many [crimes], yet it be-
> comes great, as he will receive it from the ecumenical
> synod (for does not the synod's great importance increase
> the severity in accordance with its authority?)—I also
> determine that it is appropriate that he be alien to the
> dignity of the priesthood and to the Eucharist. Let him
> also return everything which belongs to the church, so
> that his blasphemy not be profitable to him and he use
> the holy vessels wickedly.

Candidian, bishop of Antioch in Pisidia, said:

> Hiba, who lent his tongue to his father, the slanderer,
> against righteousness, was even before rightly hated by the
> Lord of all, Christ. Now also he is cut off from the priest-
> hood and from communion by your great and holy synod.
> I am a partner in your decision, both in his deposition and
> in everything determined on him by your holy synod.

Seleucus, bishop of Amusia, said:

> I also judge that Hiba, who by his blasphemies and his impiety condemned himself, be alien to the dignity of the episcopate and to communion with Christians, and that he be required [to return] whatever he dared to plunder from the sanctuary.

Leontius, bishop of Ascalon, said:

> Who would pity the snake charmer whom a snake bites? Or which Christian is able to pity Hiba, who, carrying in his soul a spiritual snake, not only dragged himself towards the pit of Sheol but also wanted to lead other souls astray in impiety? Because of this, we cast him out from the activity of the priesthood and from the communion of the laity. He is bound to restore to the poor of the church the gold that he plundered.

Dioscorus, bishop of Alexandria, said:

> Because no time remains for the God-fearing among you so that each one of you might voice his own decision, let us ratify by a common voice, if you so please, what has been determined.

The holy synod said:

> All of us say these things. This is the decision of all of us. All of us expel the contender with God. As by one mouth, all of us expel him.

BIBLIOGRAPHY

DOCUMENTS

Abramowski, Louise, and Goodman, Alan F. *A Nestorian Collection of Christological Texts. Cambridge University Library Ms Oriental 1319.* Cambridge: CambridgeUP, 1972.

Amiaud, Arthur. *La légende syriaque de saint Alexis, l'homme de Dieu.* Paris: Vieweg, 1889.

Bedjan, Paul. *Acta Martyrum et sanctorum.* Paris: Harrassowitz, 1894; repr. Hildesheim: Olms, 1968.

Bickell, Gustav. *Ausgewählte Schriften der syrischen Kirchenväter Aphraates, Rabulas und Isaak von Ninive.* Kempten: Rösel, 1874.

Burkitt, F. C. *Euphemia the Goth with the Acts of the Martyrdom of the Confessors of Edessa.* London: Williams & Norgate, 1913.

Chronica Minora. I Chronicum Edessenum. Ed. Ignacio Guidi. CSCO Scriptores Syri 3.4. Paris: e typographeo Reipublicae, Charles Possielgue, bibliopola; Leipzig: Harrassowitz, 1903.

Flemming, Johannes. *Akten der ephesinischen Synode vom Jahre 449. Syrisch mit Georg Hoffmann's deutscher Übersetzung und seinen Anmerkungen.* Berlin: Weidmann, 1917.

Hallier, Ludwig. *Untersuchungen über die Edessenische Chronik.* TU 9; Leipzig: Hinrichs, 1892.

Mansi, Giovan Domenico. *Sacrorum Conciliorum Nova et Amplissima Collectio.* Graz: Akademische Druck-u. Verlagsanstalt, 1960–61. A reprint of the 1901–1927 edition.

Martin, P. *Actes du brigandage d'Ephèse.* Amiens: Emile Glorieux, 1874.

Overbeck, J. J. S. *Ephraemi Syri, Rabulae episcopi Edesseni, Balaei aliorumque opera selecta.* Oxford: Clarendon, 1865.

Pelagius. *In defensione trium capitulorum,* ed. Robert Devreese. Vatican City: Bibliotheca Apostolica Vaticana, 1932.

Perry, S. G. F. *The Second Synod of Ephesus together with certain extracts relating to it.* Dartford, Kent: Orient Press, 1881.

Rösler, Margarete. 'Alexiusprobleme,' *Zeitschrift für romanische Philologie* 53 (1933) 508–528.

Vööbus, Arthur. *Syriac and Arabic Documents Regarding Legislation Relative to Syrian Monasticism.* Stockholm: Etse, 1960,

STUDIES

Abramowski, Louise. 'Die Streit um Diodor und Theodor zwischen den beiden ephesinischen Konzilien', *Zeitschrift für Kirchengeschichte* 57 (1955–56) 252–287.

Baarda, Tjitze. 'The Gospel Text in the Biography of Rabbula', *Vigiliae Christianae* 14 (1960) 102–127.

Barnard, Leslie W. 'Asceticism in Early Syriac Christianity', *Monastic Studies.* Bangor, Wales: Headstart History, 1991. Pp. 13–21.

Blum, Georg Günter. *Rabbula von Edessa. Der Christ, der Bischof, der Theologe.* CSCO 300. Louvain: Secrétariat du CorpusSCO, 1969.

Bowersock, G. W. 'The Syriac Life of Rabbula and Syrian Hellenism', *Greek Biography and Panegyric in Late Antiquity,* edd. Tomas Hägg and Philip Rousseau. Berkeley: University of California Press, 2002. Pp. 255–271.

Brock, Sebastian. *The Holy Spirit in the Syrian Baptismal Tradition.* The Syrian Churches Series 9; Bronx, New York (available at John XXIII Center, Fordham University, 1979).

———. 'Clothing Metaphors as a Means of Theological Expression in Syriac Tradition', *Typus, Symbol, Allegorie bei den östlichen Vätern und ihren Parallelen im Mittelalter,* edd. Margot Schmidt and Carl F. Geyer. Eichstätter Beiträge 4. Regensburg: Friedrich Pustet. 1982. Pp. 11–38.

————.'From Antagonism to Assimilation: Syrian Attitudes to Greek Learning'. *East of Byzantium: Syria and Armenia in the Formative Period,* edd. Nina Garsoïan, Thomas F. Mathews, Robert W. Thompson. Washington, DC: Dumbarton Oaks, 1982. Pp. 17–34.

————.'Hebrews 2:9B in Syriac Tradition', *Novum Testamentum* 27 (1985) 236–244.

————.'Eusebius and Syriac Christianity', *Eusebius, Christianity, and Judaism,* edd. Harold W. Attridge and Gohai Hata. Leiden: Brill, 1992. Pp. 212–234.

————.'Greek and Syriac in Late Antique Syria', *Literacy and Power in the Ancient World,* edd. A. K. Bowman and G. Woolf. Cambridge: Cambridge University Press 1994. Pp. 149–160.

Brown, Peter R. L. *Poverty and Leadership in the Later Roman Empire.* Hanover, New Hampshire: University Press of New England, 2002.

Bruns, Peter. 'Die Kanones des Rabbula', *Theologia und Ius Canonicum,* ed. H. J. F. Reinhardt. Essen, 1995. Pp. 471–480.

————.'Bischof Rabbula von Edessa—Dichter und Theologe', *Symposium Syriacum VII,* ed. René Lavenant. Orientalia Christiana Analecta 256. Rome: Pontificio Istituto Orientale, 1998. Pp. 195–202.

Camelot, T. 'De Nestorius à Eutychès', *Das Konzil von Chalkedon: Geschichte und Gegenwart,* 3 vols., edd. A. Grillmeier and H. Bacht. Würzburg: 1953–1962. I:213–242.

Chadwick, Henry. 'Eucharist and Christology in the Nestorian Controversy', *Journal of Theological Studies,* new series, 2 (1951) 145–164.

————.'The exile and death of Flavian of Constantinople: a prologue to the Council of Chalcedon', *JTS,* ns, 6 (1955) 17–34.

Chuvin, Pierre. *A Chronicle of the Last Pagans.* Cambridge, Massachusetts: Harvard University Press, 1990.

Clark, Elizabeth A. *The Origenist Controversy: The Cultural Construction of an Early Christian Debate.* Princeton: Princeton University Press, 1992.

Connolly, R. H. 'Some Early Rules for Syrian Monks', *The Downside Review* 25 (1907) 152–162, 300–306.

————.'Some Early Syriac Hymns', *The Downside Review* 35 (1916) 146–149.

Devreese, Robert. *Essai sur Théodore de Mopsueste.* Vatican City: Bibliotheca Apostolica Vaticana, 1948.

Draguet, R. 'La Christologie d'Eutychès, d'après les Actes du Synode de Flavien, 448', *Byzantion* 6 (1931) 441–457.

Drijvers, Hans J.W. *The Book of the Laws of Countries.* Assen: van Gorcum, 1965.

———. *Bardaisan of Edessa.* Assen: van Gorcum, 1966.

———. 'Edessa und das jüdische Christentum', *Vigiliae Christianae* 24 (1970) 4–33.

———. 'Odes of Solomon and Psalms of Mani. Christians and Manichaeans in Third Century Syria', *Studies in Gnosticism and Hellenistic Religions Presented to Gilles Quispel on the Occasion of his 65th Birthday,* edd. R. van den Brock and M. J.Vermaseren. Leiden: Brill, 1981. Pp. 117–130.

———. 'The Persistence of Pagan Cults and Practices in Christian Syria', *East of Byzantium: Syria and Armenia in the Formative Period,* edd. Nina Garsoïan, Thomas F. Mathews, Robert W. Thompson; Washington: Dumbarton Oaks, 1982. Pp. 35–43.

———. 'Die Legende des heiligen Alexius und der Typus des Gottesmannes im syrischen Christentum', *Typus, Symbol, Allegorie bei den östlichen Vätern und ihren Parallelen im Mittelalter,* edd. Margot Schmidt and Carl Friedrich Geyer. Regensburg: Pustet, 1982. Pp. 187–217.

———. 'Hellenistic and Oriental Origins', *The Byzantine Saint,* ed. Sergei Hackel. San Bernardino, California: Borgo, 1983. Pp. 25–33.

———. 'Jews and Christians at Edessa', *Journal of Jewish Studies* 36 (1985) 88–102.

———. 'Marcionism in Syria: Principles, Problems, Polemics', *The Second Century* 6 (1987–88) 153–172.

———. 'The Saint as Symbol: Conceptions of the Person in late Antiquity and Early Christianity', *Concepts of Person in Religion and Thought,* edd. H. G. Kippenberg, Y. B. Kuiper, and A. E. Sanders. Berlin–NewYork: Mouton, 1990. Pp. 137–157.

———. 'Syrian Christianity and Judaism', *The Jews Among Pagans and Christians,* edd. Judith Lieu, John North, Tessa Rajak. Routledge: London, 1992. Pp. 124–146.

———. 'The Man of God of Edessa, Bishop Rabbula and the Urban Poor: Church and Society in the Fifth Century', *JECS* 4 (1996) 235–248.

————.'Early Syriac Christianity: Some Recent Publications', *Vigiliae Christianae* 50 (1996) 159–177.

————.'Rabbula, Bishop of Edessa: Spiritual Authority and Secular Power', *Portraits of Spiritual Authority. Religious Power in Early Christianity, Byzantium and the Christian Orient.* Leiden: Brill, 1999. Pp. 139–154.

Drijvers, Jan Willem. 'The Protonike Legend, the *Doctrina Addai* and Bishop Rabbula of Edessa', *Vigiliae Christianae* 51 (1997) 298–315.

Ehrmann, Bart. *The Orthodox Corruption of Scripture: The Effect of Early Christological Controversies on the Text of the New Testament.* New York: Oxford University Press, 1993.

Esbroeck, Michel van. 'La Vie de saint Jean le Pauvre ou le Calybite en version géorgienne', *Oriens Christianus* 82 (1998) 153–183.

Fowden, Garth. 'Bishops and Temples in the eastern Roman Empire, A.D. 320–435', *JTS* 29 (1978) 53–78.

Frank, Georgia. *The Memory of the Eyes. Pilgrims to Living Saints in Christian Late Antiquity.* Berkeley: University of California Press, 2000.

Gaddis, Michael. 'There is No Crime for Those Who have Christ: Religious Violence in the Christian Roman Empire'. PhD Dissertation, Princeton University, 1999.

Gaiffier, Baudoin de. 'Note sur la date de la légende grecque de S. Alexis', *Analecta Bollandiana* 19 (1900) 254–256.

Gray, Sherman W. *The Least of My Brethren.* Matthew 25:31-46. *A History of Interpretation.* SBL Diss 114; Atlanta: Scholars Press, 1989.

Guillaumont, Antoine. *Les 'Képhalaia Gnostica' d'Évagre le Pontique et l'histoire de l'Origénisme chez les Grecs et chez les Syriens.* Paris: Seuil, 1958.

Halkin, François. 'Une légende grecque de saint Alexis BHG 56d', *Analecta Bollandiana* 98 (1980) 5–16.

Harvey, Susan Ashbrook. 'The Holy and the Poor: Models from Early Syriac Christianity', *Through the Eye of a Needle. Judeo–Christian Roots of Social Welfare,* edd. Emily Abu Hanawalt, Carter Lindberg. Kirksville, Missouri: Thomas Jefferson University Press, 1994. Pp. 43–66.

Hunt, E. D. *Holy Land Pilgrimage in the Later Roman Empire (A.D. 312–460).* Oxford: Clarendon, 1982.

Kelly, J. N. D. *Jerome. His Life, Writings and Controversies.* New York: Harper & Row, 1975.

Lagrange, M. J. 'Bulletin: Nouveau Testament', *RB* 40 (1931) 120–129.

Macmullen, Ramsay. *Christianity and Paganism in the Fourth to the Eighth Centuries.* New Haven: Yale University Press, 1997.

Markus, Robert. *The End of Ancient Christianity.* Cambridge: Cambridge University Press, 1990.

Martindale, J. R. *The Prosopography of the Later Roman Empire. Volume 2. A.D. 395–527.* Cambridge: Cambridge University Press, 1980.

McGuckin, J. A. *St. Cyril of Alexandria: The Christological Controversy, Its History, Theology, and Text.* Leiden: Brill, 1955.

McLeod, Frederick G. 'The Stranger as a Source of Social Change in Early Syriac Christianity', *Christianity and the Stranger. Historical Essays,* ed. Francis W. Nichols. Atlanta: Scholars Press, 1995.

————. 'The Christological Ramifications of Theodore of Mopsuestia's Understanding of Baptism and the Eucharist', *JECS* 10 (2002) 37–75.

Millar, Fergus. *The Roman Near East 31 B.C.–A.D. 337.* Cambridge: Harvard University Press, 1993.

Monceaux, Paul, and Brossé, Léone. 'Chalcis ad Belum. Notes sur l'histoire et les ruines de la ville', *Syria* 6 (1925) 339–350.

Mounayer, Joseph. 'Les canons relatifs aux moines, attribués à Rabboula', *Orientalia christiana periodica* 20 (1954) 406–415.

Murray, Robert. *Symbols of Church and Kingdom: A Study in Early Syriac Tradition.* Cambridge: Cambridge University Press, 1975.

————. 'The Characteristics of the Earliest Syrian Christianity', *East of Byzantium: Syria and Armenia in the Formative Period,* edd. Nina Garsoïan, Thomas F. Mathews, Robert W. Thompson. Washington, DC: Dumbarton Oaks, 1982. Pp. 3–16.

Nau, François. 'Les "belles actions" de Mar Rabboula', *Revue de l'histoire des religions* 103 (1931) 97–135.

Neyrey, Jerome, and Rohrbaugh, Richard. '"He Must Increase, I Must Decrease" (John 3:30): A Cultural and Social Interpretation', *CBQ* 63 (2001) 464–483.

Niditch, Susan. *Folklore and the Hebrew Bible.* Minneapolis: Fortress, 1993.

Norris Jr., Richard A. 'The Problem of Human Identity in Patristic Christological Speculation', *Studia Patristica* 17 (1982) 147–159.

Odenkirchen, Carl. *The Life of St. Alexius in the old French version of the Hildesheim manuscript the original text reviewed, with comparative Greek and Latin versions, all accompanied by English translations.* Brookline, Massachusetts: Classical Folia Editions, 1978.

O'Keefe, John J. 'Kenosis or Impassibility: Cyril of Alexandria and Theodoret of Cyrrhus on the Problem of Divine Pathos', *Studia Patristica* 32, ed. Elizabeth A. Livingstone. Louvain: Peeters, 1987. Pp. 358–365.

Peeters, Paul. 'La vie de Rabboula, évêque d'Édesse', *Recherches d'histoire er de philologie orientales* (Brussels: Bollandists, 1951) 139–170.

Pereira, F. M. Esteves. 'Légende grecque de l'homme de Dieu Saint Alexis', *Analecta Bollandiana* 19 (1900) 241–253.

Price, R. M. *A History of the Monks in Syria.* Cistercian Studies Series 58. Kalamazoo, Michigan: Cistercian Publications, 1985.

Rösler, Margarete. *Die Fassungen des Alexius-Legende mit besonderer Berücksichtigung der mittelenglischen Versionen.* Vienna: Braümuller, 1905.

Russell, Norman. *Cyril of Alexandria.* London: Routledge, 2000.

Segal, Judah B. 'When did Christianity come to Edessa?', *Middle East Studies and Libraries: A Felicitation Volume for Professor J. D. Pearson.* London: Mansell, 1980. Pp.179–191.

———. 'A Note on a Mosaic from Edessa', *Syria* 60 (1983) 107–110.

———. *Edessa, 'The Blessed City'.* Oxford: Clarendon, 1970.

Stebbins, Charles E. 'Les origines de la légende de saint Alexis', *Revue belge de philologie et d'histoire* 51 (1973) 497–507.

———. 'Les grandes versions de la légende de Saint Alexis', *Revue belge de philologie et d'histoire* 53 (1975) 679–695.

Teixidor, Javier. 'Deux documents syriaques du IIIe siècle provenant du moyen Euphrate', *CRAI* (1990) 144–166.

Theokritoff, Elizabeth. 'The Life of Our Holy Father Alexander', *Aram* 3 (1991) 293–318.

Vööbus, Arthur. *Investigations into the Text of the New Testament Used by Rabbula of Edessa.* Contributions of Baltic University 59. Pinneberg: 1947.

———. *Studies in the Gospel Text in Syriac.* Louvain: Secrétariat CSCO, 1951.

———. 'Das literarische Verhältnis zwischen der Biographie des Rabbula und dem Ps.–Amphilochianischen Panegyrikus über Basilius', *Oriens Christianus* 44 (1960) 40–45.

————.'The institution of the *benai qeiama* und *benat quiama* in the ancient Syrian church (rules of Rabbula, Pseudo–Nicaean canons)', *Church History* 30 (1961) 19–27.

————.'Solution du problème de l'auteur de la "Lettre à Gemillinos, Évêque de Perrhé"', *L'Orient syrien* 7 (1962) 297–306.

————. *History of the School of Nisibis.* Louvain: Secrétariat CSCO, 1965.

————. *A History of Asceticism in the Syrian Orient.* CSCO Subsidia 17. Louvain: Peeters, 1960.

Wilken, Robert L. *The Land Called Holy: Palestine in Christian History and Thought.* New Haven: Yale University Press, 1992.

SCRIPTURE INDEX

GENERAL INDEX

INDEX OF NAMED RELIGIOUS PERSONNEL IN EDESSA

CISTERCIAN PUBLICATIONS
Texts and Studies in the Monastic Tradition

TEXTS IN ENGLISH TRANSLATION

THE CISTERCIAN MONASTIC TRADITION

Aelred of Rievaulx

- Dialogue on the Soul
- The Historical Works
- Liturgical Sermons, I
- The Lives of the Northern Saints
- Spiritual Friendship
- Treatises I: Jesus at the Age of Twelve; Rule for a Recluse; Pastoral Prayer
- Walter Daniel: The Life of Aelred of Rievaulx

Bernard of Clairvaux

- Apologia to Abbot William (Cistercians and Cluniacs)
- Five Books on Consideration: Advice to a Pope
- Homilies in Praise of the Blessed Virgin Mary
- In Praise of the New Knighthood
- Letters
- Life and Death of Saint Malachy the Irishman
- On Baptism and the Office of Bishops
- On Grace and Free Choice
- On Loving God
- Parables and Sentences
- Sermons for the Summer Season
- Sermons on Conversion
- Sermons on the Song of Songs, I-IV
- The Steps of Humility and Pride

Gertude the Great of Helfta

- Spiritual Exercises
- The Herald of God's Loving-Kindness, Books 1 and 2
- The Herald of God's Loving-Kindness, Book 3

William of Saint Thierry

- The Enigma of Faith
- Exposition on the Epistle to the Romans
- Exposition on the Song of Songs
- The Golden Epistle
- The Mirror of Faith
- The Nature and Dignity of Love
- On Contemplating God, Prayer, Meditations

Gilbert of Hoyland

- Sermons on the Song of Songs, I-III
- Treatises, Sermons, and Epistles

John of Ford

- Sermons on the Final Verses of the Song of Songs, I-VII

Other Cistercian Writers

- Adam of Perseigne, Letters, I
- Alan of Lille: The Art of Preaching
- Amadeus of Lausanne: Homilies in Praise of Blessed Mary
- Baldwin of Ford: Commendation of Faith
- Geoffrey of Auxerre: On the Apocalypse
- Guerric of Igny: Liturgical Sermones, I-II
- Helinand of Froidmont: Verses on Death
- Idung of Prüfening: Cistercians and Cluniacs. The Case of Cîteaux
- In The School of Love. An Anthology of Early Cistercian Texts
- Isaac of Stella: Sermons on the Christian Year, I-[II]
- The Letters of Armand-Jean de Rancé, Abbot of la Trappe
- The Life of Beatrice of Nazareth
- Mary Most Holy: Meditating with the Early Cistercians
- Ogier of Locedio: Homilies [on Mary and the Last Supper]
- Serlo of Wilton & Serlo of Savigny: Seven Unpublished Works (Latin-English)
- Sky-blue the Sapphire, Crimson the Rose: The Spirituality of John of Ford
- Stephen of Lexington: Letters from Ireland
- Stephen of Sawley: Treatises
- Three Treatises on Man: A Cistercian Anthropology / Bernard McGinn

EARLY AND EASTERN MONASTICISM

- Besa: The Life of Shenoute of Atripe
- Cyril of Scythopolis: The Lives of the Monks of Palestine
- Dorotheos of Gaza: Discourses and Sayings
- Evagrius Ponticus: Praktikos and Chapters on Prayer
- Handmaids of the Lord: Lives of Holy Women in Late Antiquity and the Early Middle Ages / Joan Petersen
- Harlots of the Desert. A Study of Repentance / Benedicta Ward
- Isaiah of Scete: Ascetic Discourses

- John Moschos: The Spiritual Meadow
- The Life of Antony (translated from Coptic and Greek)
- The Lives of the Desert Fathers. The *Historia monachorum in Aegypto*
- The Spiritually Beneficial Tales of Paul, Bishop of Monembasia
- Symeon the New Theologian: The Practical and Theological Chapters, and The Three Theological Discourses
- Theodoret of Cyrrhus: A History of the Monks of Syria
- Stewards of the Poor. [Three biographies from fifth-century Edessa]
- The Syriac Book of Steps *[Liber graduum]*
- The Syriac Fathers on Prayer and the Spiritual Life / Sebastian Brock

LATIN MONASTICISM

- Achard of Saint Victor: Works
- Anselm of Canterbury: Letters, I–III
- Bede the Venerable: Commentary on the Acts of the Apostles
- Bede the Venerable: Commentary on the Seven Catholic Epistles
- Bede the Venerable: Homilies on the Gospels, I–II
- Bede the Venerable: Excerpts from the Works of Saint Augustine on the Letters of the Blessed Apostle Paul
- The Celtic Monk [An Anthology]
- Gregory the Great: Forty Gospel Homilies
- Guigo II: The Ladder of Monks and Twelve Meditations / Colledge, Walsh edd.
- Halfway to Heaven
- The Life of the Jura Fathers
- The Maxims of Stephen of Muret
- Peter of Celle: Selected Works
- The Letters of Armand-Jean de Rancé, I–II
- The Rule of the Master
- The Rule of Saint Augustine
- Saint Mary of Egypt. Three Medieval Lives in Verse

STUDIES IN MONASTICISM / CISTERCIAN STUDIES

Cistercian Studies and Reflections

- Aelred of Rievaulx. A Study / Aelred Squire
- Athirst for God. Spiritual Desire in Bernard of Clairvaux's Sermons on the Song of Songs / Michael Casey
- Beatrice of Nazareth in her Context, I–II: Towards Unification with God / Roger DeGanck
- Bernard of Clairvaux. Man. Monk. Mystic / Michael Casey
- The Cistercian Way / André Louf
- Dom Gabriel Sortais. An Amazing Abbot in Turbulent Times / Guy Oury
- The Finances of the Cistercian Order in the Fourteenth Century / Peter King
- Fountains Abbey and Its Benefactors / Joan Wardrop
- A Gathering of Friends. Learning and Spirituality in John of Ford
- Hidden Springs: Cistercian Monastic Women, 2 volumes
- Image of Likeness. The Augustinian Spirituality of William of St Thierry / D. N. Bell
- Index of Authors and Works in Cistercian Libraries in Great Britain / D. N. Bell

- Index of Cistercian Authors and Works in Medieval Library catalogues in Great Britain / D. N. Bell
- The Mystical Theology of Saint Bernard / Etienne Gilson
- The New Monastery. Texts and Studies on the Earliest Cistercians
- Monastic Odyssey [Cistercian Nuns & the French Revolution]
- Nicolas Cotheret's Annals of Cîteaux / Louis J. Lekai
- Pater Bernhardus. Martin Luther and Bernard of Clairvaux / Franz Posset
- Rancé and the Trappist Legacy / A. J. Krailsheimer
- A Second Look at Saint Bernard / Jean Leclercq
- The Spiritual Teachings of St Bernard of Clairvaux / John R. Sommerfeldt
- Studies in Medieval Cistercian History
- Three Founders of Citeaux / Jean-Baptiste Van Damme
- Understanding Rancé. Spirituality of the Abbot of La Trappe in Context / D. N. Bell
- William, Abbot of Saint Thierry
- Women and Saint Bernard of Clairvaux / Jean Leclercq

Cistercian Art, Architecture, and Music

- Cistercian Abbeys of Britain [illustrated]
- Cistercian Europe / Terryl N. Kinder
- Cistercians in Medieval Art / James France
- SS. Vincenzo e Anastasio at Tre Fontane Near Rome / J. Barclay Lloyd
- Studies in Medieval Art and Architecture, II–VI / Meredith P. Lillich, ed.
- Treasures Old and New. Nine Centuries on Cistercian Music [CD, cassette]
- Cistercian Chants for the Feast of the Visitation [CD]

Monastic Heritage

- Community and Abbot in the Rule of St Benedict, I–II / Adalbert de Vogüé
- Distant Echoes: Medieval Religious Women, I / Shank, Nichols, edd.
- The Freedom of Obedience / A Carthusian
- Halfway to Heaven [The Carthusian Tradition] / Robin Lockhart
- The Hermit Monks of Grandmont / Carole A. Hutchison
- A Life Pleasing to God: Saint Basil's Monastic Rules / Augustine Holmes
- Manjava Skete [Ruthenian tradition] / Sophia Seynk
- Monastic Practices / Charles Cummings
- Peace Weavers. Medieval Religious Women, II / Shank, Nichols, edd.
- Reading Saint Benedict / Adalbert de Vogüé
- The Rule of St Benedict. A Doctrinal and Spiritual Commentary / Adalbert de Vogüé
- Stones Laid Before the Lord [Monastic Architecture] / Anselme Dimier
- What Nuns Read [Libraries of Medieval English Nunneries] / D. N. Bell

Monastic Liturgy

- From Advent to Pentecost / A Carthusian
- The Hymn Collection from the Abbey of the Paraclete, 2 volumes
- The Molesme Summer Season Breviary, 4 volumes
- The Old French Ordinary and Breviary of the Abbey of the Paraclete, 5 volumes
- The Paraclete Statutes: *Institutiones nostrae*
- The Twelfth Century Cistercian Hymnal, 2 volumes
- The Twelfth Century Cistercian Psalter [NYP]
- Two Early Cistercian *Libelli Missarum*

MODERN MONASTICISM
Thomas Merton

- Cassian and the Fathers: Initiation into the Monastic Tradition
- The Climate of Monastic Prayer
- The Legacy of Thomas Merton
- The Message of Thomas Merton
- The Monastic Journey of Thomas Merton
- Thomas Merton Monk
- Thomas Merton on Saint Bernard
- Thomas Merton: Prophet of Renewal / John Eudes Bamberger
- Toward An Integrated Humanity [Essays on Thomas Merton]

Contemporary Monastics

- Centered on Christ. A Guide to Monastic Profession / Augustine Roberts
- Inside the Psalms. Reflections for Novices / Maureen McCabe
- Passing from Self to God. A Cistercian Retreat / Robert Thomas
- Pathway of Peace. Cistercian Wisdom according to Saint Bernard / Charles Dumont
- Poor Therefore Rich / A Carthusian
- The Way of Silent Love / A Carthusian

CHRISTIAN SPIRITUALITY PAST AND PRESENT

Past

- A Cloud of Witnesses. The Development of Christian Doctrine [to 500] / D. N. Bell
- Eros and Allegory: Medieval Exegesis of the Song of Songs / Denys Turner
- High King of Heaven. Aspects of Early English Spirituality / Benedicta Ward
- In the Unity of the Holy Spirit. Conference on the Rule of Benedict

- The Life of St Mary Magdalene and of Her Sister St Martha [Magdalene legend]
- The Luminous Eye. The Spiritual World Vision of St Ephrem / Sebastian Brock
- Many Mansions. Medieval Theological Development East and West / D. N. Bell
- The Name of Jesus / Irénée Hausherr
- Penthos. The Doctrine of Compunction in the Christian East / Irénée Hausherr

CISTERCIAN PUBLICATIONS Titles Listing

- Prayer. The Spirituality of the Christian East II / Tomás Spidlík
- Russian Mystics / Serge Bolshakoff, Introduction by Thomas Merton
- Silent Herald of Unity. The Life of Maria Gabrielle Sagheddu [Patron of Ecumenism] / Martha Driscoll
- The Spirituality of the Christian East / Tomás Spidlík
- The Spirituality of the Medieval Latin West / André Vauchez
- The Spiritual World of Isaac the Syrian / Hilarion Alfeyev
- The Venerable Bede / Benedicta Ward

Present

- Bearers of the Spirit: Spiritual Fatherhood in the Romanian Orthodox Tradition
- The Call of Wild Geese / Matthew Kelty
- The Contemplative Path. Rediscovering a Lost Tradition
- Drinking from the Hidden Fountain / Tomás Spidlík

- Entirely for God. The Life of Michael Iwene Tansi / Elizabeth Isichei
- Grace Can Do More. Spiritual Accompaniment / André Louf
- Interior Prayer / A Carthusian
- A Hand On My Shoulder. Memoirs of John Willem Gran, I–II
- The Hermitage Within / A Monk
- How Far to Follow. The Martyrs of Atlas / Bernardo Olivera
- Memoirs. From Grace to Grace / Jean Leclercq
- Mercy in Weakness / André Louf
- No Moment Too Small / Norvene Vest
- The Prayer of Love and Silence / A Carthusian
- Praying the Word / Enzo Bianchi
- Praying with Benedict / Korneel Vermeiren
- Sermons in a Monastery / Matthew Kelty
- Tuning In To Grace / André Louf
- Words To Live By. Journeys in Ancient and Modern Egyptian Monasticism / Tim Vivian

EDITORIAL OFFICES

Cistercian Publications • WMU Station
1903 West Michigan Avenue
Kalamazoo, MI 49008-5415   USA
tel 269 387 8920   fax 269 387 8390
e-mail cistpub@wmich.edu

CUSTOMER SERVICE—NORTH AMERICA: USA AND CANADA

Cistercian Publications at Liturgical Press
Saint John's Abbey
Collegeville, MN 56321-7500 USA
tel 800 436 8431   fax 320 363 3299
e-mail sales@litpress.org

CUSTOMER SERVICE—EUROPE: UK, IRELAND, AND EUROPE

Cistercian Publications at Columba Book Service
55A Spruce Avenue
Stillorgan Industrial Park
Blackrock, Co. Dublin, Ireland
tel 353 1 294 2560   fax 353 1 294 2564
e-mail sales@columba.ie

WEBSITE
www.cistercianpublications.org

Cistercian Publications is a non-profit corporation.